Paul,
with best wishes
Paul ....
_17/1/01_

Blair's Britain
England's Europe

A View from Ireland

Edited by
Paul Gillespie

IEA

IRELAND
2000

INSTITUTE OF EUROPEAN AFFAIRS

Published by
The Institute of European Affairs
Europe House
8 North Great Georges Street
Dublin 1
Ireland
Tel: (353) 1-874 6756
Fax: (353) 1-878 6880
website: www.iiea.com   e-mail: info@iiea.iol.ie

ISBN 1-874109-54-0
£15.00 – €19

Origination by Alan Hodgson
Printed by The Brunswick Press, Dublin, Ireland

Contents

CONTRIBUTORS

PAUL GILLESPIE, EDITOR

Paul Gillespie is Foreign Editor and a duty editor of *The Irish Times* with overall responsibility for international policy and foreign news coverage. He has travelled and reported extensively in Europe, the Middle East, North America and Japan. He is leader of the Institute of European Affairs' (IEA's) project on Britain. Paul Gillespie was one of the principal authors of the IEA's studies *Maastricht Crisis of Confidence* (1993) and *Constitution Building in the European Union* (1996), and was co-author (with Rodney Rice) of *Political Union* (1991). He was editor of the precursor of this study, *Britain's European Question: the Issues for Ireland* (1996).

RONAN FANNING

Ronan Fanning is Professor of Modern History at the National University of Ireland, University College Dublin. He was joint editor of the premier Irish history journal *Irish Historical Studies* from 1976 to1987. In 1989 he was elected a member of the Royal Irish Academy. His main research interests are in twentieth century Irish and British history and in international relations. His major publications include *The Irish Department of Finance 1922–58* (1978) and *Independent Ireland* (1983). Ronan Fanning is also a regular political columnist for the *Sunday Independent.*

GARRET FITZGERALD

Dr FitzGerald was Taoiseach from June 1981 to March 1982 and from December 1982 to March 1987. He was a Co-signatory of the Anglo-Irish Agreement in 1985. Dr FitzGerald was a member of Seanad Éireann (Irish senate) from 1965 to 1969 and of Dáil Éireann (Irish parliament) from 1969 to 1992, Minister for Foreign Affairs from 1973 to 1977 and Leader of Fine Gael from 1977 to 1987.

BRENDAN HALLIGAN

Brendan Halligan was General Secretary of the Irish Labour Party from 1967 to 1980, a member of Seanad Éireann (Irish senate) from 1973 to 1977, Dáil Éireann (Irish parliament) from 1976 to

1977 and the European Parliament from 1983 to 1984. He was a founder member of the Institute of European Affairs (IEA) in Ireland and has been Chairperson since its foundation in 1991.

BRENDAN KEENAN

Brendan Keenan is Group Business Editor of Independent Newspapers Ltd. He began his career as a reporter for the Belfast Telegraph in 1963, bcoming Deputy Political Correspondent there in 1973. He joined RTE in 1976 and in 1981 became the Economics Correspondent for the RTE News team. Between 1983-86 he was the Ireland Correspondent for the Financial Times. He was appointed Business Editor for the Irish Independent in 1986.

GERARD O'NEILL

Gerard O'Neill is Managing Director of Amárach Consulting, which he founded in 1989 as the Henley Centre Ireland after working as a senior consultant at the Henley Centre for Forecasting in London. He is Ireland's best known futurist and commentator on the business implications of technological and social change. Gerard O'Neill was appointed as a special advisor to the Irish government's Information Society Initiative in 1996. His publications include *The Future of Offices* (1992), *Ireland 2000* (1994) and *The Coming Boom in Direct Marketing* (1996) and he is the author of a number of reports on economic, social and technological trends in Ireland.

LOCHLANN QUINN

Lochlann Quinn is Deputy Chairman of Glen Dimplex, a privately owned Irish industrial group with annual international sales of over $1 billion. He is a former partner with Arthur Andersen. Lochlann Quinn has been non-executive Chairman of Allied Irish Banks since 1997.

Preface

Paul Gillespie

This study is a follow-up to the book published in September 1996 by the Institute of European Affairs, *Britain's European Question: the Issues for Ireland*. Given the moment at which it was published, in the run-up to the 1997 UK general election campaign, it is not surprising that Labour's sweeping parliamentary majority and subsequent broad reforming agenda should have looked like a laboratory of political change to test the conclusions and scenarios put forward in that book.

The group of authors kept informally in touch; by early 1998 there was a consensus emerging on the need to track the process of change in Britain's domestic and European policies, not least because of the Blair government's extraordinary activism on, and commitment to, reaching a settlement in Northern Ireland, which bore fruit in the Belfast Agreement. That consensus crystallised into a decision to reconstitute the group and to describe and analysis the progress made by the British government in addressing the dual sovereignty question – concerning domestic and external policies – identified in the 1996 book, and its implications for Ireland. The new government's more positive attitude towards joining the euro held out the prospect that this would help resolve its outstanding difficulties in bringing Britain to the core of European integration. Since whether sterling is strong or weak directly affects the Republic's economic performance and well-being, Ireland retains a clear interest in that question.

Deeper study of these issues in 1998 and 1999 convinced us of the validity of such a follow-up exercise and of the need to make a more far-reaching assessment of it than could be contained in an interim report. This book is the result of that evolving awareness. The pace of events in 2000 meant the emerging text was chasing a moving target: it will be up to the reader to decide whether a satisfactory balance between narrative and analysis has been achieved. That is both the attraction and difficulty of contemporary policy studies. The perspectives and scenarios outlined in the following chapters offer a guide to a fascinating and complex process of change, as the United Kingdom changes its constitutional arrangements irreversibly, debates its future role in Europe intensively, and pursues a normalised relationship with Ireland through the Belfast Agreement.

The authors have been fortunate indeed in the help and back-up made available by the Institute of European Affairs as this project evolved and matured. We were fortunate too in being able to maintain contacts built up during the preparation of the previous book and to explore new lines of enquiry with many authoritative policy-makers and analysts in Britain, Ireland, Europe and the United States. We are particularly grateful to Ted Barrington, Ambassador of Ireland in the United Kingdom, for facilitating a richly rewarding briefing visit to London last year, during which we met senior officials in the Treasury, the Foreign Office, No 10 Downing Street, the Bank of England, the Houses of Commons and Lords and in the policy studies, media, industrial and banking worlds. The Irish ambassador's colleagues, Dan Mulhall, Consul General in Scotland and Conor O'Riordan, Consul General in Wales, likewise facilitated visits to Edinburgh and Cardiff, during which we met an extraordinary range of people in a short space of time. Their work should be recognised as especially valuable for developing and consolidating the transformed British-Irish relationship which this study is intended to explore in its European dimension.

In Dublin we have also been fortunate to have had the encouragement of the British Embassy with contacts and advice. Baroness Veronica Sutherland and Sir Ivor Roberts, who succeeded her as ambassador to Ireland in 1998, have been unfailingly helpful. They and their staff have made a succession of visitors to Ireland available to us for briefings and discussion, giving us a privileged insight into the evolution of British policy and political debates.

We would like to record our appreciation to Charles Grant, director of the Centre for European Reform in London, for his continuing interest in our project. John Osmond, director of the Institute of Welsh Affairs in Cardiff, was equally helpful. Gordon Leicester, director of the Scottish Council   Foundation in

Edinburgh, retained a sympathic interest in our work. We would also like to thank Brigid Laffan, Jean Monnet Professor of European Politics at University College Dublin, Rory O'Donnell, Jean Monnet Professor of European Business Studies at University College Dublin, Elizabeth Meehan, Jean Monnet Professor of Politics at The Queen's University of Belfast, and Tony Brown, until recently a Director of the European Bank for Reconstruction and Development, for reading the text and making valuable suggestions to improve it.

The work could not have been completed without the resources and commitment of the Institute of European Affairs in Dublin. Terry Stewart took a close interest in our work as Director General and continued to advise us after retiring from that post. His successor, Joe Brosnan, has shown himself to be equally committed and enthusiastic. Jill Donoghue, Research Director, and Pete Glennon, Administrator, encouraged us to persevere as the project expanded. Conall Quinn, the UK project's serving officer, deserves a special word of thanks for his efficient and patient administrative work and his engagement with our theme. Iain MacAulay and his editorial team have been equally helpful and more than willing to facilitate updates and changes to the texts. The authors are grateful, too, for the understanding of their families and working colleagues as we endeavoured to pin down such a complex and rapidly evolving subject, which took up much more time than was originally anticipated to bring to a conclusion.

PG
19 October 2000
Dublin

CHAPTER ONE

Introduction

Garret FitzGerald and Brendan Halligan

BACKGROUND

Ireland is linked to Britain in a complex relationship influenced by geography, history, economics and a common language. Membership of the European Union has added an extra dimension to that relationship and has introduced a range of additional strategic problems for Irish policy-makers. These would have required considered responses in any event, because joint membership of the Union transformed Ireland's previous relationship with Britain from one of dependence to independence and, subsequently, interdependence.[1] But this process of adaptation to a fundamentally changed relationship has been made more complicated by the divergent strategies which the two countries have pursued in Europe, whereby Ireland rapidly became a psychological insider within the Union, and Britain emerged as the awkward partner in Europe.[2] Generally speaking, Ireland has been comfortable with the overall thrust of integration, from which it has derived many economic and other benefits; Britain has been unhappy with what it has perceived to be the continuous erosion of national sovereignty, for which it has received little tangible compensation. For Ireland, integration has meant an enhancement of sovereignty; for Britain, a dilution.

This divergence in the general orientation towards Europe[3] has been matched by differing approaches towards common EU policies[4] which have often placed the two countries on opposite sides of the debate, such as on the Common Agricultural Policy, the Community Budget, and the Social Chapter. The most striking manifestation of these differences has concerned monetary union. Ireland joined the ERM in 1979 and eventually went on to become a founder member of the euro; Britain initially declined to participate in the ERM and when it did so, belatedly, was later forced to leave. It then refused to move to stage three of EMU having been given an opt-out in the Maastricht Treaty. This raised questions about Britain's long-term perspective in the EU since monetary union was generally understood to be the precursor of political union. This also opened up the possibility of a sharper cleavage between Irish and British interests and the manner in which they were to be pursued in Europe.

NEW CHALLENGES FOR IRELAND

In the wake of the Maastricht Treaty it was already evident that the Irish economy would face new challenges were Britain to remain outside EMU indefinitely. In particular, the issue of competitiveness caused widespread concern at that time. It was feared that the decline in the value of sterling would continue and would confront Irish business with what would amount to a series of competitive devaluations – a threat all the more worrying in the light of the Single Market then emerging. In the ensuing debate, monetary union also became an issue in terms of whether it would be an optimal currency area for Ireland.

At that point, the options open to Ireland regarding membership of the monetary union were limited to continuing with its commitment to enter the third stage of EMU, as endorsed in the referendum on the Maastricht Treaty, or postponing membership until Britain ended its opt-out. The Institute of European Affairs (IEA) believed that the implications of each option needed careful assessment so that Irish public opinion could make an informed judgement on which choice best suited the national interest. A project on EMU[5] had been established by the IEA in 1991 and it was felt necessary to complement its analysis by another project specifically devoted to a study of the UK's European policy for the purpose of working out scenarios over the medium to long term for Britain's relationship with Europe. The project was initiated in 1993 under the chairmanship of Dr Garret FitzGerald, former Taoiseach and Minister for Foreign Affairs, who had a particular expertise in UK affairs, and with Paul Gillespie, Foreign Editor of *The Irish Times* and an established commentator on the EU, as Project Leader.

The project group that was assembled to monitor and analyse UK policy on Europe produced a study in 1996, *Britain's European Question: the Issues for Ireland.*[6] This necessarily went beyond the immediate concern with EMU to examine the causes of Britain's perennial problem with Europe and to identify a number of scenarios for the future. The main theses of the study are set out for ease of reference in the panel on pages 10 to 14 but can be summarised as follows.

BRITAIN'S SOVEREIGNTY PROBLEM

The root cause of Britain's problem with Europe was that it had not yet found a role to compensate for its loss of empire. This had, in turn, contributed to an identity crisis about the nature of Britain itself in terms of the state, society and peoples. While the use of the word "crisis" was debated within the group of authors contributing to the study (and after publication was in fact subject to some external criticism), it was used throughout in the absence of an acceptable alternative and was taken as a synonym for a moment when there is neither consensus nor clarity within a society on crucial decisions to be taken about its future. In that sense, the British crisis of political and state identity was seen as having four dimensions: internally within Britain, externally with Europe, and, to a lesser degree, internationally with the US and, closer to home, with Ireland.

In one of that book's main conclusions, sovereignty was identified as the nub of the problem. Britain was simultaneously confronted with pressure to devolve sovereignty internally to the Celtic nations and, possibly later, to the English regions, and with pressure to share it externally with other nation states in Europe – moves that could also necessitate some modification of its other international relations, such as those with the US and the Commonwealth. This combination of issues was described as Britain's dual sovereignty problem. Lying behind this British problem was England itself, so often confused with Britain – an England whose presence was being made increasingly apparent with the unravelling of the British identity into its component parts.[7] The cause of the British problem with Europe, resulting in missed opportunities for positive engagement, was the negativism towards devolving or sharing sovereignty that is inherent in English nationalism.[8] Until the state structure of the United Kingdom had been rearranged to accommodate the demands for devolution internally, there would be problems about conceding additional demands coming from Europe.

Solving the problem of sharing sovereignty in Europe was seen by the authors of this earlier work as being contingent on devolving it within Britain. That did not, of course, preclude solutions being pursued on the two fronts at the same time, but it implied that, until the British identity crisis had been satisfactorily resolved in terms of the state and society, there could be no final determination of Britain's vocation within Europe or with regard to the rest of the world.

SCENARIOS UNDER MAJOR

At the time of writing the earlier volume in 1996, John Major led a Conservative government which was wracked by dissension on Europe to the point where the IGC then in session was conducted *à quartorze*[9] and the flexibility clause later incorporated in the Amsterdam Treaty was being fashioned substantially as a response to British opposition to any deepening of the integration process. These realities influenced the identification of five scenarios outlined in the conclusions to the study and set out in the panel in this chapter. The spectrum of scenarios ranged all the way from Britain being an outsider to it becoming a leader in Europe, and they included intermediate points involving Britain being a chooser of selected policies or competences, a belated joiner in each successive stage of integration, or a gambler which first agreed to new competences but later sought to change the rules.

Past experience indicated that with the exception of the Single Market (and even on that issue Margaret Thatcher initially voted against calling the IGC needed to bring it about), Britain had been a perennial late joiner in Europe, as with the decision on entry itself. In view of the serial inconsistency of its political leadership towards Europe[10] it had also proved to be a gambler, exemplified by the referendum in 1975 and the subsequent renegotiation of its contribution to the Community Budget.

Ireland could survive the consequences of the late-joiner syndrome on the grounds that Britain would always eventually face facts and become part of each new phase of the integration process, however reluctantly. But the substance of the debate on EMU indicated that the matter was so fundamental to the British perception of sovereignty that the outsider scenario might apply rather than that of the late-joiner or gambler.[11] In those circumstances, Britain would remain outside an EMU in which

Ireland would be participating from the outset. Were integration to proceed as anticipated the implications for Ireland would then be profound. The economy could be exposed to the threat of sterling depreciation without the possibility of recourse to compensating devaluations of the Irish currency. Difficulties could also be anticipated in the bilateral trading relationship with Britain. And an even more troubling problem could arise in relation to Northern Ireland where the two governments had painstakingly built an alliance of interests in ending violence and installing political institutions acceptable to the two communities. In that policy area, the repositioning of British-Irish relations in the multilateral context of Europe had come to be recognised as a benign development. It promoted a sense of interdependence and also allowed for frequent ministerial contact *en marge* of various Council meetings. Were that interdependent relationship to be jeopardised, the consequences could be damaging to the peace process in Northern Ireland, which at that time had reached a sensitive stage. The study dealt with these implications in some depth.

NEW LABOUR, NEW BRITAIN

In 1996 New Labour held a substantial lead over the Conservatives in the opinion polls, and while it was reasonable to predict that a change of government was in the offing, the authors' analysis had to stick to the facts as they then were. The election of New Labour in 1997 changed those facts. The Blair government immediately introduced a series of policy departures which on the surface heralded a new era for Britain's constitutional order and for its relationship with Europe. Commitments to hold referendums on devolving power to Scotland and Wales virtually coincided with the announcement of a positive approach to Europe in place of that pursued by the Conservatives. Within weeks of taking office, the New Labour government ended Britain's opt-out on the Social Chapter, reversed its predecessor's hostility to Treaty changes at the Amsterdam IGC, and took the first tentative steps towards joining EMU. In those circumstances, there seemed to be good reason for believing that Britain's dual-sovereignty problem was being aggressively addressed and, furthermore – if election promises were to be taken literally – that reform of society and the economy were both underway.

These developments suggested that Britain's European
question should be reviewed and that the scenarios previously
formulated should be tested against the strategic thrust of Britain's
new European policy, provided, of course, that a strategy could be
identified. Subsequently, in 1998, the IEA decided to re-establish
its UK project team under the same chairman and project leader,
and invited it to produce a sequel to the first study. This book is
the outcome.

Summary of *Britain's European Question: the Issues for Ireland* (1996)

Britain faces a crisis of national, state and political identity
concerning its position in the world, in Europe and in
relation to its internal constitutional arrangements after the
end of the Cold War. Four dimensions of this crisis
intersect with one another:

- Changing global and transatlantic relations
- Changing relations between Britain and Europe
- Proposals for changes in Britain's constitutional and
  institutional structures
- Changing relations between Britain and Ireland.

Because of the history and political structure of British-
Irish relations it is clear that if Britain faces such a crisis it
will affect Ireland as well.

The term crisis implies a moment of crucial decision in
the face of acute difficulty or danger. It usefully denotes not
only a political condition of psychological uncertainty, but
of changing historical conjunctures requiring innovation
and resolution as well. Political identity includes territorial
boundedness, shared myths of origin, a common culture
and common legal rights and duties.

Britain's place in Europe is but part of a larger
conundrum: how to manage a decline in political prestige
and economic power? How is Britain to be reinvented? It is
a paradox, tragic both for Britain and Europe, that in the
post-war period reinvention has proved easier for the
vanquished than for the victorious. Adaptation to the role
of an intermediate, but respected, world power pursuing its

destiny within Europe would be painful even if British society were internally cohesive and, at least, at ease with itself in domestic affairs. However, this is far from being the case, which accentuates the problems of Britain accommodating to radical change in its external relations.

Britain faces a dual sovereignty problem. At European level, it centres on the extent to which sovereignty is to be shared externally with other nation states. At national level, it revolves around the question of how sovereignty is to be shared internally with the UK's nations and regions. Looked at from the vantage of the British state as currently constituted, sovereignty could be drained from the centre outwards towards Europe and internally towards the nations and regions. To yield sovereignty in one direction could create the preconditions for conceding it in the other. The key to the dual constitutional problem lies in the debate about Britain rather than the debate about Europe. The solution to the first is the precondition to the solution of the second.

Ireland and Britain are linked by a long history of political engagement, occupation, colonial rule and partition. A pattern of dependence, independence and interdependence characterises their relationship. These factors are overlaid upon extremely close social, familial, cultural and artistic links between the peoples of these islands, both historical and contemporary. They are complicated by the cauldron of identity problems facing Northern Ireland, as Britain is transformed in ways that will change the political entity to which Unionists have devoted their loyalty.

Ireland and Britain have had very difference experiences of European integration. For Ireland the multilateralisation of economic, political and diplomatic relations with the EC/EU has been something of a liberation, reducing post-colonial dependence on Britain and setting the scene for a normal interdependent relationship with the neighbouring island if the Northern Ireland question is resolved. Ireland gained influence as a small state by pooling sovereignty in a law-governed international setting. By contrast Britain, with its absolutist conception of sovereignty exercised by the crown-in-parliament, has been constantly reluctant to cede it.

But precisely because of their close relations Ireland has a profound interest in seeing Britain's European and domestic sovereignty questions resolved in ways that will promote normalised relations between the two states. The prospect that the UK could remain out of the EMU indefinitely posed real problems for the Irish economy, exposed as it could be to competitive devaluations. This would be the case even if it was confirmed that the long period of relative economic decline suffered by Britain had indeed come to an end, as analysis tended to show. In the same way, the prospect that Britain would choose to opt for maximal flexibility in its relations with Europe, combined with the inevitable political volatility as it made its dual sovereignty transition, posed difficult choices for Irish policy-makers on whether to opt for the EU core group or an alliance with Britain. In this perspective it could take up to ten years for Britain to resolve its European question satisfactorily.

The study analysed these issues in detail by way of an overall essay, *Britain's European Question: the Issues for Ireland*, and then with chapters of commentary on politics, EMU, competitiveness, Northern Ireland, security policy and the 1996 Intergovernmental conference by individual authors. In its "Summing-up and Conclusions" five broad scenarios concerning the future of the European Union in terms of British involvement were offered. Probabilities were assigned to them and they were evaluated with respect to Irish interests. They were as follows:

Mosaic Europe

A multi-tiered structure for Europe with a mosaic of policies – different member states opting for the menus of policies which would best suit their individual interests, but with no two menus identical, save in the case of those which volunteer for the full list and thereby constitute a core Europe. For Ireland that would be the least desirable scenario, since the tension between European membership and British partnership would be at its most acute.

The Outsider

Britain pursues a lone strategy in relation to the EU, as was done by the Major government in relation to the Social Chapter. In that case, the unitary structure of the institutions would be preserved for all other member states, even though there would be differences in the speed with which they assumed common responsibilities. Effectively, all states except Britain would be in the core. Here, Ireland would have to determine for itself the timing and manner of its adherence to the *acquis communautaire*, depending on its exposure to British exceptionalism; but it would be understood by other member states that its ultimate goal would be to do so. The Schengen clauses in the Amsterdam Treaty were later to provide a concrete example of this scenario.

Belated Union

The third scenario was predicted to be the most desirable for the future solidarity of the Union and even the most likely. It would consist of concentric circles with a group of the most willing and able comprising the *avant-garde* of integration and with the others free to join later by mutual agreement. In this case Britain would continue to exhibit the late-joiner syndrome, and for Ireland the dilemma would not be so acute as in the first two scenarios, since Britain would be committed to eventual membership of all aspects of integration. The problem would be one of timing rather than of eventual goals.

The Gambler

A fourth scenario foresaw that the UK's strategy might take a change of direction and decide to opt-in with each new initiative, but gamble on being able to change it later from the inside. To some extent, that has been the UK's broad strategy since joining the EC/EU; the Community budget or the CAP are cases in point, although the Social Chapter revealed the limitations of this approach. Britain as a gambler would be the cause of unpredictability within the broad integration process but, at least, the problem would be shared in common with all other member states.

A Leader

The final, most benign scenario for the Union as a whole foresaw a Britain fully committed to playing a leading role in shaping the future of Europe. Although it was considered to be the least likely in 1996, the prospect was deemed so inherently attractive that other member states would persist in pursuing it as the desired end goal. This scenario would ensure balance between the large states, inject a plurality of values into the system which most would welcome, and ensure a robust cultural diversity which some believe could otherwise be lost. For Ireland, this would be the best of all worlds. British-Irish relations could then be optimised and the benefits from EU membership maximised, providing large sate-small state relations were not detrimentally affected through the emergence of a *directoire*.

IRELAND'S ROLE

It would be in Ireland's interests to foster those circumstances that could allow Britain to match the pace of its constitutional reform with its involvement in Europe. The internal debate would dictate what may be possible in relations with Europe. The minimal acceptable scenario for Ireland is a belated union. The pursuit of a strategy designed to keep Britain in the integration process would require great sensitivity by other member states to Britain's constitutional conundrum, which is not widely understood elsewhere. Ireland could best pursue its interests and those of the Union as a whole by acting where possible as the mediator between the UK and other member states, or, more accurately, as the privileged interpreter of two agendas which could easily prove contradictory rather than complementary. The twin aims of Irish policy, peace in the island and prosperity within Europe, have created an interdependence with Britain which needs to be nourished and sustained.

METHODOLOGY

The methodology adopted in the following chapters mirrors that pursued in *Britain's European Question*. Each author reviews a particular aspect of UK policy in the form of a narrative, draws conclusions based on what the narrative discloses and, finally, offers some pointers for the future. The study is broken into three broad sections. The first focuses on "Blair's Britain" and covers the Labour project in the round. The second concerns "England's Europe" and deals with European policy in general, and with security and defence in particular. The third examines the relationship between Britain and Ireland in the light of the preceding sections.

In keeping with the methodology of the previous study, the findings of the three sections are synthesised and various conclusions are drawn for Britain's long-term perspective in Europe and their likely consequences for Ireland. Where appropriate, the implications for the Union as a whole are examined. Whereas each author is responsible for the material under his name, the Synthesis and Conclusions reflect the authors' deliberations throughout the project and in that sense can be said to represent a collective view.

The analytical approach adopted by the authors was that generally employed by a public policy institute, drawing on contemporary material from a variety of sources and using a combination of research techniques. Primary sources consisted of statements by political parties and leaders, the policy position of various public bodies, everyday reports by journalists and ongoing analysis by commentators. These primary sources were supplemented by academic analysis and studies on modern Britain. Field visits were undertaken to London, Edinburgh and Cardiff where discussions were held with various individuals engaged in the policy process and briefings received from authoritative sources. These findings were then synthesised and tested in debate within the Institute and elsewhere with analysts and practitioners. This combination of sources and techniques led finally to this study of *Blair's Britain, England's Europe* as seen in the light of developments as of autumn 2000.

But since policy is always open-ended it is the actions of decision-makers which are the stuff of policy analysis. Therefore, the main political actors were themselves the raw material for the study, with all the limitations that implies for offering reflections on a moving target. As the title of the study implies, Blair, in his capacity as the Prime Minister, was taken to be the central actor in a government bent on reforming Britain irreversibly and is consequently placed centre stage throughout.

BLAIR AS BRITAIN

This methodology can be justified on two counts: the extraordinary concentration of executive power in Britain and the dominance of a government with a large majority in parliament. To these can be added the fact that the party enjoying an unprecedented majority for one of the Left is largely of Blair's making.[12] Furthermore, his personality is a political phenomenon and his managerial style one of control going beyond the previous experience of Labour governments. The only apt analogy in this regard is Mrs Thatcher. Power, however, is not the issue in this study; rather it is the use of power to realise political ambitions. For this purpose, vision and strategy are essential and since power is largely concentrated in his hands, Blair's vision and strategy must necessarily dominate any policy analysis of contemporary Britain.

Vision is, of course, a nebulous enough topic at any time and furthermore is not generally associated with the British (or rather English) cast of mind – although Mrs Thatcher would give the lie to that. The question as to whether Blair has a vision for Britain, especially one of the grand variety, has considerably exercised the authors. As events have unfolded during the preparation of the study they have concluded that, notwithstanding what appeared at times to be some incoherence between action and thought, Blair is indeed animated by a vision, even though it is not always admitted or expressed. Speeches and writings, in opposition and in government, strongly indicate a vision of a self-confident Britain, constitutionally reordered to preserve the United Kingdom, structurally reformed to meet globalisation, socially more equitable in a way that would narrow class differences, economically more dynamic to create greater wealth, and positively proactive in European and world affairs so as to promote its national interest; in short, a Britain which is thoroughly modernised. The values underpinning this vision are more personal to Blair than they are representative of those traditionally held by his party and they thus make the focus on him all the more necessary.

There are those, including some of the authors, who dispute the existence of an overarching vision, or, who, conceding either that it exists or is being developed in reaction to events, doubt that it can be achieved. This, in turn, has brought up a point fundamental to the study; whether Blair is a political strategist. To mimic his own style of rhetoric: no strategy, no point in having vision. It has been argued within the group that by a process of induction it could be inferred that Blair, or those constituting the collective leadership of New Labour, have in fact been putting a series of mutually reinforcing strategies in place.

In politics it is often the case that while the ends may be clearly discerned the means remain somewhat obscure. From observation, Blair comes across as a leader who, when it comes to strategy, either reveals little or has little to reveal. Nevertheless, the conclusion which has eventually informed this analysis, is that Blair is best understood as a strategist. The fact that the strategy, say on constitutional reform, might be obscure in terms of its end goals, did not imply there was none. On the contrary, it could be that, either by deliberate choice or instinct, little was being revealed. In the case of Europe, the position seems to be reversed; the strategic goal of ending Britain's previous isolation can be clearly discerned but the means of ending it seem less clear cut. Nevertheless, the strategic direction of Britain's new European policy is, for the most part, marked by a hitherto absent coherence and consistency. Throughout the study there is, consequently, an underlying assumption that strategic goals exist and that the means of meeting them are being systematically pursued, albeit with a mixture of daring and caution. Whether this thesis is true remains for the reader to decide but, if it is, then the implications could be of long-term significance for Britain, for Europe, and for Ireland.

BLAIR'S BRITAIN

This realisation has influenced the choice of format, beginning with the section on "Blair's Britain". The adversarial nature of British politics leads to two considerations which are of importance here: periodically, a brave new world is inaugurated and, as often, reversed. Blair follows this pattern. His government is committed to the fundamental reform of politics, the state, society and the economy, and vows that the changes will be irreversible. It is crucial in these circumstances to measure the depth and breadth of these ambitions and to form a judgement on the extent to which they will prove irreversible in the normal course of politics. Since success with the state, society and the economy forms the political platform for European and international policy, and will determine its thrust and duration, it follows that Blair's Britain is key to an understanding of the new role for Britain in Europe.

The failure to find a role for Britain commensurate with that of empire was identified in the previous study as the main cause for exposing its *raison d'être* as a composite state to the sort of questioning that was then particularly evident in Scotland, and to a lesser extent, in Wales. The resultant identity crisis, as it was described, meant that, as Scotland[13] and Wales[14] each worked out a distinction between its own nationality and Britishness, and sought to establish a new equilibrium between them, there was a corresponding pressure on England to do likewise. Initially, there was a reluctance to explore what a difference between England and Britain entailed, although there was widespread acceptance that it existed at the level of popular culture. But the decision by the Blair government to introduce forms of self-government for Scotland and Wales, as well as for Northern Ireland, meant that the issue could not be avoided.

The particular form of quasi-federalism resulting from devolution has highlighted the incongruity and asymmetry between England and Britain. If the process of state reform is to stop short of an English parliament then the parliament in London will continue to perform two distinct constitutional roles: one for the United Kingdom as a whole and the other for England (and partly for Wales, unless and until its Assembly is given powers similar to those of the Scottish Parliament). That this has led to discussion on the future governance of England is only to be expected and one consequence has been to stimulate debate on English nationality[15] and to take it in a new direction, which could involve the possible emergence of a nationalism[16] that could counter-weigh those in Scotland and Wales and, conceivably, in Northern Ireland.

ENGLAND'S EUROPE

The discussion on these developments in the first section of the book is taken as a point of departure for the analysis in the second. The title, "England's Europe", presupposes that the English national instinct is not only distinctive but has been predominant in the formulation of British international policy. The priorities of the overwhelming majority within the United Kingdom have prevailed, as was unavoidable in the absence of symmetric federalism. The inescapable consequence has been that British and English policy on Europe, to take the example most relevant to this study, have been synonymous in style and content, and co-incident in terms of orientation and aims.

This equivalence provides the key to an understanding of Britain's long-standing problem on Europe; there are some Scottish, Welsh or Northern Irish reservations about Europe,[17] but they are minor in comparison to the scale and intensity of the English aversion to sharing sovereignty with European partners. It is hardly surprising that a once great world power should have profound difficulty in adapting to a role which puts it on a par with medium-sized European states and requires a partnership with the very countries that it persistently sought to divide historically. The concept that there are no permanent alliances in international affairs, only interests, has taken a long time to die. As a result, membership of the European Union is psychologically humiliating to English nationalists almost in the same sense that Ireland's membership of the United Kingdom of Great Britain and Ireland was humiliating to Irish nationalists. This explains why the English national identity so frequently demands a self-definition which is intrinsically anti-European; it explains too why a large majority of the population in Britain, mainly English, neither feels, nor wants to feel, European.[18] The thesis which underpins Section Two is that the British problem on Europe, which has led to serial inconsistency on the part of successive British governments and has created the awkward partnership, is essentially an English one.

From the analysis of "England's Europe" there would appear to be strong reason for believing that the Blair government, either consciously or instinctively, accepts that this is the problem. In order to placate English public opinion the decision on joining the euro, for example, has been postponed. Meanwhile, the image of "Europe" is being modified by representing the Union as a system of cooperation which protects rather than threatens the nation state. To the extent that integration may be beneficial then it is to be accepted but, it is argued, integration has virtually run its natural course. Henceforth, any new aspects of the European model will be predominately intergovernmental, although admittedly more intense and structured than in a conventional international organisation. It will be nowhere near as threatening as to impair national sovereignty, any more than NATO does (to take one example where sovereignty is pooled to the extent necessary to ensure its preservation).

BRITAIN AS LEADER

Here again vision and strategy are germane, as is the case with "Blair's Britain". The "England's Europe" now being sought would play to the English instinct to be a state in Europe more equal than others – or at least, first among equals. Europe would hopefully desist from the federalist goal and settle down to pragmatic forms of cooperation whenever common sense dictated that hanging together was better than hanging separately. Since this vision would contest that generally attributed to France and Germany, its achievement would require Britain to take on a leadership role in Europe, with a particular responsibility for success falling on Blair himself.

The issue of whether Blair aspires to *the* leadership role for himself and Britain in Europe as distinct from *a* leadership role was debated throughout the preparation of the study. It was concluded that while the first may be an aspiration, the second is more probably the expectation. What Blair is trying to achieve is that Britain should enjoy a level of influence and weight within Europe commensurate with its size. Britain on its own, not least because it has come into the European adventure late in the day, cannot hope to displace the Franco-German alliance as the engine pushing the process forward. At best, Britain can aspire only to being part of a *triad* providing a collective European leadership. Although such leadership could be greatly diffused by enlargement, nonetheless for Britain to be part of it is an ambition way beyond anything previously experienced. Its achievement would end the awkward partnership of the past and replace it with positive leadership in the future.

REDEFINING THE UNION

Blair's strategy towards that end is identified as using time and space; time to postpone the euro issue, lest it undo his goal of a second term, and space to construct a network of alliances within the Union in order to attempt to shape it to his own design. Central to such a strategy would be the task of redefining the core of EU membership and of preventing new circumstances arising which would again consign Britain to the margins. Since the Maastricht Treaty, the core has been defined as membership of the euro, a fact of which Blair and his government are acutely aware. Security could provide an alternative core, conceivably even of equal weight, and this explains the systematic attempt to make the European Security and Defence Policy the next grand ambition for the Union alongside enlargement.

Because of the other interests which have to be accommodated, in particular those of the US, this latter ambition may not succeed, however. Security and defence on their own may not become equivalent to the Community Pillar as a core competence. Moreover, enlargement has been threatening to push institutional reform to the top of the Union agenda, and since flexibility, or enhanced cooperation, could emerge as a defining issue for France and Germany in terms of maintaining momentum for further integration, Blair could be confronted with the dilemma of either going too fast for his (English) public opinion or going too slowly for his European partners. The resolution of that dilemma, should it arise, would provide further insights into the strategy by which "an unwaveringly pro-European government" can square this circle.[19]

REASSESSING THE SCENARIOS

It is our belief that, in terms of Britain's future role in Europe, the probability to be assigned to each of the five scenarios identified in the previous study (and described in the accompanying summary of its contents) has altered under Blair. In particular, the prospect of Britain being an Outsider has been firmly rejected; instead, the role of a Leader has become the preferred option. Leadership cannot, however, be credibly assumed by Britain except as part of a triad involving France and Germany, and then only on terms which satisfy the Franco-German alliance. But until Britain enters the euro, the necessary conditions cannot be satisfied, unless – and this appears unlikely to some of the authors – the Union were to take on an additional ambition of equal weight to which Britain made a unique and indispensable contribution. That could compensate for Britain's absence from the monetary core around which the Community Pillar is being constructed. In the meanwhile, Britain is constrained from being a full member of the triad. It would have to await, or engineer, a new European project on the grand scale in which it would indisputably be part of Europe's collective leadership. Britain has become, as it were, a leader-in-waiting.

The evidence accumulated during the study indicates that the leadership scenario, despite the handicap of being outside the euro, best explains the long-run orientation of the Blair government's policy on Europe. Consequently, the Outsider, Opportunist and Gambler scenarios can be dismissed for such time as New Labour enjoys office. This conclusion constitutes a significant shift in the analysis. Britain under Blair can legitimately be regarded as playing the complex role of a Late Joiner and potential Leader, with hopes of shedding the former and realising the latter.

As the study progressed, however, the popularity of the Blair government waned in the opinion polls. This raised a doubt about the general assumption that it would win a second term of office and so be able to consolidate its programme of domestic reforms, thereby largely solving the identity crisis in respect of the state and society. It also introduced a certain measure of circumspection in the minds of the authors with regard to the eventual solution of England's identity crisis over Europe.

OLD BRITAIN

Two possibilities became increasingly germane; the return of a (seriously) weakened Blair government or, less likely, of one led by William Hague. The persistence of opposition within England to EMU membership, and its increasing strength as time went on, suggested that if its current majority were to be greatly reduced another New Labour government could lack the authority to win over English public opinion. Accordingly, the possibility was raised that the referendum might be postponed. This may explain why some advocates of entry became increasingly strident in their demands that the issue be put to the test during the next election, especially after an OECD report in June 2000 concluded that the British economy adequately fulfilled the chancellor's five tests for entry.[20] This also raised the prospect that Britain might continue as a late joiner beyond what had been the most pessimistic time forecasts for EMU membership and it appeared that aspirations to be a leader in Europe could in these circumstances be severely jeopardised.

The demise of New Labour after only one term of office, were it to happen, would, of course, dramatically alter all forecasts for Britain's future in Europe. A Conservative government would maintain sterling and reject EMU; it would presumably also live up to its promise to employ its own singular version of flexibility by picking and choosing among new EU competences.[21] As a result, Britain would revert to being an awkward partner, except that it would be more likely to become an outsider rather than be permitted to dine indefinitely *à la carte* from an increasingly expansive EU menu. Were that to be so, the whole range of our original five scenarios would remain as a robust analysis of the possibilities for Britain's relationship with Europe and the probabilities previously assigned to each would be restored to those set out in the first study.

VOLATILITY

The fact that the future scenarios for Britain in Europe can still range from one extreme of the spectrum to the other has forced some British commentators to reflect on the root cause of such volatility. The British electoral system, as can be imagined, is sometimes identified as the chief culprit for systematic instability.[22] Indeed, it is argued by some that until such time as an element of proportionality is introduced into that system, it will prove impossible to eliminate the endemic polarisation of British politics and to reach a durable settlement on the European question.

Undoubtedly, the electoral system facilitates (or exaggerates) the adversarial nature of politics in Westminster, and it is instructive that forms of proportional representation were introduced into the Scottish, Welsh and European Parliament elections, as they had been earlier for Northern Ireland, as an antidote to the excesses of the majoritarian system. But when no fundamental consensus exists in a society about itself (as it generally does in Scotland and Wales) it is doubtful if consensus politics can be manufactured at parliamentary level. England, it would seem from contemporary discourse, is still far from that state of mind which makes broad coalitions of interests possible at different levels of governance.

This somewhat sombre conclusion sheds light on Blair's determination to win at least one more term of office and even to put the Conservatives out of government for a generation. His objective is to make them unelectable, either by transforming the nature of politics, or by reforming the electoral system, thus making coalitions with the Liberal Democrats inevitable – or both. If, however, a significant minority of opinion were to see itself manoeuvred out of power on a permanent basis the result would be deeply divisive and the reaction to that exclusion could accentuate the steady drift of the Conservatives towards an English nationalism. Under certain circumstances that nationalism could put the coherence – even the existence – of the new United Kingdom at risk and place positive engagement in Europe out of sight. For these reasons, there can be no guarantee that progress towards Blair's Britain is irreversible – or that his England's Europe is assured.

A CAUTIONARY NOTE

These conclusions prompt two further considerations; the fragility of New Labour's electoral base and the ideological nature of English politics. Chapter Three opens with a salutary reminder that Blair was elected by less that one-third of the adult population, which obviously means that two-thirds of those entitled to vote did not support him. In view of the fact that the turnout was the lowest since 1935 it is clear that abstentions were above normal and analysis suggests that two million of these were Conservative voters. A further two million who had previously voted Conservative switched to New Labour. In addition, the Referendum Party drained Conservative support, and tactical voting by Liberal Democrat supporters increased the New Labour vote. This combination of factors resulted in a huge – but deceptive – parliamentary majority for New Labour, even though the party's actual vote nationally was below that of the three previous Conservative governments. The first-past-the-post system, together with the geographic distribution of the votes, leveraged New Labour's plurality amongst the electorate into an overwhelming majority in terms of parliamentary seats. Were differential abstention to be reduced among Conservative voters in the next election, and were former supporters to be won back, the overall effect could be leveraged in the opposite direction, with the final outcome dependent on the vagaries of tactical voting and the particular geographic spread of each party's support.

The euphoria which initially greeted New Labour's victory and the size of its parliamentary majority masked those electoral realities and led many, including some of the authors it must be admitted, to assume that a new era had been ushered in and that Britain's long-term prospects could be predicated on New Labour being in office for at least two terms (perhaps involving a coalition with the Liberal Democrats). With the dissipation of the euphoria and the belated appearance of mid-term jitters, these electoral realities bore in on most commentators. This in turn led to a greater understanding of the caution with which Blair has approached Europe and of the determination with which he has pursued some domestic policies which might traditionally be regarded as right-wing.[23] The Blair team have, no doubt, always been alive to the narrow base on which the party's victory has rested, and have been aware of the exceptional electoral circumstances that transformed a minority popular vote into a huge parliamentary majority. The mixture of daring and caution which has puzzled some observers may have sprung from a realisation that the New Jerusalem has been founded on shifting sands. Perhaps it is wise to conclude an analysis of "Blair's Britain" on this cautionary note.

PRAGMATIC OR DOGMATIC?

In respect of "England's Europe" a quite different note is necessary. The English portrayal of themselves as pragmatic and reserved has been taken by other Europeans at face value as representing the national character and, by extension, the nature of English politics. But to accept this self-portrait unquestioningly would be as unwise as to assume that the Blair government had been given a lease in perpetuity on Downing Street. Even the most casual observation of English politics reveals deep ideological cleavages which are expressed in competing views of society and the state, generally held with a passion which is at variance with the traits of pragmatism, tolerance and stolidity that are said to grace the English character. The disjunction between the reality of politics and the representation of the national character is striking.

Outside observers need to reflect on this paradox. Britain has been the one major member state which persistently adopted what can only be described as a dogmatic position on Europe; most other member states have been pragmatic. The history of integration demonstrates that the member state claiming to be pragmatic has generally been ideological (John Major's "game, set and match", as it were), while those accused of being ideologically driven have, in the main, been accommodating and prepared to compromise. This more than suggests an element of self-deception at work in England, one which may be dangerous for other Europeans who accept it without qualification. Monnet, no less, may have been guilty of this fault when he argued that the "pragmatic British" should always be confronted with the facts rather than with grand ambitions.[24]

But outside observers need to reflect on another phenomenon; despite the predilection for the late-joiner syndrome there has always been a sizeable volume of support within England for a positive engagement in Europe. The contemporary debate proves this still to be the case. While the Eurosceptics appear to dominate and to control much of the media commentary there are many individuals, groups and organisations in favour of membership of the eurozone and of a positive commitment to EU membership. Across the political divide and throughout business and academia the case for such commitment is made in the face of what often amounts to a torrent of anti-euro and anti-Europe propaganda. Key political figures, from Edward Heath and Ken Clarke to Robin Cook and, indeed, Tony Blair himself, speak regularly in this vein; the Prime Minister's passionate statements on both Europe and the euro during his solo appearance on BBC TV's final edition of "Question Time" in mid-2000 was the visible example of such advocacy.

As this volume illustrates, the European debate in Britain has been divisive in both main political parties and in public opinion as a whole. However, it must be recognised that there has always been pro-European sentiment within all parties, as well as business and trade union circles. The appearance of Jacques Delors at the Trades Union Congress in 1988, and the consequent shift of trade union opinion to a pro-European stance based on the attractions of European social policy, was a defining moment within the wider labour movement. As this change in orientation was taking place on the centre-left the opposite tendency was emerging in Conservative circles, culminating in the near disintegration of the

Major government in the mid-nineties. Nonetheless, the CBI has generally been pro-European, thus giving balance to the support from the social partners for the European project.

Many pro-Europeans seem troubled, however, by the policy stance of the Labour administration and frustrated at the "wait and see" position of the Chancellor of the Exchequer, Gordon Brown, on the euro. Within the *Britain in Europe* movement there has been considerable controversy over the appropriate pace and intensity of activity in a situation where the government appears unwilling to take a firm, positive stance. Resignations have occurred within some pro-European bodies because of continued uncertainties over the policy framework within which their activities have to be planned.

Despite these uncertainties and frustrations, the *Britain in Europe* organisation and the *European Movement* spearhead a range of information campaigns, seminars and public meetings on current European themes and have achieved considerable publicity – not always of a positive nature. The difficulties connected with the public launch of *Britain in Europe*, arising from arguments about the precise role of Prime Minister Blair, detracted from the fact that the event brought together a powerful cross-party grouping on a pro-European platform on 14 October 1999. With the Prime Minister were the Chancellor and Foreign Secretary, former Conservative ministers, Ken Clarke and Michael Heseltine, and the leader of the Liberal Democrats, Charles Kennedy, together with leading figures from business, trade unions and the media. Richard Branson, Adair Turner of the CBI and Ken Jackson of the ETU made clear their commitment to the dual cause of the euro and Europe. The Campaign Director of *Britain in Europe*, Simon Buckley, claimed that "we have assembled a truly historic coalition behind the *Britain in Europe* campaign. We represent the mainstream common sense view of the vast majority of British people that Britain is better off as a strong and influential player in Europe". Whether that is the case may be questioned in the light of the opinion poll results but many analysts hold the view that there are limits to the influence of Euroscepticism – in other words, that Britain will not leave the Union notwithstanding the widespread aversion to the need to share sovereignty.

The fundamental question of continued British membership of the Union has, nevertheless, surfaced as an issue. Debate has been fuelled by political and media campaigns based on the proposition that Britain should cut adrift from the European project, with one media tycoon, the Canadian owner of the *Daily Telegraph*, Conrad Black, strongly arguing the case for UK membership of NAFTA. The pro-European groupings have reacted by tailoring their activities to more effective communication of the basic message that EU membership is vital to British interests. Well organised and professional bodies, such as the Federal Trust and the Centre for European Reform, have developed programmes of research and communication on European themes which are of the highest quality and which provide both a rationale for pro-European policies in government and for a distinctive British input to Europe's many contemporary debates. Charles Grant's vision of *Europe 2010* is a case in point. The recently formed think-tank, the Foreign Policy Centre, has published an important tract, *Network Europe*, written by its Director, Mark Leonard – which is another example of the sort of innovative analysis Britain can bring to the wider European debate. Business-centred organisations, such as *Europe-21*, headed by former Commissioner Stanley Clinton Davis and Commission Secretary General, David Williamson, play an influential role in building links between UK commerce and industry and the European institutions.

Furthermore, British academic work on major European themes is of a high standard with a current Economic and Social Research Council project, *One Europe or Several?*, devoting substantial public funding to a programme of research, publication and seminar organisation involving many university faculties and leading researchers. Directed by Professor Helen Wallace, this impressive programme covers topics ranging from identity and citizenship to globalisation and, even, the policy options available to Ireland within the eurozone. UK universities, such as the South Bank University in London and the University of Sussex, are generating significant work on many European themes. The European Programme of Chatham House (The Royal Institute of International Affairs) has continuously contributed to British understanding of European matters, with particular reference to the twin issues of security and enlargement. It can be concluded that there is no shortage of informed analysis of European affairs or advocacy of a pro-European position.

It must also be underlined that there are interesting, and sometimes significant, differences in attitude within Britain's regions. *Britain in Europe* launches in Scotland and Wales were strongly supported across the political spectrum and in both nations the goal of an enhanced autonomy within closer European integration has received widespread support.

These references to the various strands of opinion favouring a positive and self-confident role in Europe are necessary lest it be inferred that Euroscepticism is a universal British phenomenon, particularly in England. A more nuanced conclusion is necessary. Although antipathy to Europe may represent the majority view, an influential minority holds an opposite but equally trenchant belief that Britain cannot prosper in a state of detachment from Europe. As the previous analysis suggests, these differences can be reduced to competing, and contrary, visions concerning identity. It could be the case that the weight of informed opinion will prevail and that the more popular attitude will be modified by a process of persuasion led by those who view British and European interests as largely coincident. This implies a dynamic rather than a static analysis of the forces contending for the British, and particularly the English, identity, But for the moment, the implications of the current state of public opinion have to be assessed in terms of the political weight of those who are negative on Europe, since the democratic system must ultimately reflect the views of the majority and nuanced analysis, however valid, must give precedence to political realities. These realities, of necessity, inform the following conclusions.

IMPLICATIONS FOR EUROPE

The English identity crisis is real, unresolved and problematic for Europe. It is being debated on terms which intimately involve Europe: sovereignty, destiny and cultural identity. It is overlaid with history and contextualised by the future – the very parameters which define Europe. In the case of England, the focus is different from that in other member states; integration is seen as a retreat from a great past. Elsewhere, however, it is more normally seen as an advance into a better future.

Other Europeans need to grapple with the social realities of an England which has put its vision of Europe at odds with theirs and need to work out the implications. The specific differences which define the English national character need to be understood with a sympathy grounded more on detached analysis than on a ready acceptance of caricature; and they need, too, to be accommodated with patience and finesse. The late-joiner syndrome should be seen for what it is: a deeply troubled search for a new order internally and externally – a search which history, as well as geography, has made singularly difficult. The adversarial nature of English politics does not help in finding solutions; neither does the confrontational intensity with which this debate is all too often conducted there.[25]

The authors have become increasingly aware of these obstacles to a settled consensus on Britain's future role in Europe, and more convinced that these issues must be finally resolved in the heartland of England itself. From this, they have concluded that other member states should proceed with particular caution at any future IGC lest the speed at which the European convoy advances proves too fast for Britain. As time went on, this conclusion began to apply to the IGC scheduled for completion at the end of 2000 because of increasing demands to amend the Amsterdam Treaty's provisions on flexibility. These resulted from concerns that widening and deepening the integration process were irreconcilable unless provision was made for an *avant-garde*, or a pioneer group of member states, to sustain the momentum of deepening.

Such developments added force to a consideration which was uppermost in the minds of the authors: Britain adds immeasurably to the European project and without a full British presence Europe will be incomplete and deficient. Consequently, nothing should be done that would force Britain prematurely and perhaps unnecessarily to make choices for which it is not yet equipped, and for which it will not be ready for at least some time to come. In dealing with Britain, patience is not only a virtue other Europeans should practise, it is a political necessity which they should accept. This applies with particular force to proposals for developing a hard core within the Union or creating a Europe of concentric circles, as were advanced by the German Foreign Minister, Joschka Fischer, and the French President, Jacques Chirac. If expressed as a medium-term ambition, a hard-core Europe need not exclude Britain; if presented as a short-term goal, it could. That fear seemingly led the Italian Prime Minister, Guiliano Amato, to echo the argument that a core without Britain was inconceivable, even while conceding that an *avant-garde* was ultimately necessary. This did no more than emphasise the prime necessity for getting the timing right when embarking on any new phase of integration. In an attempt to buy time and postpone further debate on a multi-speed Europe, Blair indicated that

Britain would be willing to support greater flexibility. This tactic can only work if other member states suppress their impatience at the slow speed of the European convoy and defer consideration of the core until the next IGC. The question of timing is all the more important because, as was always likely, the next general election will be fought on Europe, with the issue being joined on the euro despite the Blair government's desire to defer the matter by employing a "prepare and decide" strategy. This policy became less tenable as controversy grew throughout 2000 over the negative effects of a strong sterling on inward investment and manufacturing competitiveness, and as senior ministers expressed different views on the electoral practicalities of the strategy. Furthermore, if the IGC keeps to the timetable already agreed, ratification of the Treaty amendments flowing from it will place Europe on the political agenda immediately prior to the general election, thus making it all the more likely that Europe will figure as a major campaign issue, perhaps even the main issue should the Conservative Party be so disposed. Those considerations make it all the more necessary for other Europeans to take account of British domestic politics when debating the future of the Union.

This is in no way to argue that Britain should be given a *carte blanche* in determining the pace and direction of integration. On the contrary, greater understanding by other Europeans demands a corresponding response from Britain. Use will have to be made of the space afforded to lay the awkward partnership finally to rest. But the time-frame is relatively short, given that enlargement will necessitate a fundamental reassessment of the Union within a matter of years. This consideration suggests that, if progress towards ever closer union is to proceed without periodic disruption from a key member state, a more informed dialogue between Britain and Europe is essential, and vigorous leadership within Britain is indispensable. That is easier said than done, of course. The next IGC could coincide with the UK referendum on the euro. This would add to the difficulties of conducting an open dialogue on Europe's future since the British public, particularly its English component, will be prey to fears of a "superstate", and more prone to believe the worst. National and European politics could pull in opposite directions and their competing demands would prove unusually difficult to reconcile. If they are not, then the prospects for Britain's future engagement with Europe will be more malign than has been accepted conventionally since the election of the Blair government.

IMPLICATIONS FOR IRELAND

For Ireland, the most benign scenario is that Britain should progressively resolve its dual-sovereignty problem and thereafter play a positive role in Europe. Although the threat of a weak sterling has receded since the previous study was completed and the Irish economy has strengthened competitively in the interim, joint participation with Britain in the eurozone would eliminate the possibility of competitive distortions induced by exchange-rate movements and this could only be beneficial. The assumption would be, of course, that the rate at which sterling entered the euro was set somewhere around or above its equilibrium level of DM 2.70 and vigilance will have to be exercised to ensure this. Blair's evident determination to move security to the core of the Union need not pose dangers to Ireland's policy on neutrality. In all likelihood, a European security policy will reside alongside a separate and distinct European defence policy based on NATO and, hence, will not require a commitment on mutual defence, to which the Irish government remains opposed.[26]

A benign scenario of full-hearted British participation in the Union and in EMU also has its particular debits. The European Union favoured by the Blair government would be likely to be more intergovernmentalist than that experienced up to the Amsterdam Treaty. It is of course accepted that intergovernmentalism as classically understood is no longer entirely apt as a description of cooperation under the Second Pillar, or what remains of the Third, and should be taken instead as a form of enhanced and continuous co-ordination of national policies within permanent Treaty-based structures. It might better be understood as trans-governmentalism or trans-nationalism.[27] Nevertheless, a long-term repercussion of this particular form of intergovernmentalism is that the Community method could become diluted by complementary, but competing, systems of governance, and that the role of the common institutions could be altered to the detriment of the Commission and to the benefit of the Council. Ireland would stand to suffer from the first and could lose from the second, especially if a de facto *directoire* were to emerge as a consequence of enlargement. It would be in Britain's direct interest that it should; but not in that of Ireland.

As the Tampere, Helsinki and Lisbon Councils suggest, the European Council is slowly assuming a leadership role not intended for such a body by the original Treaties, and this correspondingly alters the role assigned to the Commission and reduces the weight of that body's influence as the motor of integration and guardian of the Treaties. Inevitably, this gives the large member states greater potential to determine the common European future, and Blair has been quick to recognise this opportunity, and even quicker to seek to exploit it. As a reaction to the greater diversity stemming from enlargement, it is conceivable that the larger member states will use their political muscle to the maximum in a common accord to impose coherence on divergent interests, thereby changing the rules of the game as they have applied to date: no winners and losers – just winners. The outcome could well be the emergence of losers.

IMPLICATIONS FOR BRITISH-IRISH RELATIONS

These predictions could, quite naturally, be upset were the response to enlargement to take another course and lead to the creation of an *avant-garde* intent on deepening integration by extending the Community method, and possibly centred on a perceived need for closer macro-economic co-ordination inside the eurozone. Undoubtedly, such a development would be at odds with Blair's long-term vision of a Europe of nation states and would be in conflict with his ambition to neutralise the effects of Britain's non-participation in the euro. Should an *avant-garde* emerge with Ireland as a member and Britain a late joiner at best, this could pose the very strategic dilemma which successive Irish governments have sought to avoid; convergent interests with Britain on Northern Ireland but divergent interests on key European questions.

These debits, serious as they might be, would be greatly magnified were Britain to resume its more familiar role of the awkward partner following the return of a Conservative government. The most obvious threat then could be that which in the face of a strong sterling and a weak euro seemed most remote – British over-competitiveness. At some point over a ten-year cycle, to take William Hague's own time-frame, sterling would depreciate against the euro and it is conceivable that it could again sink to the levels which caused such concern in Ireland in the early 1990s. Unlike then, devaluation of the Irish pound would not be an option. The capacity of the Irish economy to cope with such a situation would be totally dependent on domestic policy responses and would place even greater emphasis on the continuation of the consensual model based on social partnership.

As an additional debit, a logical consequence of the Conservative Party's policy on Europe is that Britain would become an outsider. In a sense not yet fully appreciated, the Blair government is Britain's last chance on Europe and a reversion by Britain to something smacking of the era of Mrs Thatcher would meet with little understanding and less sympathy in other member states. The flexibility clause would then take on its originally intended role, and the European convoy would steam ahead, with Britain veering off on another course. The options for Ireland, if past policy is any guide, would be limited: the national interest of the Irish State would require it to stay with Europe. As a consequence, the new north/south relationship in Ireland would come under pressure and interdependence with Britain, which common membership of Europe has helped to create, could arguably give way to a mix of relationships, the full intricacies of which it is difficult to identify at this remove. It is unlikely that the implications of this would be as benign as those experienced to date in the shift of relationships from dependence to independence and then to interdependence. The implications could be even more complicated if a new Conservative government failed to win majorities in Scotland and Wales leading to tensions over devolution which threatened the integrity of the United Kingdom, or even its very existence.

CONCLUSION

The sub-title of this study is *A View From Ireland*. Two comments are necessary, perhaps, by way of explanation. The first has been largely dealt with earlier, where the origins of the previous and current studies were recalled. It is self-evident that a small country should keep a weather-eye on a large neighbour. But aside from the insights which might prove helpful for the development of Irish strategy on Europe, it is hoped that the analysis may also assist strategists in other member states. The Irish are, by the nature of things, privileged outsiders when it comes to Britain, as the opening of this Introduction confirmed, and may be in a better position than most to analyse developments in Britain and to draw necessary conclusions, without suffering from the disadvantage of partisan engagement.

The second comment relates to the nature of the study itself. It may well be argued that it suffers from a defect inherent in policy analysis; it may presume patterns of political behaviour where none exist and so be too abstract in its conclusions. Those engaged in the hurly-burly of British politics might not accept that their actions described here have quite the same degree of coherence as the study presents. For them, as for politicians and senior officials everywhere, crisis management is the everyday norm, rather than a measured pursuit of long-term goals.

Yet, as the experience of most of the authors would suggest, politics generally has a purpose going beyond the mere management of events. And it is the goals generated by a sense of purpose that impose patterns of behaviour which, from a privileged position of detachment, allow for order to be discerned in the midst of what may appear, from the inside, to be more akin to chaos. In the last analysis, there can hardly be dispute over two key assertions made throughout this study. The Blair government is demonstrably trying to create a New Britain and to fashion a new policy on Europe. In the face of these two historic developments, this study is offered as an aid towards understanding the future of Britain and assessing the implications of what has been happening there since 1997. If it proves to be both timely and helpful then the task of the project group will have been accomplished.

---

1 Gillespie, ed. (1996).
2 George (1994).
3 FitzGerald (1997).
4 IEA (1996).
5 O'Donnell, ed. (1991); De Buitléir and Thornhill (1993).
6 Gillespie, ed. (1996).
7 Marr (1999); Paxman (1999).
8 Denman (1998); Siedentop (2000), Chapter 4.
9 IEA (1996).
10 Young (1998).
11 Gillespie, ed. (1996).
12 Gould (1998).
13 Nairn (1999).
14 Gray and Osmond (1997).
15 Paxman (1999).
16 Millar (2000).

Section One

BLAIR'S BRITAIN

Section One

Blair's Britain

BACKGROUND AND CONTEXT

The impression of a landslide in the 1997 general election was much more apparent at Westminster than in the country at large. This explained Labour's boldness and caution in office, making for a presidential style of government and a centralised control of the party apparatus and media relations. Popular perceptions have been affected by these characteristics, contributing to disenchantment with Labour in office. These characteristics also have made it more difficult to devolve power to the UK's nations and regions – or even within the Labour Party itself.

The transformation of Labour's ideology through the so-called Third Way accompanied the transformation of the party itself, which has made it much more professionally organised as a machine to win parliamentary elections. Class and interest-based groups were seen as increasingly irrelevant to political change. This was in keeping with the appeal to middle-England voters through the pledge not to increase Conservative levels of taxation for two years; but it underestimated the need to hold on to core Labour supporters and the commitment even of middle-England voters to welfare and social cohesion.

New Labour accepted globalisation as a central reality of today's world, to which governments have to adapt or perish. Supply-side reforms are taken to be the only realistic means of asserting competitive advantage in a much more interdependent world. Education, training, labour flexibility, welfare-to-work reforms, deregulation and privatisation are the major policy instruments available to governments. Their capacity to change those international conditions is limited because of capital's mobility.

New Labour accepted European integration as the legitimate and appropriate means of governing a globalised world. Britain's international position and interests are best protected in that setting; outside, its influence would be much reduced, not least in

Washington. But integration must reflect the realities of globalisation and its policy constraints, just as national policy does. Hence the pressure to reform the EU in the Anglo-British image.

Blair aimed to perpetuate Labour in government by realigning British politics through forging an accord between his party and the Liberal Democrats, thus putting the Conservatives out of office for a generation. This would require electoral reform as the price. But he could not be sure of bringing the party along with him when he had such an unexpectedly large parliamentary majority. Such a strategy would have to be disguised until after the next election, when it would be easier to implement, assuming the Labour majority would be smaller.

Blair is a convinced unionist with a commitment to preserve the United Kingdom from disintegration. Labour's programme of sweeping constitutional change is intended to address this crisis of political and state identity in the four dimensions dealt with in the IEA's 1996 book. The centralised state, constructed to run an empire as well as to conduct wars and subsequently to deliver welfare in the twentieth century, still faces a dual constitutional question as it suffers the combined impact of European integration and subnational devolution. The key question is the relationship between internal domestic and external European change, with the resolution of internal issues affecting the pace of the resolution of the external ones as well as the coherence with which that task is addressed. Until both are resolved Britain is likely to remain an uncertain, even a volatile partner in the EU.

The instinct to preserve conflicted with the desire to reform by devolving the UK state apparatus. The New Labour leadership's centralist instinct to maintain control over the pace of change, its preservationist attitude to the central state, and the parameters of Labour's internal policy debates, together, threatened to contradict the formal commitment to constitutional transformation. The minimum reforms necessary to devolve were difficult to reconcile with the maximum that it was possible to do within the Labour Party and its electoral politics. Half-hearted reforms rebound by radicalising demands and increasing dissatisfactions, because they deliver too little too late. There was a failure to articulate a coherent programme of change to voters and party activists, even if a coherent strategy existed to relate them. Blair remained preoccupied with winning battles against Old Labour antagonists in order to prevent the emergence of a power base which could compete politically with the mainstream in a second term with a reduced majority.

In these circumstances the media assumed particular importance. Given the weakness and disarray of the Conservatives after the election they have fulfilled many of the functions of a political opposition. The systematic Europhobia of large sections of the media has consequently profoundly affected the political arena and public opinion. Blair's government has had to take strategic account of that fact, which helps to explain its emphasis on media management.

But the media were also responding to ambiguities in the government's objectives of securing a second term, realigning British politics and bringing Britain to the heart of Europe. Indecision, hesitation and disagreements in pursuing them were quite legitimate news stories – especially as it is hard to identify one big idea in the Third Way programme, which relies rather on the accumulation of small- to medium-sized ideas about supply side, labour market and welfare reforms.

The failure to assert decisive leadership on many of these issues made the government vulnerable to a new electoral volatility that Britain shares with other developed democracies. Party identification is much weaker than before; so is the association between voting behaviour and class. Electoral volatility benefited Labour in 1997; but if core voters switch or abstain, that would dangerously erode its electoral base. The Conservatives staged a political and organisational recovery in the first half of 2000, as Labour suffered from belated mid-term blues and something of a crisis of political confidence.

Changing political and national identities also affect political choices. That made political management more difficult and helped to explain the emphasis on style and image, essentially consumer values - characteristic of the New Labour machine – and the emphasis on youth and novelty, which could become vacuous if not part of a communicable big idea.

The radical constitutional changes introduced in Blair's first year in office are well defined as "fundamental alterations in the arrangements of the United Kingdom, which amount to a reshaping of the British state". It is a work in progress, but a process rather than a settled event. Crucial elements of the change, including electoral reform, freedom of information, House of Lords' reform, regional assemblies in England and constitutional entrenchment, are as yet unresolved and quite ambiguous – and therefore difficult to communicate clearly.

The Scottish question is crucial for the future of the UK, as its national and political identities cohere through devolution, and develop and deepen the process, creating neuralgic points with Westminster over shared or disputed competences and relations with Brussels. If this is mishandled, disintegration rather than reintegration of the UK is put more clearly on the agenda. Similar, if less well-developed, processes are at work in Wales. The Scottish question could be resolved in good part through the Labour Party, which has become the unionist party, but an election as a result of which the Conservatives ruled Westminster, and Labour Scotland and Wales, would exacerbate such neuralgia – as, of course, would a euro referendum defeated by an English majority.

The English question, if conceived as an exercise in national identity, could open up the spectre of a nationalism centred on an English parliament. That has been avoided so far. Regional assemblies within England, which seem likely to be driven by increasingly resented regional inequalities, would not resolve this problem; they would be an expression of democracy, but not of national identity.

Because of the sheer size of England within the UK it is useful to conceive these constitutional changes in terms of an asymmetric quasi-federalisation, as in Spain and Canada, rather than the classical federal models familiar in states such as Germany, Belgium and Austria. If they are carried through successfully, Britain will have the opportunity to contribute to the EU debate, and a rolling programme of asymmetric quasi-federalism – on what could become the British as well as the Spanish model – would better reflect the actual processes at play in European integration than would misconceived polarities of federalism and national sovereignty, superstate versus the nation state. If the alternatives on offer are better described as somewhere between what Jacques Delors has called an unprecedented federalism of nation states, and Jacques Chirac's formula of a united Europe of states, then such a British debate could have much to contribute, and could even lead the discussion.

But it would be a great mistake to underestimate the difficulties involved for Britain in making the transition from a polity defined by an unwritten constitution, absolute parliamentary sovereignty, adversarialism and centralised power to a more European one based on devolution of political authority, consensualism, coalitions and entrenchment of rights.

The British economy has been characterised for most of the twentieth century by poor economic performance, relative to

Germany and the USA in particular, and by higher inflation. The trend became more acute after 1950, when most of the rest of Europe also outpaced the UK. There seems to have been a change in the 1980s and 1990s, with growth rates and inflation converging towards those of the rest of the EU. However, claims that the structural reforms carried out in Britain mean that it will outperform the EU average over the long term look premature. The fundamental problems of poor productivity, and lack of innovation and skills remain. So does the resulting imbalance between supply and demand in the economy. The low-inflation objective of the independent Bank of England is being bought at the price of higher interest rates and an overvalued exchange rate which threaten to make the underlying problems worse.

New Labour has specifically targeted these fundamental weaknesses, but they can only be cured over many years. The key question, but one which seems to have received little mention in the debate on joining the euro, is whether membership would help or hinder this essential process of strengthening the productive capacity of the economy.

CHAPTER TWO

The Labour Project

Paul Gillespie

INTRODUCTION

Tony Blair's Labour Party was swept into office on 1 May 1997 with 419 parliamentary seats out of 659. The Conservatives, with 165 seats, had not lost so badly since 1906. In terms of popular votes, Labour secured 43 per cent, 13.5 million votes – but this was a smaller share than at any election in the 1950s and 1960s, on a turnout of 71.5%, the lowest since 1935. Labour's overall vote was only the eighth largest in the twentieth century and was lower than that of the Conservatives in 1992, 1987 or 1979, although the average national swing to Labour was the highest since 1945. Two million voters actually switched from the Conservatives to Labour – most of them among the lower middle class C1 group, including clerical workers and lower managerial staff, teachers and nurses, and among semi-skilled manual workers.[1] Overall, 31% of the qualified electorate gave Labour its triumph; just 22% backed the Conservatives, while almost 29% did not vote at all. The Conservatives suffered from a reduced turnout of their supporters much more than Labour. In elections since then, notably the European elections in June 1999 and the local elections in May 2000, there was a marked tendency for traditional Labour voters to abstain, in what many said was a protest against the failure of New Labour to deliver on expectations and promises.

The impression of a landslide was, therefore, much more apparent at Westminster than in the country at large, which helps explain the combination of boldness and caution that became characteristic of Labour in office. Blair's leadership was spectacularly confirmed by the result, as was his ideological programme of New Labour reformism. These have made for a presidential style of government and office-holding, based on a huge parliamentary majority but one requiring perpetual reconfirmation among the voters. Blair's preference for centralised control of his party apparatus – together with what opponents say is his neglect of the cabinet and parliament[2] – were confirmed in office by his emphasis on tactical media management and obsessive concern with reproducing his pre-election victory over his Old Labour opponents. Commentators and political observers underlined the resulting evangelical approach to political communication and populist method of political consultation, in which referenda and focus groups assumed equal importance with parliamentary authority.[3] The approach contains unexpected streaks of arrogance and authoritarianism. Despite its undoubted brilliance in communications skills, the tendency to hyperbole can be irritatingly vacuous, particularly when there is no big idea to communicate.

THE THIRD WAY

These characteristics have affected the implementation of Blair's programme in government and the forward projection of it towards the next election; they have increasingly, too, affected popular perceptions of him and his government. To determine that programme's coherence and consistency, in theory and practice, it is necessary to understand Blair's own political beliefs and statements in and out of office. This especially applies to those concerning the so-called Third Way between traditional corporatist social democracy and the neo-liberal laissez-faire individualist conservatism exemplified by Margaret Thatcher. Calling this the radical centre, Blair insists on the "need to reform the European social model, not play around with it. Make it work in the long term to achieve the values it stands for. That's what we mean by New Labour. New in our means. But Labour in our aims."[4]

This new model of state-market relations is the centrepiece of his assault on Old Labour positions within the party. It is accompanied by a new approach to Britain's state and political identities and to modernising its society. The government sees itself as reconstructionist, much in the style of the Liberals in 1905, Labour in 1945 and the Conservatives in 1979. Three strands can be discerned in its programme of modernisation: constitutional (including devolution of power to Scotland, Wales and Northern

Ireland, House of Lords reform, electoral reform and European affairs); policy management (including the machinery of policy-making and the process of "joined-up" government); and service delivery (including outcome achievement).[5]

The autumn 1999 political season brought a new urgency to Blair's strategy, with reinforced emphasis on health and education expenditure and an assault on the traditional conservatism of Britain's socio-economic, administrative and political structures, which were seen as inhibiting his modernising agenda. In his speech to the 1999 Labour Party conference in September, Blair attacked "the cynics, the elites, the establishment, those who will live with decline, who yearn for yesteryear, those who prefer to criticise rather than to do" in the public service. Teachers, doctors and senior civil servants were subsequently identified as targets of his government's ire for their failure to adapt to the necessity of continuous modernisation in a world marked by global financial markets, shifting political alliances and fragmented social groups. Delivery on New Labour's electoral promises thus became intimately associated with adapting the public service to these new realities.

The Third Way programme draws variously on liberalism, communitarianism and Christian democracy within the lexicon of political theory.[6] These are undoubtedly eclectic influences; but they are capable of being rendered coherent if understood in terms of a social-liberalism with the following characteristics: renunciation of egalitarian collectivism in favour of a more thorough-going liberal individualism; a shift from equality of outcome to procedural fairness as the principle of redistribution; an emphasis on fairness as the central value defining social justice in a market society; an emphatic insistence on equalising opportunity, especially in education and employment, rather than equalising outcomes.[7]

Blair has been particularly influenced by the Christian communitarian political philosopher, John Macmurray, who taught in London during the 1930s and 1940s, notably by the idea that individuals are defined by their relationship to the community, not in isolation from it – in contrast with Thatcher's belief that "there is no such thing as Society. There are individual men and women, and there are families."[8] In keeping with a long-standing revisionist socialist tradition beginning with Bernstein, it is argued that ownership of the means of production is not the central issue in politics. Class has lost its salience as a criterion of socialist commitment and an agency of social change. Hence the overturning of Clause IV of the Labour Party's constitution, which asserted the contrary, is central to Blair's ideological critique of Old Labour. It follows that class and interest-based groups are increasingly irrelevant to political change, as more and more people are absorbed into a meritocratic middle class with far broader ambitions than their parents or grandparents. It follows, too, that privatisation, deregulation and market mechanisms are legitimate means for a modern social democratic government – an acceptance of neo-liberal political economy in continuity with the Thatcher period.

So are the encouragement of risk and flexibility. Both of these are central to the globalisation of economic forces, which is taken fully, indeed fatalistically and acquiescently, on board in Third Way theorising. This account of globalisation is associated with a vision of national competitiveness which seeks to compensate for the loss of control involved in discarding Keynesian demand-style, corporatist or protectionist methods of economic management. governments' capacity to change such international conditions is assumed to be limited because of capital's mobility. Supply-side resources are seen as the only realistic means of asserting competitive advantage in a much more interdependent world economy. Education, health and welfare-to-work reform are central to that endeavour as human capital. So is budgetary prudence. It is the role of governments to steer rather than row economies – not, in Blair's words, by "picking winners, heavy-handed intervention, old-style corporatism but: education, skills, technology, small business entrepreneurship."[9]

How a government spends money and what it spends it on are as important as how much it spends. Political power should be devolved as much as possible; a strong civic society rests on responsibilities as well as rights – hence the need to be tough on crime and its causes. Governance takes on a special importance. Drawing on a body of literature on "re-invented government", more emphasis is put on: consumer rather than producer interests; outcomes rather than inputs; partnerships between the public, private and voluntary sectors; the regulation rather than direct delivery of services by government; decentralisation of government, including privatisation; and stakeholding democracy, in which power would be dispersed, sovereignty shared and authority negotiated directly through multiple forms of representation.[10]

This is the theory; the practice has, as always, been more difficult to implement. But "joined-up government" became a major preoccupation for New Labour in office, driven by Blair's hands-on/centralist style of governing, together with significantly stronger resources in the Cabinet Office. In Blair's words, "joined-up problems need joined-up solutions". It is partly a question of overcoming the fragmentation created by the previous Conservative governments' public-sector reforms, which led to services being delivered through a combination of local government, special-purpose bodies, the voluntary sector and the private sector. There are now estimated to be 5,521 special-purpose bodies spending at least £39 billion a year to which ministers make 70,000 patronage appointments – this sector is larger than local government.[11]

Important initiatives have included a White Paper, *Modernising Government*, published in March 1999, designed to provide an agenda for modernising policy-making through networking and co-ordinated "holistic governance" rather than hierarchies or markets, providing responsive and high-quality services, introducing new technology, meeting citizens' needs and using public servants as agents of change; the creation of a new Performance and Innovation Unit in the Cabinet Office to develop electronic commerce in the UK, to streamline central government's role at the regional and local level and to develop incentives and overcome accountability barriers in achieving joined-up government; a Social Exclusion Unit to examine neighbourhood renewal, teenage pregnancy and opportunities for 16-18 year olds; a Centre for Management and Policy Studies as a centre of expertise in policy evaluation and policy-making, to conduct comparative administrative research and advise on better implementation of policy; a Regulation Impact Unit to gauge the effect of imposing new regulations on the private sector; and a Quality Management Task Force to develop benchmarking and best value as crucial elements in a modernised system of central government.[12] Taken together, such initiatives in the Prime Minister's and Cabinet Offices have been described with justice as creating an executive office in all but name.[13] One prominent researcher on governance and public administration finds there is "much to welcome in New Labour's modernising programme for central, local and devolved government. But the government lacks the trust it seeks to inspire. It fears the independence it bestows."[14] Much more will be heard of this criticism in the following pages.

This political project is undoubtedly internationalist – a central aspect too of New Labour's commitment to European integration as a means of governing these global trends. There is also the emergence of what Blair describes as "the beginnings of a new doctrine of international community…As problems become global – competitivity, changes in technology, crimes, drugs, family breakdown – so the search for solutions becomes global too."[15] Blair has put much stress on orchestrating centre-left strategy internationally in European and transatlantic settings, having been especially influenced by – and influencing – President Bill Clinton; Brazilian and South African leaders were also drawn into these debates. A crucial concern is to demonstrate for British voters that economic reform in the EU economies can prepare the way for Britain to join the euro. He has concentrated on achieving more flexibility in capital and labour markets, encouraging entrepreneurship and thereby getting unemployment down; he worked closely with the Portuguese EU presidency to get such a package accepted at the European Council in March 2000 and continued to advocate such an approach at the Council in June of that year, notably in cooperation with the conservative Spanish prime minister, Jose Maria Aznar.[16] Similarly Blair put much store on achieving reform of the European Commission, an initiative headed by the British Commissioner, Neil Kinnock.

THIRD WAY ASSESSED

The Third Way programme is an ambitious critique of traditional social democratic positions and a compelling platform from which to attack contemporary conservative ones. But it is not as invulnerable to criticism as its advocates often assert when they say – in a curious echo of Thatcherism – that there is no alternative to their approach and that it is the only possible programme for contemporary government. Such a response may help to marginalise or categorise critics of the Third Way from left and right; but it made for an intolerance that did not serve them well when harder times came, as they clearly did in mid-2000 after the setbacks in London and local elections that are examined in more detail in Chapter Three. Blair and his colleagues found then that their self-criticisms were greeted with *schädenfreude*, even by sympathisers, because of a previous overweening confidence. It is, therefore, worth examining some of the principal critical assessments of the Third Way project so as better to understand the belated mid-term difficulties faced by the New Labour government. Such criticisms animated not only dissident intellectuals but also disenchanted Labour officials, activists and voters. Anthony Giddens, the major theorist of Third Way policies, demonstrated an openness to them in a timely response to the critics, published in spring 2000, which was enthusiastically endorsed by Blair.[17]

Liberal critics such as Ralf Dahrendorf accepted that "in fact, the Third Way debate has become the only game in town – the only hint at new directions for Europe's politics in a confused multitude of trends and ideas." He found it nevertheless curiously lacking in "the fundamental value of a decent life – liberty", however much it caters for fraternity and cohesion.[18] Talk of outmoded parliamentarianism, the need for referenda and focus groups, compulsory welfare-to-work programmes and the withdrawal of benefits are all too tempting for political leaders when confronted with public apathy and a lack of democratic accountability in international fora. Undoubtedly, however, New Labour's approach to governing benefits from having a broader wind in its sails. Throughout much recent writing on governance and democracy, there is an assumption that partisan politics have been superseded by a model of good governance "in which objective solutions to social, economic or cultural problems are most likely to be found after you have established a judicious mix of institutional correctness and expert, non-partisan judgements." Blair has added to that model the idea of popular consultation and arbitration, in which the people "via elections and plebiscites, serve as the ultimate checks on their governors, endorsing or rejecting policies and programmes designed by the inner circles of relatively autonomous political institutions."[19] Sanctions are, therefore, invited for election pledges that go unmet in a contract with voters.

But there was much soul-searching among Blair's own governing team and its advisers over the failure adequately to translate their cohesive political approach in opposition into an effective manner of governing capable of delivering on promises and engaging their supporters. For example, a devastatingly frank critique of Blair's style of governing by his close adviser Philip Gould was leaked to the *Sunday Times*. Typical of the criticisms passed on by him, based on focus group research and intended to summarise popular attitudes rather than Gould's own beliefs, it asked "why does TB have a problem with Middle Britain?" and went on to say: "TB is not believed to be real. He lacks conviction, he is all spin and presentation, he just says things to please people, not because he believes them. TB has not delivered. He said he would improve the NHS and public services, he said he would change Britain, but instead things have got worse... all we have got is more of the same. Too little change, not too much. TB is out of touch – he does not really care about the [the ordinary voter]."[20]

Other critics cited New Labour's acceptance of the imperatives of globalisation, without regard for the real capacity to regulate them more effectively than Blair thinks is either possible or desirable. David Held, the theorist of cosmopolitan democracy, for example, found Blair accepted too readily the hyper-globalist conception of globalisation, distinguished by its emphasis on the overarching nature of global capitalism, the inescapability of global competition and the weakening capacity of states to regulate their economies. Adjusting to the international economy – above all to global financial markets – becomes a fixed point of orientation in economic policy. But there are alternatives, Held argued, including taxes on turnover in foreign exchange markets, new forms of economic co-ordination, entrenching new regulatory norms for child labour, trade union activity and environmental protection – allied to more ambitious schemes for extending democratic forms and processes across territorial borders.[21] Such criticisms were echoed in exchanges between the French Prime Minister, Lionel Jospin, and Blair; but the regulatory activity and policy of the European Union tend to encourage a convergence of their approaches, as was made clear at the Lisbon European Council on market liberalisation in March 2000 and the subsequent evolution of liberal policies accepted there, despite continuing tension between Blair, Jospin and Schröder over the objective of controlling or regulating globalisation.[22]

New Labour in office came under quite severe criticism from intellectuals to its left such as Stuart Hall, Eric Hobsbawm and Martin Jacques, whose own critiques of traditional left-wing positions in the 1980s exerted a decisive influence on Third Way theorising, notably with respect to the idea that "new times deserve new policies".[23] They were particularly disenchanted by the way in which New Labour theorists such as Geoff Mulgan and Charles Leadbetter (and by implication Blair and his political colleagues, since such people became government advisers) transformed this theorising from an ethical critique into a political/managerial programme about how to run capitalism better, and a "kind of technological futurism".[24] Another critic, from the left-liberal camp, David Marquand, found the Blair project unacceptably populist, centralist and anti-pluralist; it was incapable of allowing that "in an increasingly cosmopolitan world, multiple identities and overlapping loyalties are an inescapable aspect of political life." He saw a paradox between New Labour's constitutional revolution (examined in Chapter 4), which disperses power across a variety of new institutions, and the Prussian-style control exerted over Labour by Blair. This suggested that they do not understand what they are doing. Mair argued that the paradox is resolved by Blair's commitment to "partyless, depoliticised democracy", opening the way to an institutionally consensual style of governing by virtually unshiftable centrist coalitions of New Labourists and Liberal Democrats, "swatting off ineffective challenges from a rump right, on the one hand and a minority left, on the other"[25] in Clinton-like triangular fashion and periodically endorsed by elections and plebiscites. Such views were echoed by Anthony Barnett of the pressure group, Charter 88, who found that Blair's corporate-populist/centralist style of government, understood as a carry-over from the imperial state machine, challenged the devolution and constitutional change programme.[26]

REACTION AND REFORM

Many of these criticisms were dismissed impatiently by Blair's advisers. Understandably they became much more concerned with governmental efficiency in office than with continuing debates on big ideas with the academics New Labour previously drew upon in opposition.[27] This is in keeping with pragmatic commitments to effective joined-up government, rather than allowing different departments to function autonomously under their own administrative inertia, producing inconsistent or contradictory policies which confuse citizens and render cooperation with the voluntary sector all the more difficult. Delivering on policies and promises is intimately bound up with this. Public Service Agreements have been central to this journey. They are conceived as quasi-contracts in which spending departments and ministers, notably in health and education, agree to a set of objectives, targets and performance improvements in return for three-year allocations of resources. They are intended to bring together service improvement and resource control under the auspices of a cabinet committee chaired by the Chancellor.[28] They were a central feature of Brown's three-year public-spending review announced in mid-July 2000, which strengthened the Treasury's role in relation to the spending departments.[29]

Another feature has been the Private Finance Initiative (PFI); inherited from the Conservatives, this is conceived as a means of relieving public-sector borrowing by transferring financial and operational risk through contracting with private-sector organisations to finance and manage public facilities in return for guaranteed revenue streams. These have been embraced comprehensively by the government and are regarded as central to its plans for balancing control of recurrent public spending with enhanced public-sector investment. Their strategic policy importance helps to explain the bitterness of the exchanges between Ken Livingstone and the Labour leadership over how to finance investment in the London underground system during the mayoral campaign. Many Old Labour activists see PFIs as an unacceptable and inefficient relinquishing of a public-service ethos.

Much effort has gone into orchestrating policy in the emerging multi-levelled structures of government within a devolved or rearranged Britain. Inevitably there will be contested jurisdictions, boundary disputes and a need for conciliation procedures. In Chapter 4 it is argued that a potential model for such constitutional rearrangement is "asymmetric quasi-federalisation" – asymmetric because some sub-national units have greater self-governing powers than others, quasi-federalist because, although devolution goes beyond delegating powers by effectively *dividing* sovereignty between the two parliaments at Westminster and Edinburgh in federal fashion, there is no written constitutional entrenchment. Theoretically and in many practical respects sovereignty still resides with the crown-in-parliament at Westminster, rather than with British voters, who remain subjects, not citizens. It very much remains to be seen whether this hybrid model, concerned as much to preserve as to reform the British state and polity, is sustainable in the longer term. The choice between such a devolution and disintegration of the United Kingdom triggered by Scottish independence is as yet unresolved by the constitutional revolution set in train by New Labour's reforms.

Other critics said there was nothing particularly new about New Labour, since it is effectively based on the ideology of New Liberalism. From 1908 to 1914 that ideology animated the reforming Liberal governments of Asquith and Lloyd-George, although New Labour is felt to be more authoritarian on criminal justice, more hostile to local government and less interventionist in economic affairs than this tradition would allow.[30] These points were echoed by the Liberal Democrat party, notwithstanding the commitment of its new leader, Charles Kennedy, to work closely with Blair. Asked whether he is an Asquithian Liberal, Blair replied that he is a modern social democrat who wants to reunite the radical tradition of reform broken by the Liberal Party split which led to the Labour Party's emergence as a party of government in the 1920s.[31] Another historical parallel was also suggested, this time with the Conservative leader of the 1920s and 1930s, Stanley Baldwin. Like Blair, he deliberately appealed beyond his party to include men and women of goodwill in a non-political embrace and was determined to present himself as a friendly, trustworthy, ordinary person. His reward was nearly 20 years of Conservative hegemony, during which that party was in power alone or in coalition for ten of the thirteen years between 1918 and 1931 and for the whole of the period 1931-1940. According to this analysis, Blair is "best seen as a Charles II, not as a Cromwell. He seeks a restoration, not a revolution. His true aim is to re-invent the Age of Baldwin, not to stride forward into a hitherto unimagined future."[32]

One of the abiding questions about Blair's policies is whether he will be able to carry his party along with an assumed plan to realign British politics by amalgamating Labour and the Liberal Democrats, based on a far-reaching programme of constitutional change encompassing not only devolution, but proportional representation, an elected second chamber, regional assemblies, revitalised local government, thorough-going freedom of information reform and a federal or quasi-federal Britain in a federal or quasi-federal Europe. The jury is still out on those questions, despite disenchantment among the left-liberal intelligentsia – and the interesting fact that so many of his immediate political advisers hail from the Social Democratic Party group that split from Labour in the early 1980s and who are more sympathetic to these ideas than many traditional Labour figures. It is out also on Blair's willingness to plump decisively for membership of the single currency in advance of the next election,

were happy with the government's record on education, 44% were not; 43% believed the old stop-go economic cycle had yet to be conquered against 40% saying that had been achieved. Significantly, most of the sceptics were outside the south-east.

The 1999 *Social Attitudes Survey* found a patchy and uneven public commitment to Third Way values as articulated by Blair and sympathetic theorists such as Anthony Giddens. Big majorities supported the view that the unemployed, young mothers and elderly people deserve government support. Voters were much more willing to pay higher taxes to improve the health service than Third Way theorising assumes, a finding confirmed by an *Observer* poll in early 2000. The health service had by then become a serious political issue, highlighting Britain's much lower spending compared to the EU average, giving it the lowest number of doctors and the fewest heart operations per capita in the developed world. The Blair government's emphasis on the work ethic and the environment attracted support; but attitudes to the EU and the euro were much more negative than the government's.[36] By June 2000 there was a 71% to 29% margin against joining the euro, with those strongly opposed rising in one year from 23% to 33%.[37] Eurobarometer findings published in July found British support for joining the euro at 22%, with only 25% of respondents saying UK membership of the EU is a positive thing (compared to 58% in 1991, and 29% in 1993 after the Black Wednesday sterling devaluation). Senior Commission officials blamed the British media for the comparatively high levels of hostility to, and ignorance about, the EU shown in the poll.[38]

There was plenty of evidence by mid-2000 that the government was aware of these potentially negative trends and determined to reinforce its delivery of domestic policies, to re-emphasise the necessity of its constitutional reform programme, and to argue more forcefully for its European policies, although there were acute tactical divisions on what to say about the euro – and when to say it. The government's major £43 billion three-year public-spending review announced in July clearly set parameters for delivering on its promises that would be central to its electoral strategy. It did so against a background of underspending on infrastructural projects; it fell by 32% in the 1999-2000 financial year from £3-8bn to £2.6bn despite the Treasury having sanctioned an increase to £5.5bn.[39] This was caused partly by Labour's voluntary freeze on public expenditure to the level of the Conservatives' for their first two years in office, partly by mismanagement and logjams. The spending review will see total public spending jump 6.7% in 2000-1 – the biggest rise since 1974-75 – to compensate for the underspend. Otherwise, increased spending was in line with taxation increases and economic growth, allowing Brown to confirm his record of macroeconomic prudence and stability, which is believed to be a central element of New Labour's electoral appeal. The departments benefiting most were education, health, transport, the Home Office, local government and defence, centrally concerned with the delivery of New Labour's programme.

STATE AND POLITICAL IDENTITIES

Britain still faces a *dual sovereignty* question. The common point at issue in its internal and external relations is the extent to which sovereignty is to be shared both with other nation states in Europe, and in the UK with its constituent nationalities and regions. As the IEA's 1996 book put it:

> Looked at from the vantage point of the British state as currently constituted, there is a dual concern. Sovereignty could be simultaneously drained from the centre in two opposite directions: outwardly towards Europe and inwardly towards the regions. Britain has a double constitutional problem.

The key to the problem, we then said, "lies in the debate about Britain, rather than the debate about Europe. The solution of the first is the precondition for the solution of the second." It suggested there was "still a considerable distance to be travelled before a verdict will be handed down on whether Britain is to remain a unitary state or be transformed into a devolved, rearranged or even a federalised one". It could take ten years to work that transformation through, over which time Britain was likely to be an uncertain or even a volatile partner within the EU.[40]

Four years on, that analysis stands despite the momentous changes in the meantime. The intensifying debates about British and English identity examined in subsequent chapters bear that out. So do those concerning parliamentary versus popular sovereignty by way of referendums; joining EMU; centralisation, devolution, separatism, disintegration, breakup or asymmetric quasi-federalisation in Scotland, Wales, Northern Ireland and the English regions; writing down the constitution; and those concerning whether Britain is a union or a unitary state.

The IEA's New UK Group's brief is to update the book published in 1996, in the light of New Labour's experience in office, its foreign, European, constitutional and Irish policies, and intervening international developments. The original study, of necessity, broadened its remit from issues related to Britain's economic performance, and prospective participation in economic and monetary union, to the country's wider political trajectory internally and externally. It argued that Britain faces a crisis of state and political identity in four dimensions after the end of the Cold War in its:

- global and transatlantic relations
- relations with Europe
- internal constitutional arrangements
- relations with Ireland.

It went on to argue that, within this context, Ireland's relations with Britain have gone through their own changes as the transition was made from post-colonial independence/dependence to a less unequal interdependence associated very much with the liberating effects of Ireland's EEC/EC/EU membership. Trade relations were radically diversified over the period 1972-99, with imports from the UK falling from 52% to 32% and exports to the UK reducing from 61.5% to 22%, a trend affecting even the domestically-owned firms which have traditionally been most dependent on that market. Politically and diplomatically, Ireland's perspectives have been broadened by participation in the more multilateral setting of the EU, where ministers meet their British counterparts on a more equal footing than in bilateral contacts. These changes have been part of an increasing internationalisation of Irish society. This has given political leaders the confidence to switch the primary focus of the Republic's policy towards Northern Ireland from reunification to acceptance of Northern Ireland's continuation in the UK, accompanied by power-sharing in the North and north-south institutions. That has facilitated the normalising of relations with Britain.[41]

The question now is whether this basic analysis still holds and, if it does, whether and how the underlying problems of the UK are being effectively addressed and resolved through objective, structural action affecting its state and political identity both internally and externally. On the basis of what has happened during the intervening years the analysis stands up reasonably well – although this is obscured by the fact that it still covers contested ground politically and culturally. It should be remembered that the word crisis derives from the Greek word, *krinein*, to judge or decide. Far-reaching decisions on Britain's internal political arrangements and external position and role are facing its leaders. This and subsequent chapters examine the inter-relationships between the four dimensions, subdivided between internal and external policies, and assess whether there is a coherent approach to them. Political and state identities are intimately bound up with the search for more democracy in these transformations. The use of the term crisis does not denote mass psychological turmoil, but rather an awareness that acute systemic problems require to be resolved by political decision-makers.

As Robert Hazell, head of the Constitution Unit in University College, London saw it, there were extraordinary paradoxes here.[42] There was no clearly articulated or apparent underlying rationale and all too little ministerial enthusiasm for a programme of change which objectively amounted to the most dramatic constitutional transformation for almost 100 years – perhaps for 300. Philip Stephens of the *Financial Times* wrote that "a revolution rolls on and the nation sleeps".[43] This may have been in keeping with the great tradition of British pragmatism, but it was a sad commentary on its lack of self-understanding. Hugo Young, the journalist and author, raised the question of whether the internal debate drives the European one, or vice versa. He believed the EMU decision to be crucial; only when it is resolved will the other sovereignty issues fall more calmly into place. Vernon Bogdanor defined the choice facing the UK as decentralisation or disintegration.[44] One must nevertheless beware of false dichotomies; devolving power is not necessarily to take a high road leading inevitably to disintegration – "refusing to devolve can be disintegrating; and resolving to devolve can be integrating".[45] Since politics is contingent, driven by events, "outcomes will depend on the capacity of elites at every level to construct procedures, and adopt habits that make cooperation rather than conflict the prevailing standard of intergovernmental relations. There is a new political culture to be learned by all sides."[46]

In spring 2000, Blair and his colleagues started to address these political realities more openly.[47] Their motivation was to remove the apparent Conservative monopoly in defining Britishness. Labour sees that as a matter of values rather than unchanging institutions or insularity from Europe. Within this context, questions of identity became highly political – a fact that seemed likely to dominate the forthcoming election campaign. Voters were presented with a choice between alternative resolutions of the dual sovereignty problem put forward by Labour and the Conservatives. Although their formulations do not exhaust the possibilities that could be offered, it is possible to draw quite a sharp distinction between these two models of Britishness at the outset of the 21st century.

The New Right or Conservative model emphasises a British Way, distinct from (and implicitly superior to) that of Europe; the traditional institutions of parliamentary sovereignty; the monarchy; maintenance of the Union; values of individualism, enterprise, social mobility and local loyalties. It draws on a long tradition of ethnic nationalism in Tory thinking, and, despite its theoretical unionism, on the long ambiguity of Englishness and Britishness, tending towards a view of Great Britain as Greater England. Hague has broadened the definition to include a more accommodating attitude to multicultural society, but combined that with an increasingly xenophobic attitude to immigration. Rather than simply reacting to New Labour's programme of constitutional reform, he proposed a series of constitutional changes himself, intended to bolster the role of parliament and to introduce referendums on EU treaty changes.

By contrast, the New Labour model is based more on values than on institutions. It is open to European integration and ready to accommodate national diversity by devolution. It is explicitly multicultural and embraces multiple identities. But it maintains a core of British patriotism. It is capable of being realised through expanding civil society and deepening citizenship. It goes beyond the imperial ethno-nationalist inheritance that still informs the Conservative vision of Britishness and moves towards an inclusive civic definition of a multinational Britain.

EXTERNAL POLICIES

Blair certainly wants to position Britain at the centre of European affairs, and in the longer term to exert a leadership role in them.

This is a constant theme. It has been accompanied by a revealing series of reflections on the relationship between power, sovereignty and influence in today's world. In his National Changeover Plan speech in February 1999, he put them as follows:

> In finance and business the world is more and more integrated. It is moving closer together. And if joining a single currency is good for British jobs and British industry, if it enhances British influence and power, I believe it right for Britain to overcome these constitutional and political arguments and the fears behind them.[48]

He refused to rule out joining the euro on grounds of sovereignty, because technology, global finance, mass communication, travel and culture show a world moving together, in which "sovereignty pooled can be sovereignty, or at least power and influence, renewed." Were euro membership to be ruled out, the likelihood was that such a decision would have to be revisited in a few years, "and in the meantime we would lose all influence whatsoever in the economic future of the EU of which we will remain a member." As he put it in his "Britain in Europe" speech on 14 October, 1999: "Europe is not marginal to the British economy. It is fundamental to it and each day becomes more so. To quit Europe would be an act of economic mutilation." He was quite happy to use the term integration to describe these processes.

This will require addressing a further paradox involved in centralist/devolutionary debates within Britain and with respect to relations with Europe. From the point of view of central government, federalism in the UK was seen as a threat to the British state because it licensed a hitherto suppressed or controlled diversity; whereas federalism in EU terms was seen as a threat because it is homogenising.[49] As is suggested in Chapter Four, such a duality is misconceived if the EU is understood not as superseding nation states but as embedding them in transnationalised multi-layered governance. The same point applies within the UK.

The contrast with existing and previous Conservative policy was sharp, notably with a formulation by the then foreign secretary, Malcolm Rifkind, who distinguished between interests and influence in an address on British foreign policy in September

1995:

> Occasionally it may be right to accept less
> influence in specific areas [of the EU] in order to
> protect key national interests...We will not
> accept proposals that damage British interests on
> the spurious grounds that otherwise we will lose
> influence, create a two-speed Europe or be left
> out in the cold.[50]

Critics queried whether the distinction between influence and
interests was valid – in what circumstances, they asked, would a
loss of influence be in Britain's foreign policy interests? From the
thrust of Blair's argument it can be seen that he agrees.
Maximising international influence is taken to be the optimal
means of safeguarding Britain's interests and exercising real
sovereignty in a globalising world. This brings Labour much more
into line with other EU member states, Ireland included. The Blair
government believes the emerging European political system
combines vigorous nation states and judiciously selected
sovereignty-pooling where common institutions have a fully
legitimate role to play. It foresees a system of overlapping core
centres of integration, in which there could be provision for
differentiated membership as the EU enlarges to cater for varying
capacities and willingness to integrate. It accepts that in order to
maximise influence it will be necessary to participate in all the core
areas of integration.

In an important speech in Warsaw on 6 October 2000 Blair
proposed a much enhanced role for the European Council, in the
belief that this is the apex of political legitimacy in a system where
democracy's principal focus remains in nation states:

> The truth is, the primary sources of democratic
> accountability in Europe are the directly elected
> and representative institutions of the nations of
> Europe, national parliaments and governments.
> That is not to say Euope will not in future
> generations develop its own strong demos or
> polity, but it hasn't yet.

That means national democracies should be represented at
European level in a second chamber. The Commission's role

should continue, as an aid to a stronger European Council charged with giving clear political direction to the whole – and as a protection for smaller states and to overcome sectionalism. Europe, he said, is deepening and widening at the same time. But the balance of political forces within it will allow the emergence of a superpower, not a superstate.[51]

The Labour government also accepts fully the advice given by Raymond Seitz, the outgoing US Ambassador in 1994, to its Conservative predecessors: "There is the simple observation that if Britain's voice is less influential in Paris or Bonn, it is likely to be less influential in Washington."[52] Blair put it like this in 1995: "The fact is that Europe is the only route through which Britain can exercise power and influence. If it is to maintain its role as a global player, it has to be a central part of the politics of Europe."[53] In set-piece speeches he returned repeatedly to the theme:

> Britain is stronger with the US by reason of being in Europe. Go to the US. Deal, as I have, over the past two years, with issues of trade and investment, war and peace, with our US allies. They value us even more as people who have influence in Europe who can talk to key European allies and who are respected both in the US and in Europe. Likewise we are stronger in Europe if strong with the US. Stronger together. Influential with both. And a bridge between the two.[54]

Major initiatives taken by the Labour government make sense when seen in this perspective. The Saint Malo defence initiative with France was a crucial influence on the developing debate on a European defence identity. As the Treaty of Amsterdam came into effect, NATO enlarged and mounted its attack on Serbia over Kosovo and the EU decided at the Cologne, Helsinki and Feira Councils in the aftermath of the war that it should undertake and equip itself to assume a significantly greater responsibility for politico-military crisis management. As Keatinge put it:

> Previously, such proposals had come from other European governments, only to be dismissed by London as cutting across the transatlantic cohesion of NATO. Prime Minister Tony Blair,

largely because he has demonstrated British solidarity with Washington's policies (particularly on Iraq), has been able to stand this logic on its head. Greater European responsibility is to strengthen transatlantic solidarity, partly through more equitable burden-sharing which Congressional critics of NATO have long sought.[55]

Thus Britain is offered a choice as to its appropriate external policies. It must decide between an increasingly Eurocentric position espoused by New Labour, in which Britain's political and state identities are expressed and reaffirmed by its participation in the EU (making it more influential in Washington) and a very different Conservative model, which emphasised its insular and global/transatlantic position and its radical distinctiveness from Europe.

INTERNAL POLICIES

Concerns with identity have been most marked on the right-wing end of the political spectrum.[56] But the historian, Linda Colley, in a lecture on "Britishness in the 21st Century" to Blair and his colleagues in Downing Street, emphasised it is "in part because New Labour is one of the few authentically British political parties remaining in these islands, that since May Day 1997 questions of Britain and Britishness have been receiving concentrated attention" across the whole political spectrum. She wondered what "all this navel-gazing" was expected to achieve, but acknowledged the ironic fact that the theoretical and political downsizing of class politics meant that as a substitute "you increasingly get the politics of place, ethnicity or religion" and that "the new, sectional-interest politics often explicitly rejects notions of a unitary Britain". This is an important point. For most of the last century the politics of class and redistribution dominated British politics. Constitutional structures and ethnic identities were essentially secondary, having been largely removed from the political agenda by Ireland's independence in 1921. It took the end of empire and the experience of economic decline to revive territorial identities, the appeal of which was reinforced by the Anglocentric and centralising thrust of the Thatcher period. In the process, and after the end of the Cold War, there was a major shift of emphasis away from class towards the politics of identity. New Labour's programme is part of that shift.[57]

Colley listed nine factors undermining the sense of a common Britishness: the erosion of Protestantism as a badge of identity; the decline of the monarchy; the end of imperial plunder and glory; reduced acquiescence in centralised government; sovereignty-sharing with the EU; Commonwealth immigration; privatisation of state companies; constitutional change; and the decline in Britain-wide class politics. She proposed an important distinction between identity and citizenship and rejected three current scenarios for the future of the UK: breakup by way of Scottish independence and Irish reunification; absorption into a European superstate; or the "complacent" assumption that Welsh, Scottish and Northern Irish devolution represent resolutions to problems, not their beginning. Instead of being so mesmerised by debates over British identity it would be far more productive to concentrate on renovating British citizenship, and on "convincing all the inhabitants of these islands that they are equal and valued citizens irrespective of whatever identity they may individually select to prioritize." She said this should be based on the following policies for a revived citizen-nation: more inspiring and accessible definitions of citizenship and constitutional rights; a transformed monarchy dedicated to popular sovereignty; abolition of titles of rank and sumptuary ceremonial customs; a continually reforming central government in association with a radical diffusion of power to multi-levelled politics and governance; much more political participation, based partly on US practices; much more commitment to ethnic and gender equality; and a new and more dynamic approach to Britain's pluralist history.[58]

Such an agenda went well beyond New Labour's current programme. But it indicated where that programme would have to be driven if its objective of reforming the UK to preserve it was to be fulfilled. Although most public soul searching about Britishness was associated with such right-wing figures among the chattering classes as the Conservative politician, John Redwood, or the editor of the *Daily Telegraph*, Charles Moore, "the chatterers are not all on the right. And they are on to something"[59] -because the cumulative impact of constitutional change in Britain will be revolutionary; there is nothing settled about such a long-term process. In early 2000, the Home Secretary, Jack Straw, said on a Radio 4 programme entitled *Brits*, that under pressure from European integration and devolution, there was a possibility that violent traditions in English nationalism could reassert themselves – stimulating another round of navel-gazing at British identity.[60] That took on a sharply defined tone during the European soccer championships in June 2000, which were marred once again by violent incidents in Belgium involving British hooligans and German and Turkish fans. According to Roy Hattersley, the former deputy leader of the Labour Party:

> Football provides the opportunity to demonstrate their brutal contempt for foreigners – a contempt which is often encouraged by politicians and journalists…Most football thugs are the sort of men who, regretting that we no longer rule the world, want us to control the penalty area – and fight the opposition on the terraces as we were once ready to fight them on the beaches.[61]

The Foreign Office went on to warn the government that England's reputation as a footballing nation risked being damaged irrevocably unless urgent measures were taken to tackle hooliganism and would certainly damage its chances of hosting the World Cup in 2006[62] – as proved to be the case when FIFA voted controversially to award it to Germany not South Africa, England receiving only minority support.

During this period of soul-searching, the Chancellor of the Exchequer, Gordon Brown, contributed an article to *The Times*, in which he argued that multiple allegiances, cultural openness to change, an enduring commitment to liberty and a determination to develop civil society in the direction of citizenship rather than subjecthood would see Britain through this period of political innovation. He rejected the right-wing equation of Britishness with institutions.[63] But in doing so he laid himself open to the charge of assuming away the realities of English expansionist nationalism in the past and attributing nationalism solely to the Celtic periphery. As Joe Lee wrote:

> By a convenient but natural degree of self-delusion, a dominant national power is not nationalist when it expands to control other peoples.[64]

As if there were never such a thing as imperial nationalism in

Britain.

CONCLUSION

Britain is a composite state-nation rather than a nation state, "a union of multiple identities", which was configured by the experience and management of empire.[65] As Nairn put it:

> "Britain" was a multinational social class before it was a multinational state; and the latter remains in essence a manifestation of the former. Britishness was a stratum phenomenon rather than a mass or popular one, but later on the elite-mass linkage was greatly fortified by an overseas command-structure in which mass participation was allowed, and indeed positively encouraged and channelled. Empire and successful warfare gave this class-forged link an iron durability. At the same time the monarchy was refashioned into an equivalent or simulacrum of nationalist symbolism. The chain was both gilded and strengthened by this transformation.[66]

Therefore, it would follow that "just because there has never been a British nation underpinning the state, the latter's decay is likely to be terminal". England's emerging identity predicament is largely the product of systematic Anglo-British ambiguity historically determined, as a result of which "a British-imperial class and ethos have been in possession for so long of its vocal chords"[67]; in that sense England, not Ireland or Scotland, is Britain's last colony. "'Blairism' is really a last-ditch attempt at maintaining the United Kingdom by the formation of a pot-noodle ruling class"[68] now that that old patriciate has been destroyed by a combination of imperial and post-imperial decline and Mrs Thatcher. It is conservationist rather than conservative – and therefore incapable of the central constitutional reform in association with devolution required to save the UK from disintegration. This is a powerful argument, difficult to rebut categorically. Only experience over the coming years will prove whether it is true.

Devolution forms part of the redefinition of the British state, in which Ireland is involved through the Belfast Agreement, irrespective of whether the Executive in Northern Ireland survives. This process "symbolises the changing power relationships in the Atlantic archipelago. Its establishment could presage the final termination of the long Anglo-Saxon hegemony in these islands."[69] The Belfast Agreement is seen by sympathetic observers in Britain as setting the scene for a radical recasting of the British state to bring it more into keeping with modern constitutional and political norms. The British-Irish Council is seen as providing a potential model for a more equal encounter between its various nations and regions than has traditionally been available through the excessively centralised Westminster/ Whitehall one.[70]

Another historian, Norman Davies, concluded his monumental survey of the history of these islands as follows:

> At bottom, I belong to the group of historical colleagues who hold that the United Kingdom was established to serve the interests of Empire, and that the loss of Empire has destroyed its *raison d'être*...It is not inconceivable, of course, that the British Establishment may yet wake up to its predicament. It may even set in motion a plan to create the structures of a British nation state and to recover pro-British sentiment. If so, it would be running against the contemporary tide. In my estimation, it would deliver too little, and too late...Even if Britain were to break up, all that is really valuable would remain. There could be a sovereign Scotland. There could be an English Republic. It could be better than the last one. There might even be a consolidated Wales, and an Ireland at peace with itself.[71]

Whatever one's view about reform and preservation of the UK as against its disintegration – scenarios explored in subsequent chapters – a great deal is therefore at stake for all the peoples of these islands as these issues are decided in coming years.

---

1   Butler and Kavanagh (1997), p. 246; Norris (1997), pp 7-8, 15-16; FitzGerald (1997); Denver and Hands (1997), pp 222-5.
2   Hurd (2000); Barnett (2000); Hennessy (2000).
3   See for example Dahrendorf (1999); Gould (1998); Marquand (1999,

1999a); Mair (2000).

4   Blair (1998), p. 6.

5   Gray and Jenkins (2000), p. 239.

6   For accounts of Third Way theorising see Blair (1996), (1997), (1998),
    (1999b); Cronin (1999); Dahrendorf (1999); Driver and Martell
    (1998); Gamble and Wright (2000); Giddens (1998), (2000); Gould
    (1998); Hattersley (2000a); Held (1998); Krieger (1999), (1999a);
    Leadbetter (1999); McKibbin (1999); Mulgan (1998); Ryan (1999);
    Smyth (1999); White (1998).

7   See Buckler and Dolowitz (2000) for a riposte to Freeden (1999).
    They argue that New Labour's ideology is more coherent and less
    eclectic than Freeden allows. Hattersley (2000a) pp 248-9 argues that
    one of the main Third Way theorists, Anthony Giddens,
    systematically fails to distinguish between equality of outcome and of
    opportunity.

8   Gould (1998), pp 233ff; Thatcher in *Woman's Own*, 31 October, 1987.

9   Blair (1999a).

10 Driver and Martell (1998), pp 126-133.

11 Rhodes (2000), pp 155-6.

12 Gray and Jenkins (2000), pp 222, 232.

13 Burch and Holliday (1999).

14 Rhodes, *op. cit.,* p. 163.

15 Blair (1999b).

16 Blair and Aznar (2000).

17 Giddens (2000). The book contains an excellent select bibliography
    of critical writings on Third Way policies, amounting to a guide to
    contemporary international debates on the future of social
    democracy.

18 Dahrendorf (1999), pp 13, 17.

19 Mair (2000), pp 32-3.

20 "Secret memo says Blair is out of touch", *The Sunday Times*, 11 June
    2000.

21 Held (1998); Held *et al.* (1999).

22 Cassen (2000).

23 Hall and Jacques (1989).

24 Finlayson (1999), p. 224.

25 Mair (2000), p. 33; for the subsequent debate on his article in *New Left
    Review* see Marquand (2000a); Barnett (2000a); McKibbin (2000a).

26 Barnett (1999).

27 Lloyd (1999).

28 Gray and Jenkins (2000), p. 230.

29 Adams (2000).

30 On Blair's left-wing and other intellectual critics see Barnett (1997),
    (1999); Marquand (1999), (2000); Ryan (1999).

31 *The Daily Telegraph* (1999).

32 Marquand (2000a), pp 75-6.

33 Travis and Wintour, *The Guardian*, 16 May 2000; *Mail on Sunday*, 11 June 2000.

34 Butler (2000); Killner (2000a).

35 *The Observer* (1999).

36 For these opinion surveys see *The Observer* (1999); Wintour *et al.* (2000); *The Daily Telegraph* (1999a), (2000); Bromley and Curtice (2000); *British Social Attitudes* (1999).

37 Webster and Riddell (2000).

38 Osborn (2000).

39 White and Elliott (2000).

40 Gillespie ed. (1996), p. 181.

41 Gillespie (2000a).

42 Hazell, ed. (1999).

43 Stephens (1999).

44 Young (1999a); Bogdanor (1999a).

45 Editorial, *The Political Quarterly* (2000), p. 2.

46 O'Neill (2000), p. 80.

47 "The Patriot Game", *The Economist*, 1 April 2000.

48 Blair (1999).

49 Meehan (1999).

50 Gillespie ed. (1996), p. 86.

51 Blair (2000e).

52 *ibid.*, p. 82.

53 Blair (1995).

54 Blair (1999d).

55 Keatinge (1999), pp 99-100.

56 George (1998), pp 27 ff.

57 Cannadine (2000), p. 7.

58 Colley (1999). She commands attention as the author of a classic study of how British identity was constructed in the eighteenth and nineteenth centuries.

59 David (1999).

60 Millar (2000).

61 Quoted in Fanning (2000).

62 Burns and Ward (2000).

63 Browne (2000).

64 David (1999); Brown (2000); Lee (2000).

65 Brockliss and Eastwood, eds (1997).

66 Nairn (2000), pp 176-7.

67 *ibid.*, p. 85.

68 *ibid.*, p. 76.

69 Bogdanor (1999).

70 Partridge (2000); Meehan (1999); Bogdanor (1999).

71 Davies (1999a), pp 1053, 1055. For a critique of Davies's historical accuracy on Ireland, see Kennedy (2000).

CHAPTER THREE

Politics

Paul Gillespie

INTRODUCTION

Following its landslide victory in May 1997 the Labour Party assumed a real hegemony over British politics. The sheer extent of the parliamentary triumph and of the Conservatives' defeat opened up many opportunities, but also created their own challenges. A large parliamentary majority makes it difficult to manage dissident backbenchers and can encourage a certain hubris about political invincibility. Indeed there was evidence to suggest that Blair and the leadership were very surprised, even felt imprisoned by, the extent of their victory, which altered the parameters of their plan to modernise and realign British politics. Part of that plan involved, for Blair, a long-term alliance with the Liberal Democrats. In a potential second or third term this might be all the more necessary to keep the Conservatives out of office. But the price of coalition would be electoral reform – a difficult project to sell to those Labour backbenchers who would lose out as a result. It would also require explicit commitments to devolve power within the UK and to resolve the long-standing uncertainties about its relations with the European Union.

Many of the main political issues and features of the New Labour government arose from these simple political realities. A central preoccupation has been the necessity to secure another parliamentary term in order to implement the party's policies. This was an often-repeated mantra of Blair's, that Labour had never achieved two full terms in office. He attributed that in good part to the split between the Liberals and Labour in the first half of the twentieth century – hence the desire to realign British politics in the twenty-first. Strategically New Labour planned their political programme with those main objectives in view – hence the shock when a belated mid-term blues afflicted them in mid-2000 with the realisation that they could face a real challenge winning the next general election. They had to take account of four main players in the British political game: the Conservative opposition; opposition from Old Labour elements within their own party; the Liberal Democrats; and the national media. While it may seem strange to include the media among these players there can be no doubting their importance and the government's preoccupation with them. Given the weakness of the Conservatives, the Eurosceptic press assumed an opposition role itself; there was widespread resentment among policy-makers that it should be so much controlled by expatriate moguls such as Rupert Murdoch and Conrad Black.

This chapter will summarily examine each of these players. It will look more closely at the two major objectives of a second term and political realignment. It will go on to look at the methods and substance of the policies pursued by the government, including its health, social and industrial relations policies. It will then examine the changing social basis of Labour support and look at whether increased electoral volatility, disenchantment among core working class supporters and falling partisan identification could affect its popularity in unexpected ways.

THE FOUR MAIN POLITICAL PLAYERS

The Conservative Party
New Labour's political hegemony was based in its first two years in office not only on its overwhelming parliamentary majority but on the disarray and ineptitude of the Conservatives in opposition under their leader, William Hague. He presided over a pronounced shift to the right in that party's positions on domestic and European affairs. In both these dimensions issues of sovereignty increasingly divided the two parties. It would suit the Conservative agenda to have them determined as much as possible at the next election by the question of whether the United Kingdom should join the euro, which Hague has ruled out for ten years ahead, but effectively in principle. This is on the grounds that euro membership would spell the end of the country's identity as a nation state and therefore as a national democracy as it became subsumed in an emerging federal superstate. Hague defined a nation as "a group of people who feel enough in common with

one another to accept government from each other's hands. That is why democracy functions best within nations." Consequently his party advocated a super-flexibility clause in the European treaties that would allow countries to opt out of certain policies: "New members should have the right to accept some EU policies on a selective basis in perpetuity and existing member states too should be free to develop a mix and match approach."[1]

This was seen by many observers and most opponents as unrealistic and tantamount to a renegotiation of the terms of EU membership or even a withdrawal from the Union. But it attracted majority support from Conservative members and supporters and tuned in to a real disenchantment among voters at large. Hague and his colleagues saw their formula of being "in Europe, not run by Europe" and "saving the pound" as potentially decisive factors in a Conservative political recovery.[2] The more evidence there was for that recovery the easier it was for Hague to maintain his Eurosceptic line, despite residual support for more Europhile positions among significant sectors of the party leadership and support base.

The return of Michael Portillo to the Conservative front bench in autumn 1999 reinforced these perceptions and also the party's emerging role as the voice of English nationalism. But Hague resisted calls for an English parliament because it would contradict the party's unionism – although he favoured letting English MPs decide on English laws and excluding Scottish ones from those decisions. The Conservatives accepted devolution as a fact of political life in Scotland and Wales. Hague said they would not seek to abolish the Scottish Parliament but to make it work effectively within the context of the UK. The Scottish Tories hoped to recover from their mere 15.5% vote in the May 1997 elections – when they failed to win a single seat – partly based on their appeal as a low-tax party.

But their fortunes will be affected by what the party decides to do on the emerging Anglo-British question: the future of England. Hague was "as yet unpersuaded" by the case for an English parliament for fear that it would undermine Westminster; he did not want to risk a sharp break with the party's traditional unionism by lurching towards an English nationalist position when constitutional reform was not a major issue in English public opinion.[3] It was considered important by only 6% of the electorate in July 2000, among whom Labour supporters outnumbered Conservative ones; in comparison, healthcare, law and order, education, taxation, unemployment, pensions, managing the economy and public transport were seen as relatively the most important issues, ranging from 67% to 27%, Europe coming in at midrange with 37%. Among these issues the Conservatives trailed Labour in all except law and order, pensions and Europe.[4] In September Hague launched a new manifesto which brought these themes together. Entitled "Believing in Britain" it put the defence of national identity at the centre of the campaign, saying it is threatened by European integration and Labour's constitutional reforms. Hague opposed regional assemblies in England, in the belief that such identities are weak, whereas local and community ones are stronger; but he favoured strengthening parliamentary arrangements for dealing with English "domestic" affairs, based on a "legitimate English political consciousness".[5] This could, however, create its own complications in a tight parliamentary situation at Westminster.

It is also likely to add to pressure to revise the Barnett formula on budgetary allocations within the UK. That was put in place by Joel Barnett as Chief Secretary to the Treasury in 1978. It apportions increases in spending pro rata to Scotland, Wales and Northern Ireland on the basis of their population as a proportion of the British total; but it provides for levels of spending that are higher than an objective assessment of their needs would suggest they should get, largely because of a political judgment that this is the price of maintaining the Union in areas where votes and seats count. Barnett himself told the Commons Treasury Select Committee he created the system purely for reasons of political expediency. Its great shortcoming was that it was not based on real needs and that the Labour government was reluctant to change it because "they fear what will happen because of devolution in Scotland. Scotland gets far more than it should."[6]

Assumptions that the Conservatives would accept a referendum in favour of joining the euro were more questionable, despite Portillo's statement that "this isn't like entering the exchange rate mechanism which we entered for a brief period and then came out".[7] The issue could have major implications for Britain's ability to join the euro, since, if that commitment was taken to be reversible, the European Central Bank would presumably recommend against admitting sterling for fear of speculative movements. Much would depend on how decisive a majority could be expected, including how closely the referendum might carry in England.

For three years after the 1997 general election the Conservative Party lagged behind Labour in the opinion polls by 15-20 points, despite the dissatisfaction of core Labour supporters with the delivery of the government's commitments on health, welfare and educational reform. It was precisely the convergence of New Labour policy with its Conservative predecessors that explained the opposition party's difficulty in distinguishing itself as an alternative with the voters and its concentration on the European issue which offered clear policy differences. The continuing deep unpopularity of Britain joining the euro seemed to justify Hague's dogged insistence on the issue, despite advice that it could not carry the burden of opposing the entire range of New Labour policies. He was underrated during this period, despite several characteristics that kept him in touch not only with his party's right-wing activists but with actual and potential Tory voters as well – notably the blue-collar *Sun*-reading voters from constituencies in and around London who swung to Labour in 1997 and who continue to figure prominently in electoral strategy and tactics. Following Labour's poor showing in the May 2000 local and London elections, and despite losing the safe Tory Romsey seat to the Liberal Democrats on the same day as a result of tactical voting by those who disapproved of the Conservatives' anti-immigration policies, it became possible for sympathetic commentators to imagine that Hague could do enough to deprive Labour of its overall majority in the next general election, and incidentally to win back the majority in England.[8]

To the anti-euro position he had by then added several more populist electoral issues, in what one commentator described as an "embrace of Poujade-Powellism".[9] Labour set out to appropriate the crime issue with the promise to be tough on it and its causes. But Hague was able to prioritise it politically by systematically demanding more illiberal measures than the Home Secretary, Jack Straw, himself no instinctive liberal, was willing to concede. This phenomenon of a "race to the right" was even more pronounced in 1999-2000 over the issue of asylum-seekers.[10] An increase in the numbers seeking asylum from 33,000 in 1997 to 71,000 in 1999 occasioned an outburst of media and political hostility and was described by Hague and his colleague Ann Widdecombe as a "massive influx" of bogus applications orchestrated by racketeers. Asylum-seekers should be held in detention camps if necessary, they argued. This became a major plank in their local election manifesto. It was accompanied by promises from New Labour to increase arrests, open new detention centres, disperse asylum-seekers throughout the country and give them vouchers instead of cash – all of which proposals influenced Ireland's political debate on the subject in the first half of 2000.

A third issue was the countryside, the subject of a strong lobbying movement combining ecological, planning and pro-blood sports positions against New Labour policies. Despite the government's efforts to appropriate some of these sentiments – based on a considerable number of new rural seats gained by Labour in 1997 – they also helped to revive Conservative organisations. A fourth issue was a sustained campaign against the baleful influence of a liberal elite supposedly foisted on Britain by the Labour government and an effort to reassert religious values. And fifthly, Hague planned to champion the National Health Service and to channel money directly to schools, bypassing local authorities, in an effort to outflank Labour's policies in those areas by accepting the new levels of expenditure but offering alternative methods of managing them. Here he was strongly influenced by advisers from the US Republican Party and their attempts to outflank President Clinton's "triangulation" techniques of appropriating opponents' policies but distancing oneself from them politically – in what came to be described as "compassionate conservatism".[11]

The cumulative impact of this apparent Conservative revival, combined with Labour's political and electoral setbacks in mid-2000, certainly rattled Blair and his advisers. This was dramatically confirmed by the leaking of two highly confidential documents in July 2000: a memorandum on "touchstone issues" written by Blair on 29 April; and a memorandum to Blair written a few days later on "Getting the Right Place in History and not the Wrong One" by his close political and polling adviser Philip Gould.[12] Blair acknowledged that on crime, asylum, the family and "sticking up for Britain" a linked series of issues had given an advantage to the Conservatives, requiring "a thoroughly worked-out strategy stretching over several months to regain the initiative in this area". Gould was characteristically more apocalyptic. He argued that the "settled pattern of Labour's lead has been broken by recent events", based not only on opinion poll evidence, but because for the "last 18 months, the government has been drifting, growing almost monthly weaker and more diffuse. Above all else, I have a sense of government which started with great strength but has seen that strength ebb away and erode as the months and years have passed." Thus "we are outflanked on patriotism and crime; we are suffering from disconnection; we have been assailed for spin and broken promises; we are not believed to have delivered; we are believed by a huge margin to be slowing down rather than speeding up; we are disliked on the left for being right-wing, on the right for being politically correct". Gould went on to argue that holding and sustaining power is far more difficult than before, because "politics has now moved on from representational democracy to direct democracy, in which there is a need to win a daily mandate, in which the public is much more fickle and discerning and the media far more hostile. This is the opposite of the old model in which you took tough mid-term decisions, lost popularity but won it back at the end." Saying Labour does not know how to handle such conditions he called for a stronger political centre, a determined effort to reach a shared agreement about what is the New Labour project for the government, and an effort to reach an emotional as well as a rational contract with the British people based on economic and cultural stability and security. In these new conditions, Labour must win "a daily mandate in which strength comes from popularity".

These are very revealing indications of Labour's style of government and the philosophy underlying it. The effort to recover from mid-term setbacks was probably obscured and deflected by the continuing effort to court popularity.

By September it appeared that Labour had fully recovered from these setbacks, as polls indicated a 10-13% lead over the Conservatives, enough to win a majority on the scale of 1997.[13] But the weeklong flash fuel price protests beginning on 11 September, which brought the country to a standstill in days, deeply dented that Labour recovery. Blair's determined assertion that he would get the fuel lorries moving again was not borne out by the record. This, together with ill-preparedness and the impression of panic, lost him and the government credibility. Public opinion, especially among middle-England voters, seemed to be with the protesters; their message, that Britain's fuel taxes are the highest in the EU, struck a real chord. So did Gordon Brown's refusal to countenance lowering them under such pressure. Hague's opportunist identification with the protesters as "fine upstanding citizens" helped him to stage a recovery which showed up in two polls, in one of which the parties were neck and neck at 37% apiece, or, sensationally for the first time in eight years, in front by 38% to 36%. This was confirmed by a *Guardian*/ICM poll which gave the Conservatives a four-point lead – 38% to 34% – and reported Blair's popularity to be in free fall.[14]

Much therefore depended on Blair's performance and reception at Labour's annual conference in Brighton at the end of September. In a powerful and widely-praised speech he set out the party's campaigning positions based on the central priorities of expenditure on health, education and the pursuit of social justice. In response to allegations of arrogance and disregard for public opinion he said: "I am listening. I hear. And I will act." He insisted that Britain faces strategic choices on economic management, its position in Europe, multiculturalism and racism; he won particular applause for saying there were certain things he could not do to win votes, including putting tax cuts before education spending, telling people that Europe is full of terrible foreigners or exploiting the asylum issue for reasons of race.[15]

The conference once more boosted Labour in the polls, a lead that was sustained after the Conservatives held their own successful conference in the following week. At it Hague effectively asserted his own leadership and attempted to broaden the party's appeal beyond the narrowly right-wing core support base he had relied upon to consolidate his position. He called for new initiatives on inner cities and cultivated the image of his party's appeal to ordinary voters such as those in Yorkshire with whom he grew up. On health, education, Europe and constitutional affairs he clarified his party's policies and priorities. But it remained vulnerable on taxation. And observers noted continuing tension between its social libertarian and authoritarian wings as it forged a more populist appeal. The former was exemplified by an appeal from Michael Portillo for the party to embrace a more inclusive multicultural society in Britain, the latter by Ann Widdecombe, who called as shadow Home Secretary for a zero-tolerance approach, including compulsory £100 fines for anyone using cannabis. Hague sat uneasily between these wings of conservatism, hoping (unconvincingly) to make them cohere through his strongly articulated Euroscepticism.[16] His own performance was more convincing than that of the team he assembled to lead the party.

The Conservative Party membership's age at the last election averaged 64. It had great difficulty adjusting to the loss of power in the years following its defeat in 1997. A trickle of defections from its Europhile and liberal wings to Labour seemed to hold out the possibility of a split. That, of course, was part of New Labour's longer-term strategy to create a centrist coalition embracing not only Liberal Democrats but liberal Europhile Tories as well. In that perspective Europe could do to the Conservatives what the Irish Question did to the Liberals in the late nineteenth century; but the more the party's prospects held or improved in the opinion polls the less likely was a split, despite the disenchantment of Europhiles with its policies. Hague seemed likely to survive to and beyond the next general election; conceivably he could do well enough in it to endanger a second Labour term.

This prospect of a Conservative return to office was tailor-made for Labour's leaders to help galvanise Labour activists and its voters out of the differential abstention which deflated Labour's mid-term electoral performance. Clearly a more effective opposition could make real dents in Labour's lead. If Blair felt imprisoned by the extent of his 1997 victory, he needed a strong, but not too strong Conservative recovery in 2001-2 to release him. Much would depend on whether dissatisfied voters turned back to the Tories in Scotland and Wales or went rather to the Scottish National Party and Plaid Cymru.

Old Labour
Blair devoted a lot of time to ensuring Old Labour personnel and policies were marginalised and was generally successful in doing so, despite the large parliamentary majority. He acknowledged his obsession with overcoming the legacy of left-wing policies from the 1980s which he is convinced made the party unelectable, admitting he may have been "too scarred" by it to realise that, when in power, he didn't need to control everything all the time.[17] Effectively his coming to power as leader represented a revolutionary change in party structures and policies, forged to make it electable and capable of responding to a much more uncertain and fluid world. These changes are graphically communicated in a book by Philip Gould, who set out the core beliefs of the New Labour leadership group in the following passage:

> When critics attack New Labour for caution, for failing to be radical enough, early enough, for making tough economic decisions, for trying to impose order and discipline, they are trapped in the conservative mind-set that kept Labour in opposition for so long. If a progressive coalition

> can govern Britain for a majority of the time then
> more poverty will be removed and more real
> change achieved than could ever be achieved by
> short, sharp occasional spasms of radicalism.
> Lasting change can only happen over time, as part
> of a progressive project for government ... New
> Labour may have won an election, but now it has
> to win a century.[18]

It is impossible to understand Blair's position on these
questions without realising fully how deep his conviction is about
the damage done by the combination of left-wing factionalism
within the Labour Party in the 1980s and the right-wing
ideological factionalism of the Thatcher governments, based on a
minority of the popular vote. That is why he wants to substitute
pluralist good governance for partisan structures. But
paradoxically, as we saw in Chapter Two, he came to power by
majoritarian means and remains under strong party pressure to
continue using them against his opponents.

After the May 2000 setback in the London and local elections
Blair defended himself against criticisms of his party leadership
style:

> But it's important that we do not allow our
> strengths to be turned into weaknesses by our
> critics. A disciplined Labour Party is a good
> thing. A Labour Party whose annual conference
> is not a beanfeast for people to tear the party
> apart is a good thing. A Labour Party that is pro-
> business is a good thing. There will be people
> who want to turn these strengths into
> weaknesses: discipline becomes control freakery;
> well-run party conferences become suppressing
> debate; Labour pro-business becomes anti-
> working people. Of course you can learn the
> lessons, but don't let us fall into a Tory trap.[19]

His obsession with discipline and the rooted belief that were it
to be relaxed Labour's position would disintegrate had indeed
threatened to rebound, however, as allegations of control freakery
attended his efforts to ensure conformity, notably in Scotland,
Wales and London. The techniques deployed continued those

used to ensure his triumph over internal party dissent after he succeeded John Smith. They included changing representative procedures, appealing over the heads of activist layers to ordinary party members, substituting policy forums for conference debates, seeking mandates on the basis of individualised postal ballots, and reinforcing the control of the party's Millbank administrative centre in selecting candidates for elections to ensure they were "on message". After the London and local results more of the internal party debate on these techniques emerged in public – and was by no means confined to left-wing critics. David Pitt-Watson, a former assistant general secretary at Millbank, warned, for example, in an inquest paper on the results that unless that centre learned to trust and respect its volunteer members it would turn Labour into a version of the US Democrats. Pitt-Wilson criticised marketing techniques, the use of focus groups as a substitute for representative democracy, and policy forums as a substitute for decision-making conferences. If the party did not devote more attention to recruitment and local campaigning a second term win could be more difficult because "as a result the electorate will simply not bother to vote". He admitted that a deep alienation had opened up between the Millbank professionals and the party's voluntary rank and file members.[20]

The Scottish and Welsh Labour parties are traditionally more collectivist in their values, some of which energy has been converted into enthusiasm for devolved government. But both the Scottish Nationalists and Plaid Cymru have deliberately sought to compete to Labour's left, drawing on these value orientations, and with considerable success. In London, Blair's campaign against Ken Livingstone was centrally concerned with preventing the emergence of an Old Labour power base which could compete politically with the mainstream in a second term with a reduced majority. Livingstone's narrow defeat in the Labour selection process, his subsequent decision to stand as an independent and his substantial victory in the election on 4 May, 2000 presented Blair with his sharpest internal political challenge since he was elected to lead the party. Blair was unused to political defeat; indeed his political career had been built on political success, transforming Labour into an electable party, winning such a famous victory and overseeing the implementation of its policies as Prime Minister. But this made him many enemies, factional as well as ideological. The question arose as to whether his colleagues would stick by him through a prolonged period of political difficulty and the slide of his personal standing in the opinion polls, during which he came under great personal strain.

Coping with these setbacks would, therefore, reveal much about Blair's political capacity. He said he would co-operate with Livingstone; the Labour Party confirmed that by accepting executive positions in the new mayoral administration. But there was no move to take Livingstone back into membership, despite his evident appeal to rank and file members and supporters who rallied to him precisely to cock a snook at the Labour leadership. In an interview as he returned from a visit to Wales in early April 2000 Blair acknowledged he had misjudged Rhodri Morgan. He added, in response to a question about his apparent urge to control, that this flowed from his experience of the Labour Party in the early eighties and said "essentially you have to let go of it with devolution".[21]

It was clear that Livingstone intends to use his base as mayor to campaign for the devolution of more power and resources to London. Asked if he was disappointed with how the position has been framed, he replied:

> Come back in 25 years time and I suspect it will be much more like the job of Mayor of New York. The Lord Mayor will run health, schools, everything. And we'll be the model for regional government in Britain.[22]

It was also clear that Livingstone's victory altered the balance of forces within Labour, providing an opening for alternative voices and more plural ways of governing, rather than a resurgence of Old Labour positions. Just as a tighter political struggle seemed set to bring New Labour and the Liberal Democrats closer together, so the possibility of electoral reform opened up the prospect that a left-wing Labour group could split from the party and establish itself in parliament. That would spur political realignment. But left-wingers complained that precisely such a prospect convinced the Labour leadership to reject any radical approach to electoral reform, so as to avoid giving those on the left a political foothold.[23]

A mood of self-criticism affected many strands of the Labour Party in mid-2000. Several cabinet ministers urged Blair to delay the election to autumn 2001 or even spring 2002 to give the party time to re-enthuse its core supporters and deliver on its key promises. There was considerable worry that the "horrible explosive cocktail" of issues which hit them in April 2000 – including negative reaction to a mere 75p budget pension increase, illiberal approaches to asylum-seekers, deteriorating crime figures, the reaction to a farmer convicted of murder for shooting dead an intruder, and the row over teaching about homosexuality in schools – had been building up unanticipated for a long time. These events sparked off the memoranda already referred to. Some ministerial voices urged a period of silence from the relentless public relations activism characteristic of Blair's leadership style, so as to allow the message of delivery, competence and trust to build up again.[24] The decision by Blair's spokesman, Alistair Campbell, to reduce his daily briefing sessions with the press lobby in order to concentrate on strategic planning and the more effective communication of the government's big themes and achievements was symptomatic of that mood. So was the decision to reorganise the Millbank operation in preparation for the election campaign. But, typically, that in turn threatened to be jeopardised by competition between different factions in the leadership, especially those surrounding the two men nominated by Blair to run the campaign, Brown and Mandelson. They were hardly on talking terms with each other and now had a significant policy difference – on whether and when to advocate joining the euro – to divide them.[25]

As Matthew Taylor, director of the Blairite Institute for Public Policy Research, put it:

> If we are to reconnect with the voters, from Halifax to Wimbledon, we must mobilise our activists with a more open style and a core progressive message.[26]

This was despite the many achievements he said the government had to its credit, including the re-invention of the tax-benefit system; the minimum wage; new employment rights; and a 28 per cent increase in the foreign-aid budget. Philip Stephens, a sympathetic but critical commentator, added to this list: a strong economy, despite the Treasury's "malign neglect of sterling and feeble policy towards the euro"; a low rate of inflation and unemployment; budgetary surpluses available to spend on public services; and an irreversible constitutional reform programme. But he pointed out, shrewdly, that, despite Blair's political ambition to build a permanent coalition behind his brand of social democracy bringing together prosperous Middle England and the less fortunate in society, the government has treated the interests of the two groups as distinct and often conflicting, rather than using its continuing strength to explain why economic prosperity and social cohesion are allies rather than enemies. Unless it addresses this issue, Stephens wrote, "the danger is not that he might lose the next election, but that in his anxiety to win it he may surrender the chance to remake the political landscape."[27]

The Liberal Democrats

The Liberal Democrats remained on board the project of cooperation with Labour against the Conservatives. But they had a difficult time holding party ranks given the government's majority and the reluctance of many Labour leaders to support Blair's plans for closer cooperation. Blair said his greatest regret was that he did not bring the then Liberal Democrat leader, Paddy Ashdown, into the cabinet in 1997; but that was made impossible by the large majority. The two parties have a structured dialogue, share membership of a joint cabinet committee on constitutional change, which discussed devolution and Lords reform, weekend polls and reform of the United Nations; they issued a common paper on the IGC 2000 negotiations and in July 2000 announced that following a consultative process they were to co-operate against the Conservatives on health funding policy along the lines laid out in the government's spending review. In Scotland the two parties went into coalition, which made that executive a laboratory of wider political change; in Wales the new assembly leader, Rhodri Morgan, was willing after his election in March 2000 to court unpopularity in London as he co-operated not only with the Liberal Democrats but with Plaid Cymru; in October it was agreed to offer two of the posts in the Welsh cabinet to the Liberal Democrats.

The Liberal Democrat leader, Charles Kennedy, said that without a firm Labour manifesto commitment to hold a referendum on PR for Westminster, he could not see "much basis for further cooperation" between the two parties. There was tension between the Liberal Democrats' activist wing in northern England (where the party took control of Sheffield and Liverpool councils from Labour before the May 2000 local elections), which wants to maximise differences and assert an opposition role by overtaking the Conservatives, and the leadership group. The

Liberal Democrats did well in the local elections, attracting significant swing votes from Labour supporters – a reminder that the parties compete with one another and will co-operate most effectively on that basis. The importance of tactical voting was underlined at the Romsey by-election held on the same day, in which Labour voters swung to the Liberal Democrats to take a safe Conservative seat. Evidence from the voting showed Labour has a major task in store to get its voters out in a general election – the party could not assume it would easily make up the difference between its 29% share of the local vote and the 50% share it enjoyed in opinion polls. A plausible reading of the results was that Labour's Westminster standing stood at 40 per cent, which might not be enough to secure an adequate majority in a general election.[28]

The former Liberal Democrat leader, Paddy Ashdown, urged his party to develop half-a-dozen distinctive policies which would form the basis of negotiations in the event of a post-election coalition with Labour.[29] Blair emphasised that he wanted to keep open the project of cooperation with the Liberal Democrats and the prospect of electoral reform. The biggest test of his commitment to this approach would be whether he would stick to his pledge to include a referendum on voting reform in his party's next election manifesto, despite vehement opposition from party traditionalists led by the deputy leader, John Prescott, and a number of trade union leaders convinced that changing the electoral system would cost many Labour seats and necessitate undesirable coalition government. There were firm indications that Blair would opt for the Alternative Vote system, in which candidates are ranked by voters in order of preference and the least popular eliminated until one has the support of half or more of the voters. Despite the fact that this tends to exaggerate the votes/seats ratio for the leading party, and continuing opposition to coalition government by leading figures such as Mandelson, the prospect that this could be a first step towards a fully proportional system and would disproportionately favour Lib-Lab tactical voting, tempted leading Liberal Democrats to welcome it.[30] At Labour's national policy forum in July 2000 it was agreed to retain the party's commitment to hold a referendum, without specifying a voting system to put to the public.

The London and local results reinforced Blair's case for working with the Liberal Democrats at the "radical centre" of British politics, using the triangulation technique developed by

Clinton to distance himself both from Old Labour represented by Livingstone and Hague's Conservatives. If the opinion polls narrow, the two parties might have to consider a pre-election pact; they would certainly be under pressure to recommend anti-Conservative tactical voting to their respective supporters, which would threaten many of the seats won by Labour in 1997. But there are paradoxes here. Liberal Democrat voters who want to see a Lib-Lab pact and proportional representation would have a reason to vote Conservative in many constituencies in order to produce the hung parliament their party needs. That would be damaging to the Conservatives, because it would increase the likelihood of a realignment designed to marginalise them in the longer term; therefore they would not want to do too well, unless they could win outright.[31] The Conservatives also had good reason to suspect the introduction of the Alternative Vote system, since there are far more Conservative-Liberal Democrat marginal seats, where the second choice of Labour supporters might prove critical, than there are Labour-Liberal Democrat ones where Tory voters would be similarly decisive. That is one reason it appeals to Labour and Liberal Democrat leaders.[32]

The National Media

The national media, specifically the national press, are a real phenomenon in contemporary British politics. Blair's government has to take strategic account of that fact, which helps to explain its obsession with media management. A relentless drumbeat of sovereigntist positions vis-à-vis Britain's relations with the EU is to be heard from key sections of the right-wing press, led by those owned by Murdoch and Black, which regularly substitute for the weakness of the Conservative opposition. The message is tied up with the two men's roles as international players in a globalising world whose interests are best served by minimal regulation. They, therefore, have much to fear from the model of trans-nationalised governance emerging in the EU, despite their ability to reap advantage from some specific state and inter-state regulatory regimes. Black, indeed, put up a case for the UK to join the North Atlantic Free Trade Agreement between the US, Mexico and Canada, rather than deepen its relationship with Europe.[33]

Euroscepticism verging on europhobia attracted much criticism from Blair and his colleagues, notably at the Helsinki European Council in December 1999, where he accused most of the national media of betraying Britain's national interests by distorting the reality of negotiations; after it he told the House of Commons a policy of opposition to Europe urged on him by sections of the media and the Conservatives amounted to "utterly bogus patriotism".[34] Anyone who attended that meeting would tend to agree; it was as if two summits took place, one dealing with British beef (which was not dealt with) and tax harmonisation (which was deferred), while the other focused on the decision to add Turkey to the list of candidates for EU membership (the lead story in most of the Continent's press, but which barely figured in most of the British reports) and the formal decision to develop the EU's defence identity by creating a 60,000-strong rapid reaction force. In his speech on European policies at Gent in February 2000, Blair cited equally distorted coverage of the Agenda 2000 European Council at Berlin in March 1999: "By making our case persuasively, we protected Britain's rebate and got a very good deal on structural funds. Yet that got a fraction of the media attention that attended the failure by France to lift the ban on British beef, even though the financial consequences for Britain were more far-reaching." If people said the argument for Europe has been lost in Britain, they were wrong, he said. "Of course our position has been made more difficult by our media. One part has abandoned all sense of objectivity and is essentially hostile to the European Union. The other part is supine in the face of that hostility."[35] Speaking in Berlin, Blair and his spokesman Alistair Campbell attacked the Eurosceptic press in detail and urged it to "grow up" on the subject of Europe, and lamented "the way that press bias and misrepresentation sets the agenda for broadcasters who endlessly repeat the cliches of isolation, division and international conflict."[36]

Nonetheless, the resulting media mindset profoundly shaped contemporary British attitudes to European integration. This helped explain why Blair placed such emphasis on securing changes in the substance and operation of EU policies, including reforms in labour markets and the work of the European Commission. If the EU could be shown to change in the direction of British preferences it would be all the easier to convince English voters of the necessity to be at the heart of Europe to preserve their country's international influence – a theme enlarged upon in the next section of this book. Similarly, Blair found it necessary to emphasise continuously that "standing up for Britain does not mean being anti-Europe. It is not pro-British to be anti-Europe."

A new modern patriotism was necessary to achieve "a Britain that is stronger, fairer, modernised to be fit for the new world we live in", in which the European Union is the most effective means of regulating globalisation together.[37] Both on the issue of the euro and the wider question of courting Middle England and its media, Blair was willing to reach understandings with Murdoch in order to neutralise the *Sun*'s attitude towards his party. The referendum on the euro is intended politically to get around the newspaper's objections by separating the decision to vote Labour from that supporting euro membership – based on the assumption that 52 per cent of *Sun* readers vote Labour, most of them oppose the euro, and that they undoubtedly represent an important swing vote.[38]

On a wider plane, Blair devoted much attention to the *Daily Mail* and its constituency in an effort to convince Middle England swing voters that their interests were not threatened by Labour and of the government's credibility and competence in economic management (the *Sun* and *Daily Mail* have 16 million readers between them). His government is nonetheless left with a basic imbalance of support and sympathy in the national press, as perceived by ministers and their advisers. There are few loyal New Labour newspapers (among them the Mirror and Express groups); on the liberal left the *Guardian* and *Observer* thrive on criticism of what they see as the government's illiberalism, factionalism, centralism and control freakery. The media are partly responding to the very success of New Labour's media management techniques, which have brought proactive response and spin-doctoring to a high art and were an important ingredient in its victory in 1997; but given this imbalance Blair insisted "we are infinitely more spun against than spinning".[39]

Efforts by Blair's team to reach out to the regional, non-metropolitan media have had some success but have been limited by the very centralism of the national media, which remain concentrated on London.

THREE MAJOR OBJECTIVES

Second Term
The media were also responding to ambiguities in the government's position with regard to the objectives of securing a second term, winning a euro referendum and realigning British

politics. We have seen how issues of core Labour turnout, delivery on promises and reconnecting with Labour activists preoccupied ministers after the May 2000 London and local elections. That involved difficult choices about arrangements with the Liberal Democrats and the timing of the election. In order to galvanise core Labour voters, it would be necessary to convince them there is a real threat of a Conservative victory which would reverse Labour's achievements. These in turn have to be delivered and understood more effectively than was the case in mid-2000. That produced an argument in favour of delaying the election into the autumn of 2001 (or even into 2002 when it must be held) despite the danger of being seen to be boxed in or of opportunistically delaying the date to maximise party advantage. So much in the New Labour programme is predicated on a second term in office as to make it certain this objective will have absolute priority over taking a lead in Europe or considering the optimal timing for a referendum on joining the euro.

Euro Referendum

The complex relationship between the next election and the euro referendum concerned ministers from the autumn of 1999. It became a very public issue in June 2000, when tactical and political differences surfaced about the best way to handle it.[40] That followed from the basic decision taken in autumn 1997 not to hold the referendum then (which some believed would prove to be Blair's greatest strategic mistake).[41] One group, centred on the Foreign Secretary, Robin Cook, and including the Northern Ireland Secretary, Peter Mandelson, and the Trade Secretary, Stephen Byers, argued it would not be credible to fight an election without adopting a positive position on the euro; to preserve Britain's international influence and protect foreign direct investment it was important to make the case as soon as possible. The other, centred on the Chancellor, Gordon Brown, and including the deputy prime minister, John Prescott, argued that to link the two organically in the manner of the 1997 referendums on devolution would risk conceding the anti-euro agenda to the Conservatives, allowing them to cash in on its unpopularity. A compromise reached in early 2000 to the effect that the government would not "bounce" the country into a referendum on the back of an election victory accepted the case for a more prolonged public debate, but did not quieten the issue. Assuming the Conservatives were defeated, and that a referendum was

carried either in late 2001 or more likely in 2002, that probably
pushes back the likely date of British EMU entry. It also creates its
own difficulties of timing, since a mid-term referendum would risk
associating the issue with normal political disenchantment.

Hence the need to conceal the strategy towards the euro behind
the mantra of prepare and decide, using the five economic criteria
set out by Gordon Brown in October 1997, concerned with
convergence between the British and euroland economies.[42] The
strategy relies on assumptions about the likely convergence of
interest rates, currency values and the performance of the
euroland economies over the medium term, at which point it
would presumably be easier to convince British voters of the
merits of joining a successfully functioning system for fear of
being isolated; the very success in establishing the government's
economic competence would also make it easier to convince them
that joining the euro is a decision framed in the national interest,
as well as being an inevitable means of adjusting to a successful
policy. But the poor performance of the euro against sterling and
the dollar made it more difficult to sustain the argument until the
international economic tide turned, as conventional economic
opinion expected it to do following sterling's sharp depreciation
against the dollar in August and September 2000.[43] On balance,
the evidence points to a continued commitment by Brown to
joining the euro, despite political and media speculation that he
had become more sceptical about it, and believed it could lose
Labour the next election; or that he had used the ambiguities
involved to bolster his political position vis-à-vis Blair (whom he
could replace as prime minister) and the Treasury's vis-à-vis the
Foreign Office presided over by his long-standing rival, Robin
Cook.

Philip Stephens described these three attitudes towards the
euro as the statecraft, politics and personal ambition approaches.
He made the following important point about the delay in holding
the referendum: "The question that will be asked in Berlin, Paris
and Brussels is what is Blair's purpose. Is this a prelude to Britain's
permanent self-exclusion from the project at the centre of
European integration? Or can Blair be believed when he says there
is a positive purpose to this new delay? How this question is
answered is of vital consequence."[44] The Treasury was acutely
aware of the distinction between the international perception of
Britain as a "pre-in" and an "out"; Japanese businessmen lined up
to warn Blair that a shift from one to the other over the next few

years would undoubtedly jeopardise the foreign investment that has been so important in Britain's industrial recovery. Leaked memos from senior officials made the same point, despite the news that foreign direct investment volumes were up on the previous year. Another commentator, Andrew Marr, warned Eurosceptics not to overlook Blair's continuing commitment to joining the euro in the next parliamentary term.[45] This would rely on the same expectation of political and economic convergence over the medium term; on a realisation that opposition to the euro is thin and capable of being turned around; and that it will be possible to make the EU more British as well as to make Britain more European – as implied by the title of Blair's lecture in Gent on 23 February 2000, "Committed to Europe, Reforming Europe". Blair himself said the whole dynamics of the argument would change once the government made a recommendation to join the euro. "I think when you get underneath it people want to keep the option open. They understand that we live in a different world today, the world's moving closer together. From 1 January 2002 the euro notes and coins are going to be in circulation. So they'll make up their minds on sensible British grounds. They always do."[46]

Much was taken on trust in these explanations of New Labour's approach to the euro. To delay a decision was to risk political derailment on such a central issue. The assumption that it would be relatively easy to engineer a major turnaround in British attitudes by converting a two-thirds plus hostility to joining the euro into a two-thirds vote in favour (having to change the minds of some 4.75 million voters[47]) seemed ambitious and questionable without a major act of political leadership – despite Blair's conviction that people do "respond to political leaders who know what they want to do". Downing Street insiders believed the lesson of the 1975 referendum on staying in the EEC was that opinion turned around in the same proportion six months after Harold Wilson called it, recommending a "yes" vote.[48] In these ambiguous circumstances the government should not have been too surprised at the nature of press commentary on their intentions. Robert Worcester, the opinion pollster, argued in a pamphlet that the key point would be political leadership in engineering a turnaround of public attitudes. Voters would not decide on the basis of detailed arguments, but according to whom they could trust – and that meant predominantly the pro-euro camp.[49] Nevertheless it should be remembered that, unlike the situation in 1975, the major parties and business interests are divided and the media overwhelmingly hostile. Given the inevitability that the euro issue will figure prominently in the election campaign, prevarication and delay looked like less and less convincing strategies. That was acknowledged in a document agreed between the different leadership factions, which adopted a much more positive line on joining the euro, stressing the transactions cost, price transparency, exchange rate and macro-economic stability benefits it would bring, but without sacrificing the principle that Brown's five economic tests would have to be met. But, speaking in Korea on 19 October after the Danish referendum rejected euro membership, Blair said he would not vote for joining if asked on that day. This was seen as damping any expectation of a campaign in favour of the euro ahead of the election.[50]

Thus what the influential commentator Martin Wolf described as his "decisively indecisive, resolutely irresolute policy towards the euro" affected Blair's credibility deeply at home and in the EU.[51] While the government dithered on the subject through the latter half of 1999, public support for joining EMU collapsed from 28 per cent in a Eurobarometer poll in July to a risible 17 per cent according to another for the anti-EMU organisation, Business for Sterling, at the end of December. Despite his optimism about swinging opinion around, on these figures if Blair were to opt for a referendum soon after a victorious election, he would have a good chance of losing; that would reinforce the surprisingly popular sentiment that Britain should pull out of the EU altogether. One way or another it looked difficult indeed to prevent the election becoming a choice about abolishing sterling and joining the euro, even if the government's instinct was to avoid the issue as much as possible before it. Hence the significance of the speech made by Mandelson in May 2000, in which he warned that a high sterling threatened jobs in manufacturing industry. Despite the rational basis of his case, he was castigated for raising the issue, thereby giving the Conservatives ammunition to make it a centrepiece of the election campaign.[52] They were also expected to secure ammunition from the outcome of the Intergovernmental Conference on EU decision-making and representation which the French EU presidency hoped to conclude at Nice in December 2000. Eurosceptics underlined the possibility that taxation would become subject to majority voting in a further transfer of sovereignty to Brussels. They made much of the renewed debate on a hard core and a more flexible federal union; but this also reinforced Blair's political case to be at the centre of Europe, although the timing of the Franco-German debate on flexibility was certainly awkward for him.[53]

To win a referendum following the next general election, it would be necessary for the government to embark on a more vigorous campaign in favour of entry. Some argued that it could also have engineered fiscal, taxation and interest-rate policy towards greater convergence with euro-zone rates, thereby weakening sterling, in preparation for entry. But such preparations for early entry had one decisive drawback: they would be dreadfully unpopular, not least with almost all the government's supporters, in the run-up to an election. In addition, they would run counter to New Labour's conviction that such changes could only be market-led. Winning a referendum could be even more dangerous than losing one, because early entry would have to be at an over-valued rate – unless, as is suggested in Chapter Eleven, there was to be informal agreement between the UK government, the Euro-12 group and the European Central Bank on an acceptable range of values within which Britain would join, in advance of the referendum. Without that, the loss of competitiveness could not be recouped even in the medium term (the IMF suggested sterling was 16-20 per cent over-valued in relation to the euro). Wolf concluded bluntly that if such a strong prime minister as Blair was not willing to court the unpopularity involved in order to make entry economically safer "it follows that the UK is not a fit candidate for membership."

Realignment

Some of the same ambiguities were to be seen in the government's assumed plans to realign British politics by pursuing a coalition agreement with the Liberal Democrats, changing the voting system and decisively devolving power to the nations and regions. If this would be a more appropriate agenda for a second or third term, voters and observers were left guessing over whether it was realistic or achievable. Undoubtedly this was an important, if studiously vague, part of the New Labour political project. It would involve a decisive shift from majoritarian democracy – characterised by a unitary state, single-party government, a majority voting system, the absence of a written constitution or judicial review, concentration of parliamentary power within a single legislative chamber and an effective fusion of powers between executive and legislature – to a pluralist, consensual democracy.[54] These issues are examined in more detail in Chapter Four.

There was also the question of how such a platform sat with Blair's centralist preferences. The paradox of a pluralist objective pursued by such ruthlessly centralist means was much remarked upon. Mair pointed out that the only element of the majoritarian model Blair seemed determined to hold on to was the executive domination over parliament; he suggested the paradox was better understood as part of a long-term plan to marginalise party rule by substituting non-partisan democracy. This would work according to a model of "depoliticised good governance" increasingly influential in western democracies.[55] But devolution within the political system does not as easily extend to delegation of control within the Labour Party. The question arose as to whether Blair's hands-on centralist political style suited the kind of Britain implied by his pluralist objectives.

There was also genuine ambiguity about Blair's renewed zeal to preserve the United Kingdom and its state apparatus through a period when Britishness was being eroded and needed re-invention. Blair and his colleagues concluded in spring 2000 that they needed to convince voters that the strategy of reforming the constitution to preserve the UK was genuinely being pursued. As he put it in a speech on Britishness in the 21st century, "Britain is stronger together than separated apart" and was best preserved through "a powerful combination of shared values and mutual self-interest". Shared values and a common purpose counted more than unchanging institutions.[56]

DOMESTIC POLICIES

The Third Way ideology committed New Labour to new state-market relations, including the acceptance of market mechanisms, risk and flexible labour markets; to new state and political identities; to more effective policy management and delivery of service outcomes; to a "modernised" social structure no longer subject to the forces of conservatism; to a realist and acquiescent approach towards globalisation, requiring supply-side changes in educational and welfare policies for optimum response; and to budgetary prudence as a means of putting these policies into effect. That is an abstract policy agenda. Translating it into practical policies proved difficult. It was hard to say what was the big idea animating the project, or to rank-order policies coherently; they looked rather like an accumulation of small- to medium-sized ideas which might add up to something big.[57]

Despite disappointment over the pace of delivery of its reforms, the government put its record on the line through publishing *Annual Reports* on how it delivered on its promises. The report published in August 1999 showed that "early pledges" to cut class sizes, waiting lists and youth unemployment, protect the economy and introduce fast-track justice for young offenders were all on track. The record looked impressive enough halfway through the parliament, with more than 177 commitments made in the 1997 manifesto having already been met. That led one analyst to observe: "It seems somewhat curious that public support has ebbed away from the government at precisely the moment progress is finally being delivered."[58] The third *Annual Report* issued in July 2000 emphasised that "we have only just begun. We need to do more", but gave an upbeat account of the record to date.[59] It was while Blair was spelling out such an achievement in the spheres of extending opportunities for the unemployed, the disabled, lone parents, childcare, Internet access, the minimum wage and family tax credits to a Women's Institute meeting in June 2000 that he was heckled and jeered for being too party political. The incident was unkindly described by *The Economist* as Blair's "Ceausescu moment" in that it recalled the day in 1989 when the obedient masses of Bucharest startled the Romanian dictator by their sudden decision to boo.[60]

In office the party maintained many of the labour market and industrial relations reforms introduced by the Conservatives. There was no return to the trade union corporatist power and confrontation of the 1970s. Trade unions are no longer as powerful institutions within British society or the reformed Labour Party; most of their leaderships have bought into the New Labour agenda. Industrial relations reform eased their role but did not turn back the clock. The results were seen in much of British industry's capacity to withstand a high sterling rate, based on some increased productivity and greater labour force participation (although it is questionable how sustainable that was in the less advantaged regions of England). Industrial structures were based on a largely post-Fordist pattern of manufacturing introduced from outside, notably by US and Japanese investors, rather than on a reinvigoration of domestically-owned industry. Krieger argued: "The UK has assumed a specialised role within EU Europe as a producer of low-technology, low-value-added products through the use of a comparatively low-paid, segmented, decollectivised, and easily dismissed workforce.".[61]

This may be a premature judgment, based on an assumption that the government's policy was to remain on this relatively low link of the value chain rather than progress beyond it through long-term investment in human capital. But, if true, that would not be the best base from which to develop innovation and competitive enterprise in high-technology projects. The Chancellor, Gordon Brown, acknowledged the need to close technology gaps with the US (36%), Germany (15%) and France (25%).[62] A study of regional competitiveness in the UK showed a big range between London and the southeast on the one hand and the north and west of England, Wales and Northern Ireland on the other, with clear implications for their differential capacity to withstand a strong sterling without losing manufacturing.[63] Another official study found disposable income inequality indices had increased under Labour;[64] the bottom 50% of the population hold just 7% of marketable wealth, the top 1% almost one-fifth. These proportions have barely changed in 20 years; they would be even wider if home ownership were removed from the equation.[65] A "map of inequality" in Britain, based on two massive tracking surveys of 16,000 people born in single weeks in 1958 and 1970, published by the government, found that the country is still a class-ridden society with the gap in educational and job opportunities between rich and poor as deep as ever.[66] A Mori poll in June 2000 found most voters thought the Labour government had failed to reduce class divisions, one-third (predominantly working class people and those living in the North and Midlands) that they had actually grown since 1997, and one-half that there was no change.[67] But a *Guardian* ICM poll in mid-October reported for the first time since Blair came to office that a majority of voters see Britain as becoming a fairer and more equal society under New Labour.[68]

Welfare-to-work schemes are central to the New Labour agenda. They are seen as part of its "inclusive" approach, whereby participation in the wider community with its rights and obligations requires participation in the workforce as a means of reducing welfare dependency. Carrots and sticks were combined in introducing these policies. Positive inducements included training programmes targeted at youth and extensive reliance on compulsory elements. These also applied to pregnant women, those with disabilities and those with dependents. There was considerable evidence that labour-force participation and potential increased as a result, including through some substitution of means-testing for universalism[69]; but there were strong regional variations – if the jobs are not available the programme cannot work.[70]

Health is also central to Labour's reputation as a social democratic party for which the National Health Service was the crowning achievement of its post-war government. It remains so for a population in which 87% have no private health insurance. But the government was severely constrained by the commitment to hold taxation to the levels set by the Conservatives in their first two years of office. As a result, it emerged strongly in autumn 1999 that this was a crucial area of disenchantment for core Labour supporters and a wider audience of voters who were prepared to accord health spending a higher priority than the government, even if taxes were to be increased. Labour organisers saw a clear relationship between reduced turnout of their supporters and the failure to deliver on expectations and promises in this domain. Structural change takes time to come through and was not apparent to most NHS users, even though it has been a central preoccupation of New Labour in office through the use of the panoply of joined-up government techniques, with a special emphasis on reducing waiting lists and changing doctors' and surgeons' working practices. Blair himself admitted it would take six years of substantially increased expenditure to bring the UK's spending on healthcare up to the EU average expenditure of 8% of GDP from its current 5.75% – a profound acknowledgment of how far it has slipped behind. Brown's February 2000 budget and his July 2000 three-year spending review made health expenditure a first priority in coming years, as the government announced a detailed programme that included more beds, consultants, nurses and general practitioners, together with extensive reorganisation.[71]

Educational expenditure was similarly comparatively low, as is made clear in Chapter Five and is to be similarly targeted. Pensions likewise suffered, as did public transport. As was argued in Chapter Two these failings, if not addressed, will endanger Labour's electoral base. Another area of the government's core commitment, competence in economic management, was much more clearly established in the popular perception; that enabled the government to prime public spending on social services as the election approached and to make the case that now the wherewithal to fund it can be found without reverting to previous tax and spend policies.

LABOUR'S SOCIAL AND POLITICAL BASE

One of the most distinctive features of contemporary politics in Britain and elsewhere in Europe is the decline in partisan identification. The proportion of British voters who say in opinion surveys that they strongly identify with either Conservative or Labour has dropped from roughly three-quarters in the mid-1960s to about two-fifths today. There is a similar decline in the smaller numbers who identify very strongly with either party. Alongside that, the association between occupational class and voting behaviour has also weakened considerably – a phenomenon described by political scientists as "class de-alignment". The resulting electoral volatility was a marked feature of the 1997 election, when it doubled, nearly reaching European averages, but without the external shocks that have occasioned such change elsewhere. This raises the prospect of an "easy come, easy go" politics, in which landslides could be easily reversed, playing havoc with Britain's first-past-the-post, winner-takes-all adversarial system. Sociologists and political scientists speculated that the very success of New Labour had inevitably blunted the edge of party identification.[72] Therefore the trend identified in Chapter Two of core supporters abstaining is potentially very dangerous. Their reduced turnout in the next election could easily erode Labour's majority,[73] thereby necessitating the political realignment that was arguably delayed by the extent of the 1997 landslide.

The more the core issues differentiating the two main parties were eroded, the more the consumer ones closer to the election assumed prominence. Hence the obsession with style over substance in New Labour's presentation and the stress on consumption values in politics. There is evidence of much stronger gender identification among the parties and age groups; parallel to that is a new emphasis on identity politics as class identification is reduced or transformed. As is the case throughout western European countries, commitments are now more revocable, allegiances more eclectic, electoral participation more uncertain and identities more plastic – all of which make electoral politics much more difficult to manage, especially for social democratic parties. When to these are added the state and national identity shifts in Britain already discussed, it can be seen to be a volatile mixture indeed.

The question needs to be asked whether New Labour can hold these constituencies together through the next election and the following one as its leaders aspire to do. There is considerable evidence that class erosion has not gone as far as is often assumed by Third Way theorists, evidenced in the behaviour of core working-class Labour supporters. There is also room to doubt whether the value systems of Middle England are all that different in their orientation than are those of traditional Labour voters, in respect of the core issues of welfare, health, education, employment and international involvement. This gives New Labour more room to manoeuvre than would be expected from its political rhetoric – an opportunity to join up its commitment to Middle England and traditional core working-class supporters, based on a warning of the consequences of a Conservative victory – the return of normal politics after the artificial interlude of such a large Labour majority.[74]

Changing political identities can also be mobilised constructively, given their classical multiple character. It would, therefore, be a mistake to agree too readily with Tam Dalyell's conclusion in a House of Commons debate on 4 March 1998 that devolution is "a motorway without exit to an independent state" of Scotland. That has not been the outcome in Spain, which devolved power without it leading to independence; or, indeed, in Canada, where Québécois remain split on whether to support a state sovereignty. These issues are examined in more detail in the next chapter. A great deal will depend on how relations are handled between Whitehall/Westminster and Edinburgh, London and Cardiff, in particular on whether the central state can indeed let go to autonomy over time. Scotland is crucial for the survival of the UK. Successive surveys show that only a minority of Scottish voters feels an exclusive loyalty to Scottish rather than British identity – that they are Scottish not British. "Most people in Britain would have no problems choosing between a Scottish or English identity, or between British or French identity. These are horizontal, non-hierarchical, basically exclusive alternatives – a few immigrants or children of mixed marriages apart. But people do have problems choosing between a British and a Scottish identity," as one writer put it.[75]

Only a quarter of the Scots said they want independence rather than devolution, though a smaller majority expected the UK to be intact by 2019. Significant minorities of SNP supporters reject independence and do not think it is a particularly important political question. But, in an indication of future tensions, there was a clear discrepancy of opinion between the two-thirds of English respondents who believed the 15 per cent higher government spending in Scotland ought to be phased out and the similar majority of Scots who thought it ought to be maintained. That issue is rapidly creeping up the political agenda and is also examined in more detail in the next chapter. A Mori survey for *The Economist* found that Britain commands less loyalty than the separate nations, as 72 per cent in Scotland and 81 per cent in Wales identify with their nations first, whereas the balance was 41 to 43 per cent in England. The picture of multiple identification was nonetheless borne out, but by a smallish 18 and 27 per cent respectively in Scotland and Wales, compared to much greater identifications with local communities and regions. It looked, therefore, as if the British identification was diminishing. Looking forward, the survey found that 44 per cent of Britons as a whole expect the European Union to exert most influence on their lives in 20 years' time, compared to 22 per cent for the Westminster Parliament.[76] A poll marking one year of devolution in Scotland found most voters believed the only parliaments to matter in 20 years time will be those in Edinburgh and Brussels; 62 per cent thought the Scottish Parliament should have more powers.[77]

Such attitudes are based on a substantial degree of social integration between Britain's main national groups. There is extensive intermixing of English, Scottish, Welsh and Irish – as well as of Commonwealth immigrants, many of whom value a British state identity, because that accommodates their other identities in a way an English identity is unable to do.[78] A major report on the future of multi-ethnic Britain, published in October 2000, argued the case for the renewal of British identity so as to accommodate black and Irish people. It urged a debate between those who support the liberal view of Britain as a community of citizens and the pluralist view of it as a community of communities. But because it queried the use of the term "British" (to describe black and Irish people) it was contemptuously dismissed in the Tory press.

Nearly five million residents of Britain have or qualify for Irish citizenship; many more have Irish ancestry and a quarter of British citizens have an Irish relative.[79] There are about 550,000 people born in the Republic living in Britain[80] many of them still suffer

from prejudice and racism, as well as material disadvantage.
Nearly 20 per cent of the population of Wales is English-born,
as is 7% of the Scottish population. The same applies to the many
Scots and Welsh living in England – 745,000 people born in
Scotland live there, equivalent to 15% of the Scottish population.
Citing these figures Blair asked: "Why should anyone want to say
to all these people that they should suddenly become foreigners in
the land they live in?"[81] This integration gave substance to the
demands for a comprehensive modernisation of British
citizenship that animate much of its debate on constitutional
change.

CONCLUSION

A great deal, therefore, is at stake for all the people of these islands
as the politics of New Labour work themselves out. There can be
no doubt of two central facts: Tony Blair and his government are
altogether preoccupied with winning the next general election and
gaining a second term; and it is seen as altogether vital that a
referendum on the euro is won and not lost. Otherwise the
question could not be reopened for at least another ten years, by
which time Britain would have thrown away its chance of leading,
let alone influencing, the direction of European integration. Blair
is driven by the grand idea of achieving a second and third term in
office, thereby breaking the political mould and banishing
Conservatives from power for a generation. But he is substantially
constrained by the size of his majority and the party pressures it
generates, the commitment to economic and fiscal prudence
which has delayed delivery of education and health reforms,
confusions and ambiguities about his intentions and longer-term
objectives, and the sheer difficulty of translating them into
electoral politics. He is reported to have demanded a more radical
approach as the election approaches. That would be well advised.
There is much truth in the view put forward by Roy Hattersley, a
trenchant critic of New Labour from the centre-left: "Unless
politicians are brave enough to say what they believe they stop
believing in the things they dare not say".[82]

---

1   Hague (1998).
2   Lynch (2000), p. 64.
3   *ibid.*, p. 65.

4 Riddell (2000d).
5 Hague (1999b).
6 Kite (2000).
7 Groom (2000d).
8 Rees-Mogg (2000a).
9 Watkins (2000).
10 Donnelly (2000a); Toolis (2000).
11 Watt and Ward (2000).
12 *The Times*, 17 and 19 July, 2000; Gould text in *The Guardian*, 20 July 2000.
13 Kellner (2000).
14 Travis (2000b).
15 Blair (2000d).
16 Shrimsley (2000).
17 Ahmed (2000); Harris (2000).
18 Gould (1998), pp 393-4.
19 Interview with *The Times*, 8 May 2000.
20 Wintour (2000b).
21 *The Observer*, 9 April 2000.
22 Rayner (2000).
23 Wainright (2000).
24 Wintour (2000b).
25 Baldwin and Watson (2000).
26 Taylor (2000), p. 43.
27 Stephens (2000a).
28 Curtice (2000a).
29 Ward (2000).
30 Baldwin (2000a); Riddell (2000b).
31 Rees-Mogg (2000a).
32 Editorial, *The Times,* 30 June 2000; Curtice (2000b).
33 Black, Conrad (2000).
34 Peston (1999).
35 Blair (2000).
36 "Media's coverage is a joke, says Blair", *The Guardian*, I July 2000.
37 Blair (2000b).
38 Seymour-Ure (1997), p. 82; Whiteley (2000a).
39 Interview with *The Times*, 8 May 2000; see also Jones (1999).
40 Watt (2000).
41 White and Elliott (2000).
42 Brown (1997a).
43 Elliott (2000).
44 Stephens (2000).
45 Marr (2000).
46 Groom (2000d).
47 Whiteley (1999), cited in Gamble and Kelly (2000), p. 25.
48 *ibid.*

49 Worcester (2000).
50 Dodd and Watt (2000).
51 Wolf (2000).
52 Watkins (2000).
53 Fischer (2000); Smyth (2000); FitzGerald (2000).
54 Mair (2000), pp 23-4.
55 *ibid.*
56 Blair (2000b).
57 Cronin (1999), p. 184; White (1998).
58 Hindmoor (2000), pp 262-3.
59 Wintour (2000c).
60 Carvel (2000); *The Economist* (2000).
61 Krieger (1999), p. 158.
62 Groom and Brown (2000).
63 Groom (2000b).
64 Sparrow (2000).
65 Timmins (2000).
66 Wintour (2000d).
67 Riddell (2000b).
68 Travis (2000c).
69 Hindmoor (2000), p. 265.
70 Erdem and Glyn (2000).
71 Carvel (2000a).
72 Krieger (1999a), pp 150 ff.
73 Whiteley (2000), Curtice (2000), (2000a), Groom (2000), Riddell (2000).
74 McKibbin (1999), (2000), (2000a).
75 Millar (1999), pp 191-2.
76 David (1999), p. 4.
77 Bell (2000b).
78 Alibhai-Brown (2000); Modood (1999); Parekh Report (2000).
79 Partridge (1999), pp 12-13.
80 Halpin (2000), p. 89; Hickman (2000).
81 Blair (2000b).
82 Hattersley (2000); see his entertainingly sceptical essay on Third Way politics, Hattersley (2000a).

CHAPTER FOUR

Constitutional Politics

Paul Gillespie

INTRODUCTION

These are fundamental alterations in the arrangements of the United Kingdom, which amount to a reshaping of the British state.[1]

Major constitutional changes are under way in Britain. The raft of 12 constitutional Bills passed through the House of Commons in 1997-8 covered devolution to Scotland, Wales, Northern Ireland and set up Regional Development Agencies (RDAs) in England; ratification of the Amsterdam Treaty; incorporation of the European Convention of Human Rights in British domestic law; independence for the Bank of England; introduction of party list systems and proportional representation for European elections; authorising a referendum on a directly elected Mayor of London; and the emergence of a hybrid form of popular sovereignty in which referendums challenge the pure sovereignty of the crown-in-parliament.

To these must be added further continuing constitutional projects: reform of the House of Lords; freedom of information legislation; a continuing joint cabinet committee with the Liberal Democrat Party on electoral reform and constitutional change; and legal and administrative reform in Westminster, Whitehall and the judicial system to render the new constitutional arrangements coherent. This reform agenda involves a radical change in political structures, which would take the Labour Party at least another term in office to complete and the consequences of which could realign the British political system decisively.

New Labour had multiple incentives to develop an agenda for constitutional change. First, it provided a clear sense of Labour distinctiveness from the Conservatives, especially when there were so few differences in social and economic policy between the two parties. There was, secondly, the need to compete with the SNP and Plaid Cymru in circumstances where Labour had lost ground to them in its electoral heartlands. By 1987, Labour, unable to restore a substantial electoral presence in middle-England, had become more dependent than at any time since 1945 on its Scottish and Welsh seats, making it much more sensitive to political forces threatening them. That was the context in which the party swung towards devolution.[2] The driving force behind the devolution project in the 1990s (unlike the Callaghan government's 1978-79 devolution legislation) may not, indeed, have been a deep conviction that the Scots and Welsh should have Home Rule, but the peculiarly dominant position of Scots within the New Labour hierarchy after the electorally disastrous Foot/Kinnock years.[3] Thirdly, the commitment to constitutional change encouraged the Liberal Democrats into a dialogue which would distinguish them from the Conservatives.

And yet much about the constitutional programme remained unclear, including its animating purpose. Was it intended to reform the British political system or to preserve the integrity of its state apparatus by making the minimum changes possible – which had priority? The instinct to preserve conflicted with the desire to reform. Likewise the continuing centralist means of controlling the Labour Party contrasted with the pluralist, quasi-federal devolution of power within the political system. Robert Hazell, director of the Constitution Unit in University College, London warned: "To be strong the story needs to be consistent; but the government's programme at present is shot through with inconsistency and hesitations. Despite the devolution programme much of the government's language is centralising in tone, and in major parts of the constitutional reform programme distinctly ambivalent."[4] It would be a difficult to exaggerate the problems involved in carrying through such a radical enterprise even if it were totally coherent and consistent.

This is, therefore, very much a work in progress. It is also, as many participants and commentators said, a process rather than an event. The phrase "a new constitutional settlement", used by its designers, is misplaced, since there is nothing settled about it.[5] There are powerful dynamics, interactions and tensions, even contradictions, between its different parts, which will combine to create new political agendas in coming years, many of them probably unanticipated by Blair and his ministerial colleagues –

assuming they remain in power to confront them. All the more is this so when account is taken of one of the most surprising aspects of the process: the comparative silence with which it was articulated and presented politically by the Labour leadership. As two students of constitutional change write:

> The process of devolution has had little resemblance to the creation of the major federal systems of the world. It has not been preceded by a constitutional convention, such as the Philadelphia Convention of 1787, nor is there a constitutional blueprint like the German Basic Law. The government has studiously avoided such high constitutional politics. Ministers deliberately decided not to issue an overarching white paper setting out a vision for the entire process of reform. They assumed that such a step would scare the electoral horses and increase the resistance from ministers less enthusiastic for constitutional reform. Instead, ministers devised the legislation for each territory on the basis of the particular circumstances of each one. Moreover, different ministers oversaw different devolution initiatives. The Welsh and Scottish legislation was co-ordinated by Derry Irvine, the Lord Chancellor (i.e. the cabinet minister responsible for constitutional matters and the judiciary), while the English regional proposals have been dealt with by John Prescott, Secretary of State for the Environment, Transport and the Regions. The Northern Ireland Assembly, too, emerged from a completely distinct process, driven by the UK government, Ireland, and the US president.[6]

Aside from Scotland and Wales, there was not a single Labour front-bench speech devoted to the constitutional changes during the 1997 election campaign. It featured at the end of the list of commitments in the manifesto under the heading "We will clean up politics". Peter Hennessy argued that, if the members of the Labour government were polled on it results would show one-third did not believe in it, one-third did not care and only one-third understood it.[7] Among the last group it was suggested that only Robin Cook and Gordon Brown were seriously committed to a coherent programme of constitutional reform; John Prescott was committed to a stronger devolution in England than most other cabinet members felt comfortable with - hence the RDA compromise, which he regarded as an interim arrangement that needs to be strengthened in the direction of regional assemblies in the next election manifesto.[8]

It is often assumed that Blair was not himself strongly committed to the constitutional changes, having inherited them from his predecessor John Smith and the party's policy review in the early 1990s. This is debatable. In an article in 1996, Blair wrote: "Contrary to the Tory canard, constitutional reform is not an issue for the 'chattering classes', irrelevant to most people. Properly done, it will go to the heart of public concerns. It is important not only for its own sake, but because it makes possible the attainment of other vital goals: a stronger economy, better transport, good schools and crime prevention."[9] But this was very much an instrumental justification, as was his further comment that "economic reconstructions and democratic renovation are not alternatives. They go hand in hand".

Blair has also, of course, presented devolution in Northern Ireland and elsewhere as a means of strengthening the Union, rather than facilitating a united Ireland, the policy tilt of his party before he took over as leader:

> Northern Ireland is part of the United Kingdom, alongside England, Scotland and Wales. The Union binds the four parts of the United Kingdom together. I believe in the United Kingdom. I value the Union. I want to see a Union which reflects and accommodates diversity. I am against a rigid and centralised approach. That is the surest way to weaken the Union. The proposals this government is making for Scotland and Wales, and for the English regions, are designed to bring government closer to the people. That will renew and strengthen the Union.[10]

Despite the extraordinary amount of time he devoted to Northern Ireland, it was generally seen as a separate issue from the rest of the programme of constitutional change in Britain. Ireland is both part of the British constitutional and political changes introduced by New Labour and separate from them. The Belfast Agreement links up all of Ireland with the devolved United Kingdom and its new constituent parts, including Northern Ireland. But much of Blair's effort was intended to get the North off the UK agenda - partly to improve relations with the Republic and to develop relations with a stable Ireland with which it can do business. In that sense both governments share an interest in stabilising the North rather than using it either to bolster the Union or facilitate Irish reunification. That motivation will survive and be tested by a collapse or prolonged parking of the Northern Ireland executive; whether in those circumstances an informal form of co-sovereignty develops will be one of the most interesting possible scenarios.[11] If Scotland were to choose the path of independence, the consequences for Ireland would be profound and probably destabilising; many unionists would be tempted to consider the option of independence themselves, rather than contemplating Irish reunification, the demand for which would presumably be reinforced on the nationalist side. Thus the prospect of reunification could come onto the political agenda more rapidly than most people in the Republic, and certainly than most of the political class, expect or desire. By the same token, the success or failure of devolution in Northern Ireland could have implications elsewhere in the UK; but these are likely to be minimised precisely because Northern Ireland is seen as separate.

CENTRALISM

As a result of the comparative lack of debate, the subject of constitutional change has been seriously under-aired among the people who eventually will have to back it if it is to succeed, the *English* electorate. G.K. Chesterton's poem, "The Secret People", was often invoked:

> Smile at us, pay us, pass us; but do not quite forget.
> For we are the people of England, that never have spoken yet.

Critics complained that the centralist instinct in New Labour's leadership to maintain control over the process of change, the preservationist attitude to the central state based in London and the parameters of the party's internal policy debates contradicted the formal commitment to constitutional transformation. So did the effort to maintain a corporate management-type control from Downing Street by its media advisers. This runs, critics said, against the commitment to democratic reform and could mean that the opportunity to achieve it was lost. As Marquand put it, "there has been no great Britain-wide debate on the rationale, implications or goal of the changes now in progress"; it is "a very British revolution. It is a revolution without a theory."[12] It was not clear to him whether Blair and his colleagues understand what they were doing: was advancement of Labour control or constitutional reform the principal objective? Or, as Mair argued, were these changes intended to create a new non-partisan, consensualised mode of governance? The centre was unwilling to relax and let go of the devolved authorities, treating them as equal partners, not subordinates. This was despite Blair's pre-election condemnation of centralism – "Britain is the most centralised government of any large state in the Western world". He did not enunciate a coherent justification of constitutional change and devoted much time to ensuring his supporters assumed office - as in Wales with Alun Michael and in London, where he went to such great lengths to prevent Ken Livingstone become the official Labour candidate.[13]

One should, however, bear in mind that political coherence, blueprints and theories are subject to the exigencies of political life and events. This may explain why, despite the cascade of constitutional Acts during the Blair government's first year in office, the tougher questions - electoral reform for Westminster elections, freedom of information, and House of Lords reform - were postponed. A referendum on electoral reform was put off until the next parliamentary term, although the government indicated it would be held - but by presenting the Alternative Vote system rather than a more proportional method to the electorate. The prime minister came under party pressure to make minimal changes. During the Kosovo war, he believed larger parties in other EU governments were prevented from taking decisive hardline action by smaller coalition parties. There was also party dissatisfaction over the necessity of having a coalition government with the Liberal Democrats in Scotland because of PR there. Surveys of party organisations showed a majority against the Jenkins Commission report in 1998 which proposed a hybrid system combining first-past-the-post and a proportional top-up element – the Alternative Vote plus. The fairness of this consultation exercise was disputed and a survey of Labour Party members showed a small majority in favour of proportional representation; a survey of voters showed 63% for a referendum, 17% against. The issue was debated intensively in the Labour Party during 2000. The new Liberal Democrat leader, Charles Kennedy, continued the close dialogue with Labour inaugurated by his predecessor, Paddy Ashdown; but in both parties there was opposition to it proceeding towards a long-term coalition or even amalgamation, as Blair was believed to favour.[14]

Freedom of information legislation severely disappointed many of the government's supporters because it gave ministers and local authorities so much discretionary power to veto an order by the new Information Ombudsman on the disclosure of information. Extremely tight control of media relations and spin doctoring were all too characteristic of Labour in office and were set to be increased.

Human rights provisions were amended in line with Labour's programme and then arising directly from the Belfast Agreement. The Human Rights Act gives UK citizens the right to claim in any UK court rights and freedoms set out in the European Convention of Human Rights (ECHR), by incorporating it into British law. It is more a matter of achieving equal access to rights available for 50 years than creating new ones, according to the Home Secretary, Jack Straw.[15] He rebutted caricatures of the provision in the Tory press to the effect that it was a further plot by Brussels to "cripple our courts and tear up our statute book", pointing out that the ECHR is a product of the Council of Europe, not the EU. But it undoubtedly represents a significant Europeanisation of British law, all the more so given the increasing convergence of legal norms between the EU and the Council of Europe. The Charter on Fundamental Rights drawn up in parallel with the IGC 2000 was expected to reinforce that process.

Lords reform awaited the government's considered response to the Wakeham Commission's report in February 2000, which argued for a hybrid system of appointed and elected peers following the abolition of the hereditary ones; despite the commission's suggestion of three different models for elected members, there was little sign of a readiness to link the House of Lords explicitly and comprehensively with the transformation of territorial politics under devolution, in order to give national and regional governments direct representation at Westminster. The report was widely condemned in the media as a disappointing compromise which would reinforce the appointment of Blair's cronies.

The prime minister stoutly resisted pressure from Scotland to amend the Act of Succession which prohibits a Roman Catholic inheriting the throne.[16] As for the monarchy, it is difficult to resist the conclusion that it was "saved by Blair. Saved and to some extent taken over really." The crucial moment was following Princess Diana's death in September 1997, when public attitudes were ready for more radical change. Instead they were citizens for a week. "It is a 'modernisation of subjecthood', rather than a replacement for it."[17] New Labour sees the monarchy as a strong symbol of continuity and preservation of the Union; there were few republican voices to be heard.[18] Although a survey in June 2000 showed growing indifference and declining support for the royal family, Blair's office was very quick to distance itself from a suggestion by the Cabinet Office minister, Mo Mowlam, that it should vacate Buckingham Palace and move to accommodation more appropriate to a modern democracy. That was clearly a step too far.[19]

Thus it is too early to say categorically what the likely direction of constitutional change is going to be. But it is certainly possible to draw up scenarios based on current positions and project them forward, as Hazell and his colleagues have done (see pages 113 and 114). Methodologically their efforts are similar to this study's. They facilitate commentary on the likely policy options and outcomes and draw attention to the interactions, dynamics and tensions involved. They throw light on the overall coherence of constitutional change in Britain as an effective means of addressing the crisis of state and political identity it faces after the end, first of the empire, and then of the Cold War, as outlined in the IEA's 1996 study. A key question is whether the internal and external elements of this process proceed in tandem and complementary fashion: Will quasi-federalisation facilitate Europeanisation, albeit in a retarded fashion? Can quasi-federalisation embed the discourse of European integration as a virtuous objective?[20] Or are they both likely to be arrested by incoherence, indecision and centralism, making it more likely that Britain will remain the belated European partner - identified as the most likely outcome in the "Summing-up and Conclusions" of the IEA study four years ago - and perhaps even the one that misses the train altogether? Will Britain decentralise or disintegrate under these pressures? Is Blair's project of preserving the world's oldest multinational state through cautious, negotiated reform, controlled from the centre, bound to precipitate much more radical change, based on the fact that revolutions always come about when changes are conceded that are supposed to modernise things in an acceptable way but fail to do so? Last - and decidedly not least - will the exigencies of electoral politics or unforeseen events deprive Labour of the second term on which so many of these constitutional reforms are predicated? A Conservative return to office would reverse many of them, and thereby - arguably - accelerate disintegration of the UK. One way or another the timescale set out in the IEA's 1996 study, suggesting the process of change could extend through to 2006-11, still looks valid.[21]

CONSTITUTIONAL SCENARIOS

The minimal and maximal scenarios shown in Figure 1 on pages 113 and 114 are projected forward for about ten years. They assume a continuation of current arguments over the constitutional settlement and provide a useful checklist of their respective political logics. Seen in this overall fashion, the need for coherence and the contradictory pull of centralism become more clear, since they will have a cumulative impact on all branches of government. From below, in the devolved assemblies and executives, there will be dynamic pressure to accelerate and consolidate the processes at work, through leapfrogging and copy-catting between the devolved assemblies and continual negotiations between the different levels of government. While the contrary pull of centralism provides ample scope for delaying or retarding decentralisation, judicial and administrative change, it seems likely that the basic elements outlined here are *irreversible* – unless there is a resurrection of atavistic Chestertonian sovereignty, for example through a movement of English nationalism mobilised by the Conservative Party revived by a prospect of Scottish independence and/or British membership of an EMU that went disastrously wrong. Such a scenario would have to assume an equally disastrous failure of the Blair government in a second term; the question of how irreversible devolution would be were the Conservatives to be returned to power at the forthcoming general election is intimately connected with its attitude to wider constitutional reform and its European policies.

FIGURE 1: Minimal and maximal scenarios
for constitutional reform

Area	Minimal	Maximal
Devolution	Scottish Parliament with legislative power, not exercising its limited tax-raising powers	Scottish Parliament exercising legislative and tax-raising powers. Independent Scotland?
	Northern Ireland Assembly with legislative but no tax-raising powers	Northern Ireland Assembly with legislative and tax-raising powers
	Welsh Assembly with secondary legislation-making powers only	Welsh Parliament with legislative and tax-raising powers
	Regional development Agencies in England appointed by central government.	Elected Regional Assemblies in some English regions; Regional Chambers elsewhere
	Elected Mayors in a few cities with limited powers	Strong elected mayors in the major cities
	Joint Ministerial Committee on Devolution meeting frequently; fire fighting only	Joint Ministerial Committee as strong part of the Devolution settlement
	Council of the Isles as token consultative body	Council of the Isles developing wider functions
Parliamentary reform	Limited reform of the House of Lords, involving removing the hereditary peers and re-balancing party numbers. House of Lords remains a nominated body.	A predominantly or solely elected House of Lords representing the nations, regions and cities. Some changes to strengthen its functions and powers
	Referendum rejects electoral reform of the House of Commons.	House of Commons elected by proportional representation
	Closed list PR for elections to the European Parliament, enabling voters only to choose between parties	Open list PR for EP elections enabling voters to choose between individual candidates

FIGURE 1: Minimal and maximal scenarios for constitutional reform—*continued*

Area	Minimal	Maximal
A rights culture	ECHR as part of UK statute law but no Human Rights Commission to promote a new rights culture	ECHR as part of UK law. Human Rights Commission, domestic Bill of Rights either in preparation or already in the statute book
Openness	Restricted Freedom of Information regime, focussed mainly on access to personal files	Liberal Freedom of Information Act enabling access to general government information
Judicial structure	Appellate Committee still sitting as members of the House of Lords. The Privy Council adapted to hear 'devolution' disputes	A new supreme court for the United Kingdom, separate from the House of Lords
Inter-governmental relations	Informal intergovernmental consultative processes based on Whitehall concordats	Formalised Council of British Isles with full-time secretariat

Source: Robert Hazell (ed.) *Constitutional Futures – A History of the Next Ten Years,* Oxford University Press, 1999, pp. 7-8.

But in Scotland it is difficult to see devolution reversed without another referendum. "Power devolved, far from being power retained [in Westminster] as implied by constitutional theory, will be power transferred, as dictated by political reality; and it will not be possible to recover that power except under pathological circumstances, such as those of Northern Ireland after 1968."[22] Thus the relationship between Westminster and Edinburgh "will be quasi-federal in normal times and unitary only in crisis times".[23]

Hazell rather assumed a programme of "rolling devolution", driven by such leapfrog pressures (to catch up on Scotland), arguments over finance, and overlapping and competing competences in such an asymmetric system, including local and city government. The Joint Ministerial Committee on Devolution and the British-Irish Council will be important institutions in that leapfrogging process, including whether and how to secure access to and representation in EU decision-making. The council, which will be primarily consultative, will represent the two governments, the devolved institutions in Northern Ireland, Scotland and Wales, the crown territories of the Isle of Man and the Channel Islands and, if they are established, regional assemblies in England. Any two or more members of the council may enter into bilateral or multilateral arrangements with each other, independently of the council itself. Common policies, from which there can be opt-outs, may be developed on questions of transport, agriculture, the environment, culture, health, education, EU issues and other matters of mutual interest which are within the competence of the member institutions. The council could, therefore, become a significant network for the development of regional interests, irrespective of what the two sovereign governments prefer. A peculiarity is that England is not formally represented. As and when English regional assemblies are developed, it can be seen that they would swamp the Irish representation – and possibly stimulate debate on the development of regional bodies in the Republic.

Five major themes are likely to emerge in Britain's constitutional changes, according to Hazell:

- the replacement of a highly centralised system of government by a form of quasi-federalism

- more checks and balances on the UK executive

- a further erosion of parliamentary sovereignty

- a tighter rule of law, with a shift of power to the courts

- the possibility that the majoritarian, two-party system will be replaced by more pluralist forms of democracy.[24]

The term quasi-federalism is appropriate because the emerging system of UK government includes the following federal characteristics: formal division of powers between the two levels of government in the devolution regime; reserved and devolved powers; overlapping jurisdiction in foreign affairs (including EU) between devolved and central governments; a new constitutional court in the form of the Judicial Committee of the Privy Council; a new structure of intergovernmental relations to be defined by concordats between central government departments and the new devolved assemblies – in time evolving into periodic summits between prime ministers and first ministers, regular meetings of ministers sharing the same portfolios and of their officials; dual nationality and multiple identities brought more into the open.

Hazell's colleague, Brendan O'Leary, argued that there are federalising aspects in the Belfast Agreement in respect of Northern Ireland and the UK and confederalising aspects in the UK-Republic of Ireland relationship. Both were strengthened by virtue of being included in an intergovernmental treaty.[25] That raised the question of whether the British government's unilateral suspension of the Northern Ireland institutions in January 2000 was a breach of international law. Indefinite suspension of the institutions would bring this question back onto the political agenda, especially if it happened through a disagreement between London and Dublin; an informal co-sovereignty arrangement through direct rule is a more likely scenario if the Northern Executive fails.[26]

But there is no written constitutional entrenchment and therefore no federation properly so-called. Devolution is asymmetric not uniform. Financial control remains highly centralised in the Treasury, which shows no sign of being willing to let it go. There remains outstanding the question of parliamentary sovereignty, which cuts across the devolution of political authority. The Labour Party distinguishes between devolution of power from the centre and a federal division of competences in which the centre would have to abrogate control. The 1997 White Paper, *Scotland's Parliament*, stated in paragraph 42: "The United Kingdom Parliament is and will remain sovereign in all matters"; while section 28 (7) of the Scotland Act says it "does not affect the power of the Parliament of the United Kingdom to make laws for Scotland". But the fact that the Scottish people have been proclaimed sovereign through the referendum vote and the political realities that make the First Minister there its representative will tend to undermine such assertions of absolute Westminster sovereignty.

> The UK is acquiring some federalist charac-
> teristics despite official denials. The federalist
> model provides invaluable signposts in a still
> largely mapless UK constitution. The new
> assemblies are now established facts of

constitutional life which are politically almost impossible to remove. The legislation underpinning the new assemblies has given part of the governance of the UK a written constitution. (The incorporation of the European Convention of Human Rights into UK law represents the other major step in the direction of a written constitution.) The country now has a system for adjudicating on the rights of the two levels of government. What the UK does not have, compared with federal systems, is an upper chamber comprised of regional or state representatives; current proposals for the reform of the House of Lords remain unformulated. The UK, too, has yet to develop a formal and, perhaps even more importantly, an informal system of intergovernmental relations.[27]

Much will depend on what happens within the political parties. Many see the question of devolution and centralism being fought out within the Labour Party itself over the coming years, especially in Scotland and Wales. On the outcome could depend the continued existence of the UK. The Union would come under great pressure when there is a Conservative majority in England and a simultaneous Labour majority in Britain. Conservatives in Wales debated whether to support the case for a Welsh Parliament if their English counterparts came out in favour of an English one. The same could happen in Scotland, in a fascinating inversion of traditional assumptions about Conservative and Labour approaches to the Union. Labour is now the main unionist party by virtue of having MPs from all the nations – unlike the Conservatives who in 1997 lost all their Scottish and Welsh seats; the question is whether power will be devolved or centralised within Labour's structures. The paradox of a decentralised polity and centralised party control cannot but be unstable in such a majoritarian system as the British one. Mair's suggestion that Blair intends to resolve it through the installation of a party-less depoliticised democracy in which voters become arbiters rather than formulators of policy is plausible; but there are many obstacles facing him before that can be achieved – not least the need for a second term in office.[28]

One of the foremost students of these issues, John Curtise,

reaches the following conclusion about Labour and devolution:

> The lesson for Labour in both Scotland and
> Wales is clear. Voters want those running their
> new institutions to advance their interests. If they
> are not to conclude that only the nationalists will
> do so, then Labour needs to show it can do
> things differently in Scotland and Wales than in
> London. Preserving the United Kingdom's
> unions means allowing the devolution child to
> grow up, not keeping it tied to its umbilical
> cord.[29]

ASYMMETRICAL GOVERNANCE

One must be careful with language. It would be wrong to assume
that federal outcomes are the only rational ones in the UK's
internal politics. Coherence need not mean symmetry or
federalism by another name; in theory it could refer to a system in
which power is devolved, not divided.[30] There is much to be said
for asymmetry as an approach to constitutional change in the UK,
as in Spain and Canada[31] – or, indeed, as a model for European
integration based on diverse national histories and sizes of the
member states.[32] There is already considerable flexibility or
variable geometry as regards participation in core activities, and
every indication that such variability will increase as the EU
enlarges over the coming generation.[33]

Asymmetrical federalism refers to a system in which some
federal units have greater self-governing powers than others. In
contrast, a symmetrical model of federalism builds a state
incorporating citizens who belong to sub-central entities with
equal rights and powers. Asymmetry has been most appropriately
applied in multinational federations, in which several groups of
individuals with separate cultural and collective identities seek
constitutional recognition for their national distinctiveness.
Symmetry implies a federal sub-division of uniform, homogenous
and equal territorial regional units. Asymmetry implies a federation
of distinct peoples, acknowledging their desire for national self-
government. It is, therefore, almost inevitable that nationality-
based units will seek different and more extensive powers than
regionally-based ones.

This situation applies in Spain, where the three nationality-based units (Catalonia, the Basque Country and Galicia) demanded greater autonomy than the other fourteen regional units or "autonomous communities" such as La Mancha or Extramadura. The Basques, Catalans and Galicians accepted a compromise system in the 1978 Constitution, which devised a model of symmetric decentralisation widely referred to as "café para todos" (coffee for everyone). Rather than directly responding to Catalan and Basque demands for recognition as nations within Spain, the constitution's drafters preferred a system of seventeen autonomous communities, some of which were historically and culturally distinct; others were artificially created, without any sense of territorial identity. While the three historic nationalities were immediately allowed to practice "full autonomy", the other regions had to undergo a five-year period of "restricted autonomy" before being allowed to do so. But, once full autonomy was achieved, the constitution made no distinctions between the communities. Article 2 of the Spanish constitution reflects the balance and tension between national unity and recognition of the historic nations. "The constitution is founded on the indissoluble unity of the Spanish nation, the common and indivisible patria of all Spaniards, and recognises and guarantees the right to autonomy of the nationalities and regions integrated in it and the solidarity among them."[34]

Twenty years' experience of autonomy has satisfied many of the demands made originally, adding a new depth to democracy in Spain. But it has not finally resolved the underlying aspirations of Catalans and Basques for a self-determination that would fully recognise their national specificity. They call for more asymmetry and increasingly reject the logic of coffee for everyone. They look to asymmetrical devolution in Britain as a possible model for Spain and call for recognition as nations within a "multinational" Spain. In July 1998, the three main nationalist parties in Galicia, the Basque Country and Catalonia signed a joint declaration demanding that Spain be defined as a multilingual, multicultural and multinational state. This was negatively received by the main Spanish political parties. Thus it can be seen that this model of differential transition periods to a symmetrical system has not resolved the issue, just as it is not resolved in Canada.

In the Russian federation there is considerable asymmetry between the 32 nationality-based units (such as Tatarstan or North Ossetia) and the other 56 federal units, which simply reflect regional divisions within the majority Russian national group. In Canada, English-speaking provinces strenuously resist the idea of a multinational federation, in which Quebec would be entitled to recognition of its separate nationality, because this would undermine Canadian national unity. This creates a bitter conflict over sovereignty and potential secession, in which the Québécois resist homogenisation, arguing that this would define the common whole by the values of the majority, which could then use majoritarian and universalist arguments against the minority. Many Québécois are prepared to contemplate secession in order to avoid such an assimilation. In Britain, by contrast, national distinctiveness is acknowledged and increasingly recognised by devolution and autonomy. It is important to understand the comparative strengths of this approach as a means of avoiding secession.[35] In the same way Britain's experience of multiculturalism is in many respects in advance of the rest of Europe's, giving its multiculturalists a "'mission' to make Europe more open to the world and to multicultural situations, perhaps to be a bridge between Europeans and non-Europeans."[36]

BRITISHNESS

Britain is a constitutionally unique entity: a union or composite state which had unitary, centralised methods imposed on it through empire, war, economic regulation and welfare. It is a union of multiple identities in which the national diversity of Scotland and Wales in many spheres of life survived their absorption into the United Kingdom; public administration and most legislation recognise these separate legal jurisdictions between England and Scotland, and to some extent Wales, as does the extensive autonomy of Scottish civil society in educational, religious and legal spheres.

But the fact that England comprises 85 per cent of the British population and has 529 of the 659 Westminster MPs makes the symmetry of national identity spurious as a criterion of constitutional coherence. The UK state's political centralism maintains its unitary characteristics despite its composite nature. The UK civil service is much more central to the working of its political system that that of most comparably-sized countries, and is widely understood to cement the union together. But the new devolution regime requires new methods of organising intergovernmental relations. That is still clearly a work in progress, both in the civil service, in politics and judicial affairs. Concordats between central departments and those in Scotland and Wales are intended to deal with these questions in the civil service.[37] In politics the Joint Ministerial Committee in Devolution has emerged as "the real gearbox of devolution, the forum for trouble-shooting, and for the UK government to negotiate policy initiatives with the new administrations".[38] Its first summit meeting was held in Edinburgh on 1 September 2000. It was convened, significantly, by the three devolved governmental leaders, Donald Dewar, Rhodri Morgan and David Trimble. It looks as if this will be a more powerful body than the British-Irish Council. The Judicial Committee of the Privy Council has emerged as the body to handle disputes between the various levels of government. Originating in the judicial relations between the UK and its imperial dependencies, it was given a similar role in the Government of Ireland Act and the Northern Ireland Act, 1973.

This clearly opens up the English question, where devolution must be conceived as an exercise in regional democracy rather than national identity – that is the stark alternative posed for the Blair government by the demand for Scottish independence.[39] The English regions, although they are not nations, face basically the same democratic deficits as Scotland and Wales.[40]

Nevertheless, the half-hearted government commitment to democratic regionalism leaves the door open to a revived Conservative programme of Little England nationalism united around a demand for an English parliament – "the much-anticipated English backlash to Scottish and Welsh devolution", as John Tomaney, chairman of the Campaign for English Regions, put it. He went on to argue:

> But the key issue for the regions of England, as it is for the Scots and Welsh, is not the achievement of a theoretical symmetry, but rather how to reduce the over-concentration of political, administrative, economic and cultural power in London and the south-east. An English parliament would do nothing to address this problem.[41]

Hague resisted the idea of an English parliament in favour of finding a formula to restrict voting on English laws to English

MPs. His position on Welsh laws remained unclear. He had to contend with a relatively strong unionist group within the party's leadership, even if he was attracted to English nationalism. Hague developed his ideas on Britishness following the 1997 election defeat. He highlighted a defence of the "British Way" from threats posed by European integration, New Labour's constitutional reform programme and "extreme nationalism within the UK". The Conservatives must be a patriotic party in touch with the identity and values of the British people. He defined Britishness in terms of parliamentary sovereignty; the monarchy; maintenance of the Union; individualism; a spirit of enterprise; the historical absence of invasion and tyranny, which differentiates Britain from other European nations; social mobility; and local identities. Hague's definition distinguished British identities from those of its component nations. He said Tony Blair's ideas on the subject are anathema to the British people.[42]

At the end of March 2000, Blair made a speech on Britishness which initiated a political debate with the Conservatives on what it means for the new millennium. It was intended to deprive the Conservatives of their assumed monopoly of patriotic sentiment. This has been a constant theme of Blair's, leading to some crass invocations of the bulldog spirit during the 1997 election campaign. But a group around Gordon Brown developed a potentially more sophisticated case, based partly on survey research. It argued that contemporary Britishness is based on such values as decency, outwardness, the work ethic and tolerance – the very ones New Labour claim for themselves. More to the point in the perspective of the discussion of asymmetric forms of government, Gordon Brown claimed that Hague, in becoming so obsessed by the breakup of Britain, missed the essential British magic: "Perhaps uniquely in the world, Britain is not just a society of many communities but also a country of nations" – so that devolution and the integrity of the UK are compatible. A Blair aide explained the thinking involved:

> For over a century, the Conservative Party has successfully wrapped itself in the flag. By contrast the left has seemed to have had a blind spot about nationalism regarding it as an awkward fault in the human psyche. But until we are sure we are sure about our own British identity, we cannot resolve our relationship with Europe. If

> we can get this right we can associate Labour
> with the values and institutions the British people
> hold most dear and regard as emblematic of
> Britishness – decency, tolerance, liberty, fair play.
> Even more, we can start to put some pressure on
> Hague. He will have to decide whether he is
> going to put himself at the helm of a new English
> nationalist party, or remain the leader of the
> Conservative and Unionist Party.[43]

Additionally, Blair argued that a true reading of British history reveals a nation committed as much to Europe as to a global empire. One of his ministers put it like this: "Britain has never been a narrow chauvinist country. From Plantagenets, Tudors, Hanoverians, Palmerston to Churchill, we have been committed to Europe. We have to assault this notion that you cannot be pro-British if you are pro-European."[44] In his Gent speech Blair added that "England was a European power long before it became an imperial one…Even in the days of Empire, Britain was first and foremost a European power, preserving the balance in Europe, opposing those who sought to dominate Europe."[45]

Thus the long shadow of empire and the end of the Cold War have thrown up the Anglo-British Question as the ghost of English nationalism returns to haunt Britain's last colony. For centuries the systematic ambiguity between England and Britain had concealed within it an identification between state and nation in the definition of Englishness. This was a state-framed nationalism, relying crucially on institutions to define it; governance, whether of Britain or the empire, was believed by many to be a central aspect of English identity. Precisely because it was formulated in the pre-democratic eighteenth century, it could tolerate diversity in civil society, notably in Scotland, without the need to impose homogeneity, as was the case in France.[46] The unravelling of the Britishness based on Protestantism, empire and war required the invention of another model. In the period following the First and Second World Wars that was accomplished through the creation of the BBC, the welfare state, the National Health Service, the creation of many state-owned industries and of the Labour and Conservative parties as Britain-wide institutions. In that sense "the twentieth century was the British century, with the mid-century of Blitz and Beveridge as the high tide of Britishness."[47]

It seemed natural at that time to write the country's history with little regard for national, ethnic or regional identities, but rather in terms of class conflict and managing imperial and post-imperial decline. The paradoxical effect of Thatcher's period in office was both to assert British strength and to oversee the re-emergence of English nationalism as a potent force. "The 'Thatcher revolution'...set out to restore British grandeur. What it actually did was to break the back of British identity."[48] Scotland and Wales responded in their own distinctive ways to the Thatcher years, which were also to see the emergence of a new multiculturalism and the increasing significance of the European Union as intruding on British sovereignty. It is only in the post-Thatcher years, and especially in the period since Labour was elected, that the full significance of the need to re-invent Britishness once again is being appreciated.

As can be seen from the summary accounts of the alternative models put forward by the Labour and Conservative parties, a very important fork in the road is being faced for the country's future. On the one side the Conservatives offer a modernised version of the traditional institutional top-down, centralised and unitary version, with an admixture of contemporary values and a systematic hostility to further European integration. This draws on themes contained in the older version of Tory ethnic nationalism, with its ambiguous elision of Englishness and Britishness, which was mediated by the construction of a state nationalism concealing itself as British patriotism in the heyday of empire. It was an exclusionary system, for Irish people in particular, by virtue of their predominant Catholicism and their assumed inferiority within this value system. Historically, Ireland has been the consistent issue on which this ethnic Anglo-British nationalism was constructed, whether at the time of the Act of Union or in the Home Rule crises of 1885-6 or 1911-14. As a result, unionism became indelibly associated with sectarian, triumphalist Protestant and imperial British ethno-nationalism for most of nationalist Ireland.

A distinction can be drawn between civic and ethnic varieties of British and English nationalisms historically and in contemporary political practice. It has to do with competing paradigms of national identity, between a universalist, inclusive model based on citizenship and residence on the one hand, and ethnic essentials and blood line on the other. British and English nationalisms have oscillated between these – just as have Irish ones.[49] As the

Conservative and Labour parties offer their competing models of contemporary Britishness, they draw on those traditions. Labour's model is consciously based on the tradition of liberal civic unionism exemplified by Gladstone. In emphasising values rather than institutions it tries to escape from the inherited Anglo-British state-framed model, in favour of multiple identities, diverse allegiances and an acceptance of Britain's necessary role in Europe. Citizenship seems to be its rational core; but its gradualist, evolutionary character contains echoes of the complacent Whig interpretation of history, which accepted and celebrated state-nation identifications. As was argued in Chapter Two, it will probably be necessary to drive it much further in the direction of citizenship if its objective of preserving Britain by reforming it is to be accomplished. It therefore remains to be seen whether the decay of the British state is indeed likely to be terminal because there has never been an authentic non-imperial nation underpinning it.

ENGLAND

There is undoubtedly a growing sense of regional identity within England, the more clearcut the further away one goes from the south-east and the home counties. The Liberal leader, Charles Kennedy, asked: "If an English Parliament was established at Westminster, as it surely would be, would the people of Newcastle or Cornwall really feel that [it would be] any less remote than the current UK Parliament?"[50] There are significant regional inequalities within England – in 2000 only two English regions (London and the South-east) exceeded the European average GDP per capita by 147% and 101% respectively. The other English regions were ranked as follows: South-west 94, East Midlands 94, Eastern 94, West Midlands 91, North-west 89, York and Humber 88, North-east 83.[51] Beyond this there were marked inequalities in terms of levels of health, educational attainment and housing conditions, as well as unemployment and access to employment.[51] In late-1999, a flurry of reports about an increasing north-south divide in living standards and state subventions illustrated the potential for material and democratic dissatis-factions to come together within the English regions.[53]

Such factors will increasingly drive demands for more regional autonomy in England, as devolution forces a disaggregation and greater transparency of taxing and spending statistics within the UK. The resignation from the government in January 2000 of Peter Kilfoyle, a loyal Blairite dissatisfied with the treatment of his Liverpool region, drew attention to that. He said Whitehall's attitude to the regions was like a "colonial raj" stamping its will on other parts of the country and pursuing "highly discriminatory financial arrangements". The north of England suffered in comparison with Scotland, Wales and Northern Ireland; he had waited in vain for a reference in the February 2000 budget to the matching government funds needed to trigger billions of EU Objective 1 funding. Inflation was being fuelled by wages and house prices in the South-east, but English regions depending on manufacturing industry were bearing the cost of high interest and exchange rates.[54] That Kilfoyle subsequently agreed to join a Labour task force campaigning for the party's re-election among core supporters amply confirmed the power of his critique. Those living in the more under-privileged English regions such as the North-east or the North-west may already consider themselves second-class citizens "because they have no territorial minister able to argue their case in cabinet. After devolution, they may come to believe they are third-class citizens, since they have no parliament either." In this way an economic imbalance could follow on from the constitutional one. Either way "the consent, or at the very least the acquiescence of England, is essential to the success of devolution."[55]

There is evidence of a growing interest in regional democratic assemblies, if not as yet of a strong political demand for them – except in the North-east. There are now Constitutional Conventions, modelled on the one that worked for ten years to bring a parliament back to Scotland, in the North-east, North-west, Yorkshire/Humberside and stirrings in the West Midlands and South-west. Labour's national policy forum agreed in July 2000 that the party had to recognise the "legitimate aspirations of the English regions and believes that the creation of elected regional assemblies is the essential next step in our programme of renewing the constitution and empowering citizens".[56] An opinion poll in *The Economist* (26 March 1999) on attitudes towards regional government reported majorities in favour of regional asssemblies in London (60 for: 21 against), the North-east (51:29), the West Midlands (46:37), the South-west (47:39), the East Midlands (40:35) and the Eastern region (43:42). Opinion was divided in Yorkshire and Humber (42:42), with majorities against the idea in the South-east (37:47) and the North-west (42:44). In the North-east pressure increased for the creation of a regional assembly and for a referendum to be held on the matter. It was stimulated by the increasing comparisons made between resources available for regeneration there and in Scotland. Deindustrialisation has affected both regions, but public spending per capita in Scotland exceeded that in the North-east sector by sector: by 24% in health and education; 18% in agriculture; 10% in transport and industry and employment; 6% in housing and law and order. In 1997, GDP per capita in the North-east was some 13% below Scotland's, but government spending was nearly 20% less.[57] Demands for a regional assembly in the North-east would become more pressing were Labour to be re-elected with a reduced majority more subject to pressure from the region's MPs. The issue will also be stimulated by Britain's success in receiving £3 billion in the EU's Agenda 2000 Objective 1 round, to be shared between south Yorkshire, Merseyside, west Wales and the Valleys and Cornwell and the Isles of Scilly. Hard negotiation was required to wring matching funding from a reluctant Treasury, increasing the case for regional assemblies to make that case. These efforts were crowned with some success for these regions and for Scotland and Wales, when Brown announced in his three-year spending review on 18 July 2000 that the government would ensure funding for EU structural funding projects, including Objective 1. The decision will increase pressure to revise the Barnett formula which allocates public expenditure to Scotland, Wales and Northern Ireland – thereby ensuring a more sharply focused political debate on territorial politics and regional assemblies to influence such allocations.

The nine Regional Development Authorities (RDAs) were put in place, co-ordinating mainly the economic work of bureaucracies and local authorities; but their most important lines of accountability were to Whitehall and they did not amount to any significant devolution of political power. They reported to the government that better co-ordination and more effective joined-up government was required, for example in bringing together the scheme for single regeneration budgets, the "New Deal for Communities" administered through Whitehall's regional offices and the new plans for neighbourhood renewal to reduce deprivation which was pledged an £800 million aid package in October 2000. A regional co-ordination unit was set up in the Cabinet Office for this purpose.[58] The government did not see the associated voluntary regional chambers developing into assemblies before referendums were held in the regions where there is most demand for them. But Brown's spending review gave the eight RDAs a boost by allocating them an extra £500m by 2003, a 50 per cent increase on their first-year budgets. They were also promised more freedom to operate outside Whitehall's control with the promise of a single budget, drawn from three main departments, giving them the ability to tailor policies to individual regions.[59]

The introduction of a "predominantly unitary structure of local government", which would require reorganisation and probably the abolition of most counties, was also envisaged. A White Paper on local government and several consultation papers emphasised that traditional modes of council operation were inefficient and that councils should consult local communities directly on the way they wished to be governed. At their annual meeting in June 2000, leaders of the Local Government Association resolved to argue the case for more local democracy in the run-up to the general election. They criticised government plans to introduce a radical "front line first" approach, under which funds from Whitehall would go directly to schools, social service units or health services, in the belief that this would prove the government was determined to remove all barriers to improving local services. Ken Livingstone was applauded for saying he had "never known any local authority to achieve the levels of incompetence and mismanagement as I have seen in central government" and for condemning the Treasury's refusal to provide proper funding for local government.[60]

Blair wants to see a system of strong mayors in the major urban centres. Legislation will provide for referendums to be held on the matter, while surveys show a margin of 59% to 32% in favour of the idea. But mayors could prove to be political rivals who might not want to see regional assemblies occupying the same political space. Thus, if elected mayors are the first to occupy the field, we might see city regions developing as an alternative model for regionalism in England. But critics said this will create more efficient executives rather than greater local democracy; elected mayors would do nothing to increase interest in town halls unless the government gave councils more freedom.[61] Strong mayors would bring yet more asymmetry to the British constitution.

Thus it remains true that "a resolution of the English question is…critical to the achievement of a stable constitutional settlement in a devolved Britain."[62] That might well be achieved on the model of asymmetry, as in Spain. If devolution is to serve the same democratic ends as in Scotland and Wales then it will have to be applied to the English regions, not to an English parliament.

SCOTLAND

A speech made by Tony Blair in Edinburgh on 12 November 1998 dwelt on how England needs Scotland to preserve the UK's global influence and role. There was no sign there of Peter Brooke's waiver of a selfish British strategic or economic role in Ireland when he spoke in Northern Ireland on 9 November 1990. Blair remained an uncompromising unionist in his dealings with Scotland. In his March 2000 speech on Britishness, he said modernisation was the key issue. "We do so on the basis of one key belief. That the United Kingdom is stronger together than apart; all the constituent parts of the Union: its great cities, regions and nations are stronger united than separate, stronger together than the sum of their parts." The intent of the devolution policy was spelled out as follows in the July 1997 White Paper:

> The Union will be strengthened by recognising the claims of Scotland, Wales and the regions with strong identities of their own. The government's devolution proposals, by meeting these aspirations, will not only safeguard but enhance the Union.

Such rhetoric can rub Scots up the wrong way if delivered insensitively, especially in Blair's favoured message of British patriotism. This was exemplified in his address to the 1997 Labour Party annual conference in which he praised the richness of the British character as "creative, compassionate, outward-looking. Old British values, but a new British confidence. We can never be the biggest, we may never again be the mightiest. But we can be the best." He mentioned Britain or the British 53 times and employed the word nation to refer to the UK nineteen times, envisaging a single united Britain.[63] Labour's heavily orchestrated barrage of propaganda against independence as supported by the Scottish National Party has on occasion reinforced its appeal. There have been many tripwires for a leadership widely perceived in Scotland to be led by a centralising elite in London obsessed with controlling dissidence.[64] But, during the campaign for the

Scottish Assembly, Labour's message, that devolution had come to stay and would be best taken advantage of by supporting their programme, convinced most of the voters. Labour emerged the strongest party, with 38.8% of the first-past-the-post constituency votes. The SNP secured 28.7%, the Conservatives 15.6%, the Liberal Democrats 14.2% and Others 2.7%. There was a fair scattering of smaller parties, reflecting the proportionality of the new voting system, which provided for a top-up of MSPs from regional lists. As a result, the overall number and percentage of the 129 MSPs was as follows: Labour 56 (46.3%); SNP 35 (27.1%); Liberal Democrats 17 (13.19%); Conservatives 18 (14.0%); Others 3 (2.3%). Turnout was 58.7%, down 13% compared to the British general election of 1997.[65]

This was, therefore, a "second order" election, more significant that a normal local government one, but less so than a British parliamentary one. The SNP's low parliamentary vote and losses in the concurrent local elections, together with the apathy evident in the low turnout, "ruled out any possibility of interpreting this election result as a step along the road from devolution to independence. Indeed it was hardly a ringing endorsement for devolution itself."[66] The result was widely interpreted as a defeat for the SNP; within that party there was an argument after the election between fundamentalists who believe there was too much ambiguity between the commitment to independence and the undertaking to make a devolution parliament work. Other SNP post mortems concentrated on bad organisation, Labour's overwhelmingly better-resourced campaign and on the party's efforts to outflank Labour on the left with a promise to restore a one-penny cut in income tax and Alex Salmond's sharp criticism of the Kosovo bombing campaign as an act of "dubious legality and unpardonable folly". But as the months passed after the elections, the SNP regrouped itself effectively, nearly won a sensational victory at a by-election in Hamilton in mid-September 1999 and thrived on Labour's teething troubles and the continued embarassments of being reined in by London, whether by concordats, joint committees or the "constant, gentle strangulation that's done in the name of consensus and the unity of the party and winning the next general election".[67] Arguments between Edinburgh and London over such issues as higher education fees, beef and BSE, teaching about homosexual relations in schools, secrecy legislation or whether to ban the boxer Mike Tyson illustrated these pressures.

Labour interpreted the election result as "an overwhelming rejection of nationalist vision", in the words of Gordon Brown and Douglas Alexander.[68] A coalition was formed between Labour and the Liberal Democrats for the next four years, as the new arrangements were bedded down. They had a rocky time in their first months in office, subject to ferocious and often cynical criticism from the Scottish media. The coalition government ran into numerous difficulties over spin-doctors, the resignation of senior officials, student tuition fees, the building of the new parliament and its cost overruns. As a result, support for Labour fell in opinion polls and the party fared badly in further by-elections.[69]

These troubles did not, however, alter one striking feature of the new dispensation: the rapid emergence of a new political identity for the executive and especially the First Minister, Donald Dewar. He effectively became the prime minister, empowered to represent the people of Scotland. Dewar saw a step-change for all concerned, and was astonished at the difference devolution made to the level of activity, the work rate and the widening horizons of Scots. Devolution, he argued, encourages confidence and adds a new political dimension to the United Kingdom, strengthening rather than weakening it. He said centralism is a rather odd charge to throw at a Labour government which had so shaken up the UK. He was to the fore in demanding more powers for the Scottish Parliament when the act was being drafted – precisely to counter SNP competition. Devolution improves and revitalises democracy, he argued, bringing it closer to the people – in fact establishing their sovereignty, rather than that of the Westminster parliament, as the touchstone of Scottish identity. His untimely death in October 2000 brought home to many people the wisdom and authority of these judgements and his political achievement in bringing them to pass.

The consequences of these new facts will take a long time to work out. But it will be the Scottish people who decide whether to opt for independence and secession or autonomy. A split in nationalism is probably more likely than a split in the UK, given that many nationalists are non-secessionist, in Catalan style. But in any confrontation between Edinburgh and Westminster, for example when there are different parties in charge, it is likely to be the former not the latter that prevails in the eyes of the newly sovereign Scottish electorate.[70]

Clearly the circumstances are potentially favourable for the

SNP, pledged to broaden the remit and mandate of the devolved assembly and its executive by continuously pushing for greater powers. An important part of its strength is its increased attractiveness to the nearly one million people of Irish Catholic background who traditionally have voted Labour, partly because they feared the SNP's historical association with Protestant and Orange sectarianism. Under Alex Salmond's leadership the SNP went out of its way to woo Irish-Scottish voters by emphasising what Scotland has to learn from independent Ireland's achievements economically and in the EU – an approach that seems set to continue with his successor as leader, John Swinney. The SNP will have plenty of opportunity to develop its case for independence in arguments over fiscal capacities, relations with Westminster and the representation of Scottish interests in Brussels. Devolution will render intergovernmental bargaining within the UK over the EU much more transparent. There will be opportunities to reflect the more positive Scottish attitudes towards the EU – across the political parties – compared to the greater reserve in English attitudes. One might see Scotland and Wales voting for joining the euro, while a majority in England is against, and carrying the overall UK vote. Were this situation to arise, "how would foreign policy in a devolved Britain then be shaped? Could it be claimed, one way or the other that it was *British*?"[71]

Short of that scenario, there will be many other occasions when Scottish and wider UK interests appear to be in conflict, for example on agriculture and fishing. The Scottish White Paper allowed for this articulation of policy, "but only so long as they adhere to and sustain the UK line." In anticipation of such conflicts, the Foreign and Commonwealth Office set up a unit to represent the interests of Scotland, Wales and Northern Ireland overseas and reached a Concordat on International Relations with the Scottish and Welsh executives, which will be reviewed annually.[72] There may also be opportunities to develop Scottish alliances with Welsh and Irish interests through the British-Irish Council. It will take considerable skill for the devolved governments to steer themselves through these obstacles without conceding too much to SNP-type objections, based on devolution as a process and inspired by Charles Stewart Parnell: "No man has a right to fix the boundary of the march of a nation; no man has a right to say to his country – thus far shalt thou go and no further." The Labour government conceived of devolution in terms of a theory of gratitude, to satisfy demands for devolution once and for all; instead it became a matter of giving democracy to nations. Thus such events set in motion a process outside centralising control – an irony indeed in the land whose eighteenth century social and political theorists invented the notion of the unanticipated results of human actions.[73]

WALES

The clash of personalities that marked the Welsh National Assembly campaign between the Welsh Secretary after the resignation of Ron Davies in November 1997, Alun Michael – favoured by Blair and the London Labour leadership – and the candidate preferred by the rank and file of the Welsh Labour Party, Rhodri Morgan, had concealed within it several of the same neuralgic points of policy difference as in Scotland. They included differences on the extent to which Whitehall and Westminster will continue to control Welsh affairs and on whether the principle of devolution applies also within the Labour Party itself. Other neuralgic points included the appointment of senior civil servants and their sceptical or hostile attitudes towards the National Assembly; fiscal policy and bloc grants from Westminster, given that the Welsh Assembly does not have tax-raising powers; the inevitable urge to equalise powers available to the Welsh, Scottish and Northern Ireland devolved executives; education policy, including the idea of changing the A-level examinations to allow a wider spread of subjects; potential competition between Welsh Assembly and Westminster MPs; the possibility of different parties controlling the Westminster and Cardiff parliaments; and Objective 1 co-financing for western Wales from the exchequer in London. Welsh relations with the EU and with Ireland through the British-Irish Council could also create tensions with Whitehall and Westminster.

All this became clear during IEA briefing visits to Wales. The Assembly was elected and an executive appointed, first under Michael and then, when he resigned in February 2000 in a row over Objective 1 funding, under Morgan. In the election campaign, Labour attacked Plaid Cymru continually for its nationalism and separatism, despite the fact that its manifesto did not include a demand for independence but rather "a full national status within Europe". There was clear evidence of Labour supporters' disenchantment with the leadership's approach, a trend devastatingly confirmed by the results, which saw Plaid Cymru do very well, notably among Labour supporters in core seats such as Islwyn, Rhondda and Llanelli. The final distribution of seats in the assembly gave Labour 28 seats, followed by Plaid with 17, Conservatives 9 and Liberal Democrats 6. Across Wales Plaid's vote increased by 18.5% while Labour's fell by 17.2%. Plaid increased its vote in real terms from 161,030 votes in the 1997 general election to 290,572, which has obviously profound implications for Westminster elections.[74] The turnout was only 46.2%, but it reflected percentage regional differences between the upper fifties and early sixties in the west and the low thirties in constituencies along the English border.

The Welsh Assembly has much fewer powers than the Scottish Parliament – no taxing power, fewer members and capacities. Westminster has primary responsibility for legislation and the Assembly is responsible for implementing it on a range of defined areas – those that have been under the responsibility of the Secretary of State for Wales. The Westminster government said it will not be able to gain similar powers as Scotland without a new referendum (the last one, on 18 September 1997, was barely carried – by just 6,700 votes and by just over half of those voting – on a turnout of only 50.1 per cent – and in stark contrast to Scotland, where turnout was 60.2 per cent on 11 September 1997, with 44.7 per cent of the overall electorate endorsing devolution). But public attitudes and politicians' commitments since the elections bind people to building the new institutions and making them work.

There are important differences between Scotland and Wales with respect to their nationality, identity and civil society, explained largely by their differing histories. Whereas Scotland was an independent nation until the 1707 Act of Union, with all the institutional trappings, including its own monarchy, parliament and church, legal and educational systems – and kept many of them after it – Wales never had any real political or institutional unity and was long absorbed into the English system. The Industrial Revolution reinforced its incorporation in a larger economy. In these circumstances a distinctive Welsh identity depended on the survival of the Welsh language and religious nonconformism, and in politics a tendency to follow a radical path of Chartism, strong trade unionism, Liberal then Labour support. But, by the 1980s, the three bases of distinct Welsh identity – the language, nonconformism and radical politics – were seriously eroded. Deindustrialisation during the Thatcher years had demoralised the communities on which they were based (except for the south-east corner around Cardiff).

During the 1990s, supporters of devolution faced an uphill task to convince Labour activists and supporters, who routinely secured up to two-thirds of the votes, that it would effectively address these problems of redevelopment within a framework of European regionalism. Despite the close referendum result, the story since then has been more positive. More and more popular support flowed towards the autonomy promised by devolution and Welsh identity has strengthened; unlike Northern Ireland, there is a much more relaxed attitude towards its expression, and very little display of competing unionist identities. But there are continuing problems over relations with London, attitudes of the London-dominated civil service towards the assembly and unresolved political factionalism within the Labour Party. "Wales is a nation, but a fractured one. It contains several distinct groups divided along socio-economic, geographical, cultural and political lines."[75] A main task of the assembly and the new executive will be to build up the new institutions and develop them incrementally. This suggests there will be continuous tension with London as to the pace of progress – and interesting knock-on effects for the English regions. There is a real determination to develop closer links with Scotland, Ireland and the European Union.

EUROPEANISATION?

The IEA's 1996 book concluded that Britain has a dual sovereignty problem, encompassing reform processes at the EU and UK levels. Do the constitutional changes underway encourage a wider Europeanisation of British politics, its structures, tone and style as well as the application of norms such as subsidiarity within its state apparatuses? Has there been a convergence of these factors internally and externally? How do the irreversibility and direction of devolution affect attitudes to European integration? Is there evidence of a process of retarded Europeanisation, through which Labour has been able "to embed the discourse of integration as a virtuous objective", after so many years when precisely this was not achieved?[76] How far has central government administration adjusted to the demands of Europeanisation?[77] These large questions cannot be answered in full here and are addressed in other chapters of this study. But there are several important pointers.

Devolution raises in sharp fashion the different national and territorial interests involved in defining the British interest and will make their orchestration both more transparent and more politically contentious. These changes stop crucially short of federalism, as we have seen; this could be their undoing. They will require defter and better-defined management of diverse interests than has so far been displayed. The dynamic between devolution and continued central control, between reform and preservation of the British state, between a consensual democracy and a centralised Labour Party apparatus, will drive further political and constitutional change.

It is possible that in the UK "the process of negotiating and agreeing domestic EU policy will come to resemble far more closely the actual processes followed by other member states in agreeing policy within the EU", with the UK coming to resemble Spain or Italy rather than the explicitly federal Germany and Belgium in this regard.[78] The major question is whether the degree of central control held in London makes it impossible to devolve power effectively. Without a more thoroughgoing transformation of central state apparatuses, citizenship and constitutional arrangements than is currently contemplated, it must be doubted whether such a devolution of power can be made to work. Reform and preservation are, therefore, probably incompatible objectives.

Reform through a process of rolling asymmetric quasi-federalisation would represent a virtuous cycle within UK policy-making, even if there was a "a painful transition from the comfort of absolute national sovereignty".[79] It is necessary to reframe British identity around new co-ordinates so as to resolve the dual sovereignty question; but preoccupation with that task will not necessarily make Britain less able to play a central part in the analogous process at European level. It is difficult as yet to make a convincing case that behind the constitutional change programme a plan can be discerned, "a root and branch incremental overhaul of each element of the constitution which in the end would reveal a thoroughly modern, balanced, democratic, devolved state".[80] Nonetheless, Blair's decision to initiate a major debate on Britishness brought the question to the centre of political affairs. Reintegration of the UK is, therefore, part of the same process as the negotiation both of a transformed UK relationship with Europe and of an EU transformed to match English preoccupations, as is argued in the next section of this book. A major source of uncertainty remains obvious: electoral politics. Were the Conservatives to return to office all bets on reform would be off. Their determination to preserve British sovereignty could accelerate disintegration of the UK through the alienation and potential secession of Scotland. That would immensely complicate politics in Northern Ireland – and probably precipitate debate on Irish reunification more rapidly than anyone currently expects.

Alternatively, it is possible that, because the United Kingdom will be addressing these issues within its own system at the same time as similar questions arise at the European level, the UK could be thrust into a pivotal position. Its role could be to gain insights from the reform process at home and reflect them in the EU debate. They would come especially from extrapolating its experience of a rolling programme of asymmetric devolution or quasi-federalisation onto the EU in recognition that "it is possible to develop a model of integration which is not federalism, which builds on existing identities and which provides a coherent framework in which practitioners and electors know who is responsible for what, and how and why the democratic elements in the system apply."[81] There may also be a case for relaunching the idea of a "Europe of small states and regions" in a "virtuous political circle where greater European integration of the appropriate sort can work hand-in-hand with the unfinished business of devolution in England".[82]

In his Warsaw speech Blair recognised such a possibility of overlapping and compatible processes of reform in the UK and EU contexts:

> In practice I suspect that, given the sheer diversity and complexity of the EU, its constitution, like the British constitution, will continue to be found in a number of different treaties, laws and precedents. It is perhaps easier for the British than others to recognise that a constitutional debate must not necessarily end with a single, legally binding document called a Constitution for an entity as dynamic as the EU.

That would help transcend a misconceived debate in the UK over the EU, which counterposes federalism to national sovereignty, on the assumption that a superstate is being planned to supersede the nation states. A better way to understand the EU is as a system that embeds or enmeshes the national in the European and vice versa, in a transnational multilevelled polity with many points of identification, including provision for multiple but non-competitive identities and allegiances.[83] That might be described as the optimistic view of the coherence and compatibility of these dual processes of constitutional change in Britain. It assumes a readiness on the part of the central British state and its political masters to permit devolution and the emergence of autonomous forces. But it is too early to make such assumptions about thoroughgoing reforms, given the centralising, preservationist impulse of Labour's actual behaviour in government. So much will depend on how these issues are managed in coming years – and on the outcome of the next general election. It would be a great mistake to underestimate the difficulties involved in making the transition from a polity defined by an unwritten constitution, absolute parliamentary sovereignty, adversarialism and centralised power to a more European one based on devolution of political authority, consensualism, coalitions and entrenchment of rights.

CONCLUSION – IMPLICATIONS FOR IRELAND

Four interlinked processes of change over the last generation have transformed relations between Britain and Ireland. There has, first of all, been a decisive shift from dependence to interdependence in their economic, political and diplomatic relations. Their relationship has become more equal, despite the evident continuing asymmetries of size and power. This transformation is best understood as a process of internationalisation within the context of the European Communities and relations with the United States. Without that there would not have been the confidence to tackle the transition from unity to stability based on inclusion and consent as the primary focus of the government's policy towards Northern Ireland, the third of these changes. This culminated in the Belfast Agreement and the closely related normalisation of relations between Britain and Ireland – the fourth theme.[84]

Ireland has emerged from a prolonged period when Irishness was perceived as being inferior, and Ireland as relatively backward – by British and unionist opinion – perceptions which concretely affected Irish people in Britain, nationalists in Northern Ireland and also psychologically the self-perceptions of Irish citizens and voters. Equalisation and parity of esteem have been delivered through European integration and are predicated on that process. As Garvin puts it:

> In these islands, Europe symbolises the end of empire and, therefore, the obsolescence of the ancient English-Irish quarrel...that has been the true European achievement in Ireland, an achievement which far outweighs the undoubted benefits of the Common Agricultural Policy, the Brussels cornucopia of grants or even European free trade. The odd thing is, we have scarcely noticed that the 800-year war is over, dying quietly and unmourned sometime between 1972 and 1998.[85]

Britain's continuing full participation in that integration process, is, therefore, a necessary condition for normalising British-Irish relations. The Belfast Agreement is a sophisticated expression of this new equilibrium (including its European dimension); it promises both to preserve and transform identities and reopen ties and friendships that had been lost sight of.

Official Ireland is strictly neutral as to the final outcome of political and constitutional transformations in the UK. Thus the Taoiseach disappointed over-optimistic members of the Scottish National Party by his failure to endorse independence when he spoke in Edinburgh in October 1998.[86] Would such independence be in Ireland's interests? Arguably it would not, given the close cooperation between the two sovereign governments in the peace process and beyond it. But the possibility that UK disintegration would provoke Irish reunification needs to be addressed. Or would a new relationship with Northern Ireland and Scotland emerge from that possibility? The British-Irish Council could be a very significant forum and network to work out such new relationships, irrespective of how the UK's future evolves.

Ireland has a profound interest in seeing Britain's dual sovereignty question resolved amicably and democratically.

Economic as well as political independence having been achieved over the last generation through pooling sovereignty in the EU, integration has gone with the grain of Ireland's civic nationalism. This is in sharp contrast to the residual Anglo-British ethnic nationalism which remains unreconciled to the loss of sovereignty. If the dual sovereignty question is tackled by reverting to such an isolating Europhobic nationalism, normalised relations between the two sovereign states will be indefinitely postponed.

After the Belfast Agreement Ireland has been coming under some pressure to engage in a closer relationship with Britain, including perhaps even to associate with a potentially emerging British-dominated group in the EU. But, just as it was important to assert by joining the euro the independence that had been won through EU membership, in order to avoid giving any impression of reabsorption in a British sphere of influence, the same may be the case in a subsequent period when Britain will be seeking to resolve its dual sovereignty questions, and seeks to build a pattern of alliances with like-minded EU states. The emerging debate on flexibility within the EU will increasingly put such questions on the political agenda by posing the question of whether Ireland participates in core activities rather than waiting for the UK belatedly to join them; but to choose core participation could have the effect of delaying cross-border cooperation with Northern Ireland and paralysing the development of north-south bodies.

1   Hazell ed. (1999), p. 4.
2   O'Neill (2000), p. 74.
3   Studlar (1999), p. 50; O'Toole (2000).
4   *ibid.*, p. 246.
5   David (1999), p. 5; Davies (1999).
6   Laffin and Thomas (1999), p. 96.
7   Hennessey (1997).
8   Hennessy (1997); Hetherington (2000).
9   Quoted in Driver and Martell (1998), p. 126.
10   Blair (1997).
11   O'Leary (1999b).
12   Marquand (1999), pp 27-8.
13   Barnett (1999); Hazell (1999), p. 247.
14   Jenkins (1998); Whiteley and Seyd (2000).
15   Straw (2000).
16   Paul (1999).
17   Nairn (2000), pp 52-3, 77.
18   But see an editorial in *The Observer* calling for a republic, 30 July 2000; and an issue of the *New Statesman* devoted to the monarchy

and a republican alternative, 4 August 2000.
19   Travis (2000); Millar on Mowlam (2000a).
20   Wallace (1997).
21   Gillespie ed. (1996); Nairn (2000), p. 9.
22   Bogdanor (1999a), p. 187.
23   Bogdanor (1999b), p. 291.
24   Hazell (1999), p. 230.
25   O'Leary (1999).
26   O'Leary (2000); Kennedy (2000).
27   Laffin and Thomas (1999), p. 106.
28   Mair (2000).
29   Curtici (2000c).
30   Hazell and O'Leary (1999), p. 21.
31   Keatinge (1998); Bogdanor (1999), (1999a).
32   Leicester (1998), pp 21-2; Hazell ed. (1999), p. 4.
33   FitzGerald (2000); Gillespie (2000b).
34   Guibernau (2000), p. 61.
35   This discussion draws on Guibernau (2000); Keatinge (1998);
     Kymlicka (1998), pp 138-143; Lancaster (1999); Safran and Maiz,
     eds (2000).
36   Laffin and Thomas (1999).
37   Hazell (2000), p. 16.
38   Modood (1999), p. 39.
39   Mawson (1998); Partridge (1999).
40   Tomaney and Mitchell (1999), p. 6.
41   Tomaney (1999), p. 81.
42   Hague (1999); Lynch (2000), pp 62-3; Parekh (2000), p. 10.
43   Wintour (2000).
44   ibid.
45   Wintour (2000); Blair (2000).
46   Wellings (2000); Siedentop (2000), p. 67.
47   Political Quarterly (2000), p. 1; see also Harvie (2000).
48   Nairn (1994), p. xxiii.
49   Kearney (2000), (1997).
50   Kennedy (1999).
51   Hetherington (2000b).
52   Tomaney and Mitchell (1999), p. 5; Hetherington (2000a).
53   Hazell (1999a); Groom (1999), (1999b); Whitehead (1999).
54   Baldwin (2000).
55   Bogdanor (1999a), p. 191.
56   Hetherington (2000b).
57   Walker (2000).
58   Financial Times survey of RDAs, 11 May 2000.
59   Hetherington (2000b).
60   Pike (2000); Freedland (2000); Hetherington (2000).
61   Weir (2000).

62 Tomaney and Mitchell (1999), p. 12.
63 Guibernau (1999), p. 168.
64 Ritchie (2000).
65 Millar (1999), pp 306-7.
66 *ibid.*
67 O'Toole (2000).
68 Quoted in Miller (1999), p. 316.
69 Bell (2000), (2000a).
70 Bogdanor (1999a).
71 Robbins (1998), p. 117.
72 FCO (1999).
73 See Nairn (1998), (2000).
74 Barry Jones (1999), pp 329, 331.
75 Loughlin (1999).
76 Wallace (1997), pp 677-8.
77 Bulmer and Burch (1998).
78 Leicester (1998), pp 15-17.
79 Mitchel and Leicester (1999), p. 30.
80 Leicester (1999).
81 Leicester (1998), p. 21.
82 Partridge (2000); Schwend (1999).
83 Gillespie (1999); Laffan, O'Donnell and Smith (2000).
84 This paragraph summarises the argument put forward in Gillespie (2000).
85 Garvin (2000), p. 43.
86 Ahern (1998).

CHAPTER FIVE

Economy

Brendan Keenan

The subject of Britain's economic standing compared with the rest of Europe has been exercising minds since the turn of the century. British politicians and economic thinkers were aware by 1900 that the country had lost is pre-eminence. They have been arguing about the reasons ever since. Like others before him, the historian Patrick O'Brien traces the period from 1870 as the start of the rot.[1] Contemporaries noted that by 1901, both Germany and the USA were producing more steel than the UK. By 1912, its share of world steel production had fallen from 40% to 34%. Among the varied explanations, though, is one that the very reliance on the old staples of steel, coal and textiles, prevented Britain moving sufficiently into the new industries such as electrical engineering, chemicals and plastics. Employment in the traditional industries grew by 40% from 1901-21, against 20% in the workforce as a whole.

Behind that, a deeper concern was being expressed early on in the century. It was claimed that the German government paid more attention to technical and commercial training, and the merits of Germany's technical education system were already being noted. The relative failure of Britain to link the work of the scientific laboratory to industry was lamented before the First World War – and it still is. Relative decline in the UK's economic performance accelerated after the Second World War, but this owed much to the extraordinary growth rates achieved on the continent in that period. From 1950 to 1970, growth in the UK averaged 2.7% per annum, versus 4.8% on the continent, where growth averaged 5.2% in 1960-70 – a staggering differential. Even on a more flattering per capita basis, continental economies grew at twice the British rate. In 1950, Britain was still a leading economic power, accounting for a quarter of the world's manufacturing exports and almost 40% of its shipbuilding. By

1980, it was a minor player. In his recent book, former *Financial Times* Editor Geoffrey Owen suggests cause and effect, saying that Britain could have shared in the European boom had it joined the Common Market at the outset.[2]

Even this speed of decline compared with most of Europe might not have been so damaging had it occurred in a steady manner. What really distinguished the British economy was its extreme volatility. This reflected the higher inflation which was such a marked feature of the economy. This higher inflation, particularly when compared with Germany, could only result in a steady depreciation in the currency. The deutschmark started life at over 11 to the pound sterling. Now, 50 years later, its equilibrium rate seems to be around DM2.5-DM3 to the pound. One explanation for this inflation may be the various attempts to increase Britain's growth rate closer to that of Europe. In line with much of the Keynesian orthodoxy of the time, these attempts usually took the form of fiscal stimulus such as the "Barber Boom", named after Chancellor Tony Barber, and Ted Heath's "Dash for Growth" in the 1970s. Modern orthodoxy would predict that these policies could only end in inflation.

THATCHER'S STRUCTURAL REFORMS

Modern orthodoxy would also say that the only cure is structural reform; improvements in the functioning of labour and capital markets, more competition and less involvement by the state. Mrs Thatcher carried out the structural reform. Among the key changes were liberalisation of capital markets and the abolition of exchange controls. This undoubtedly contributed to the disastrous credit boom of the 1980s, but it is now a transition which all EU countries have made or are having to make. Thatcher's labour reforms are more unusual in an EU context. The closed shop, which encompassed five million workers in 1979, was abolished. Secondary picketing was banned and compulsory ballots before strike action were introduced. Individual workers could not be victimised for ignoring even majority-approved industrial action, while employers had no obligation to recognise trade unions or engage in collective bargaining. Most of these changes have remained, with only modest moves by New Labour to reverse them, in areas such as union recognition. Along with the decline of traditional industry, they have contributed to a fall in union membership from thirteen million to around eight million.

With this radical labour restructuring went the privatisation of state industries and increased competition. Deregulation and the contracting out of government services have probably had more effect than the privatisation programme, but the state industries probably could not have survived in de-regulated markets anyway. These changes would seem to have made the UK a more flexible economy, rather than a low-wage one. There have been difficulties with earnings statistics but, according to the OECD, annual earnings grew by an average of just under 8% a year from 1982 to 1992.[3] The rise has been closer to 3% since then, somewhat below the EU average and marginally above the eurozone average. Employers' social security contributions are typically much lower than in the richer EU states. However, most of the credit for Britain's lower rates of unemployment is given to the greater flexibility of its labour market where it is easier and cheaper for employers to hire, and more critically, fire employees.

Attempts to provide statistical evidence for the proposition that flexibility reduces unemployment have been inconclusive. It has also been noted that other EU countries, notably Austria, Denmark and the Netherlands, have achieved high employment growth and low unemployment in recent years. The success of the Netherlands' "Polder model" means it now faces labour shortages on an Irish scale. Employers' social security contributions have been cut for the lower-paid, the national minimum wage has been reduced, entitlement to unemployment assistance curtailed and part-time work encouraged. And all within a structure of social partnership.

Adding in the effects of the economic cycle, the UK's "Anglo-Saxon" model may not have as big an employment advantage over the more successful EU economies as is sometimes claimed. At the same time, in British terms the improvement is considerable. It would appear that what is known as NAIRU (non-accelerating inflation rate of unemployment) has fallen from around 7% to 5% (at most). Despite these changes – or, it may be, because of them - the fact is that the British economy has been more volatile since 1979 than in any period over the previous 30 years. Figures show the UK following the European business cycle quite closely from 1975, but with more extreme swings. In the recession of 1981, the UK output gap between production and capacity reached 7%, versus 2.5% in the EU as a whole. At the peak of the 1989 boom, the reverse gap was 4%, again versus 2.5%.

Does this mean that nothing fundamental has changed? It may still be too early to say. The impact of the Thatcher era seems clear in the unemployment figures. Despite various changes to the methods of counting which make it difficult to make comparisons, unemployment is undoubtedly at 20-year lows. OECD standardised figures for March 2000 show UK unemployment at 5.9%, compared with an average 6.6% in the OECD but 9.6% in the eurozone. In addition, Britain has one of the highest rates of employment in the EU, at over 70% of the working-age population. The Labour government has no doubt where the blame for the volatility of the last 20 years lies - at the feet of its Conservative predecessors. There is a good deal of truth in this. But the problems which caused the Tories to make policy errors have not gone away, and may already be returning to haunt New Labour.

In its Stability Programme presented to ECOFIN in late 1999, the Treasury says volatile interest rates in the past partly reflected the fact that monetary policy targeted variables other than inflation. The Tories famously moved from one kind of money supply target to another and, when both proved poor predictors of inflation, abandoned targeting altogether. Labour, in what is still its most dramatic economic action since taking office, gave the Bank of England monetary independence and a pure inflation target. The Bank must aim to keep inflation within one percentage point either side of a 2.5% rate, as measured by the retail price index, excluding mortgages (RPIX). Should RPIX exceed the one point margin, the Governor of the Bank must write a letter to the Chancellor explaining why. The programme also says that the volatile fiscal deficit reflected "a lack of clearly defined and consistently applied fiscal policy objectives. Moreover, a failure to take account of the effects of the economic cycle at times gave a misleading picture of the health of public finances, leading to a lack of caution and inappropriate policy decisions."

There may not be much doubt about that. The question is whether the success of the UK economy in recent years represents a truly structural change, which will put it more on a par with general EU performance, or whether it is due to temporary factors, which for the time being are masking underlying. In this context, the *Financial Times* columnist and economist, Samuel Brittan, has pointed to the impact of the 1992 devaluation of sterling, which followed the currency's departure from the ERM. Along with the 10% devaluation of the punt, which followed as a consequence, this can be regarded as one of the most successful devaluations on record. The reason is that they were not followed by the usual burst of wage and price inflation. This seems to have been because they coincided with a period of low global inflation, even deflation. The rise in import prices was not fully passed on, reducing the pressure for compensating wage rises. Both countries enjoyed a real improvement in competitiveness, from which they are still benefiting. As Brittan puts it, "if this (inflation) happens again – and it need not – then the UK will be seen to have a *real competitiveness* problem, and one which cannot be tackled by monetary or exchange rate manipulation."[4]

Brittan thinks it need not happen again, and so far it has not. Consumer price inflation averaged 2.8% a year from 1992 to 1997, about the same as for the euro area. However, real GDP grew by an average 2.6% a year, as against just 1.9% in the euro area. Over this period, there is not much doubt about who out-performed whom. The UK also seems to have thrown off its traditional burden of fiscal imbalance. The 1999-2000 budget surplus of around one per cent of GDP compares with deficits of 2% of GDP in the euro area, including those of France and Germany. There was, however, a serious "blip" during 1992-95, when the deficit averaged over 6% of GDP, indicating again the volatility of past performance. The Treasury sees the Exchequer returning to a small deficit in 2001-02. Chancellor Brown hopes to avoid a recurrence of "blips" with his "Golden Rule", which says that the deficit should not exceed net government investment over the cycle – another version of the old rule that the current budget should be in balance. With the "cycle" now in its seventh year of expansion – the longest continuous expansion in 45 years - this is not proving too onerous at present. Britain's debt ratio - one of the lowest in the EU at 48% of GDP – should continue to fall towards 40%.

This is the evidence for a sea-change in the UK's economic performance. It is, after all, more than ten years since the OECD observed that "the persistence of high rates of output and productivity growth through an exceptionally long recovery phase, judged by past performance and that of other countries, suggests that the improvements on supply-side performance are more than a transitory phenomenon."[5] In its policy review published in June 2000[6], the OECD seems now to have made up its mind. It is impressed by the success of the UK authorities in ensuring a "soft landing" in 1998-99 and, it would seem, in forestalling a consumer boom and rapid rise in house prices in 2000, through frequent, small increases in interest rates. The economy seems to be less prone to "boom and bust" than in the 1980s, the report observes. The report also notes the effect of the changes to the labour market. Increased flexibility - a euphemism for the fact that it is easier and cheaper to both hire and fire workers than in most, if not all, of the EU - means the NAIRU rate has fallen since the 1980s and seems to be around 5%, at most. The report's author, Vincent Koen, thinks these changes refute many of the objections to Britain joining EMU. "The UK seems to be as close, or even closer, to the economic centre of gravity of the euro area than some of the existing members," it says. "If Greece can be a member, why not Britain?" Koen not unreasonably asked.[7]

Yet there are other signs, and other voices, warning that not as much has changed as appears to be the case. They say that the UK still lags seriously behind the major EU states in terms of underlying economic performance, as measured by things such as productivity, investment, research and educational qualifications, and that these deficiencies will show up again in the medium to long term.

One of the more bearish outlooks comes from the London office of the US stockbrokers Salomon Smith Barney.[8] They see the evidence of trouble ahead in the swelling current account deficit on the balance of payments, which reached a ten-year high in the early months of 2000. For them, the Will Hutton thesis still applies; that British consumption outstrips the economy's capacity to deliver.[9] The only reason the economy has performed so well so far is that the supply side *did* respond - on a scale not seen since the 1950s. Real investment in machinery and equipment has increased 70% since 1994, against output growth of 12% over the period. But even this has not been enough to match booming domestic demand. This was growing at an annualised 3.5% in the second and third quarters of 1999. The Bank of England Monetary Policy Committee is again wrestling with the old British dilemma – the necessity to have interest rates above EU averages, so as to curb domestic demand, leading to a soaring exchange rate and problems for UK manufacturing. It is the same combination which wrecked the Conservatives' economic policy in the 1980s. It leaves Brown in a difficult position. He has a healthy surplus with which to prime an election campaign, but the high exchange rate and strong demand calls for fiscal tightening, not loosening, so as not to leave monetary policy taking all the strain of curbing demand. The 1999 Budget was criticised for loosening policy, with the three-year projections calculated to loosen it by 1.6% of GDP. (Forward sterling rates rose in the week after the March Budget, implying that interest rates would peak at 7% next year, and remain at these levels into 2002). Yet the political pressures for more public spending, especially on health and education, grew after the local election defeats in May 2000 and were confirmed in the July three-year spending review.

A study by the International Monetary Fund suggested sterling is around one-third higher than its fundamental equilibrium rate. Faced with the same dilemma in 1987, Chancellor Nigel Lawson disastrously cut interest rates. The independent MPC, with its clear inflation target, will not do so but the consequences for sterling seem clear.

The potential damage to British industry from a prolonged period of sterling strength is less clear. Brittan has argued that it is too simplistic to say that sterling's forced departure from the ERM in 1992 proves that its central parity of DM2.95 was too high. Interest rates were inappropriately high because of the costs of German unification. These strains gave currency speculators their opportunity. Without them, UK manufacturers might have adjusted, and coped, knowing they had no choice.

The evidence since then suggests that UK manufacturing can cope with sterling at around 2.9DM (or 65p to the euro) but that it suffers above those levels. Sterling's trade-weighted index rose another 10% in 1999, and this seems to have snuffed out what looked like a manufacturing recovery. Instead, output has remained more or less flat since 1997, despite strong growth at home and in several key export markets. The imbalance which bedevils policy can be seen in the contrast between the 500,000 increase in services employment, and the 340,000 fall in manufacturing jobs, in the two years 1998-99.

Some argue that the UK is already a post-industrial economy, and that manufacturing does not matter very much. A paper from brokers Smithers and Co., summed up this situation with the title: "Britain, the World's Largest Hedge Fund." Although the UK had net liabilities of stg£145bn in 1998, it earned a positive return, with assets yielding 5.1%, while the cost of liabilities was 4.3%. This, they say, represents a successful investment strategy, but future net income from this source cannot be taken for granted. It has been suggested that a continuation of this success might amount to a "sixth test" for membership of the euro, in addition to the five official ones. This characteristic of the UK economy was on display in figures which showed that British companies were the world's biggest overseas investors in 1999, beating even the USA into second place – a feat they also achieved in 1988. Outward investment came to stg£132bn, led by mergers and acquisitions by firms such as Vodafone and Zeneca. Britain was the third biggest recipient of inward investment, at stg£39bn, after the USA and Sweden, where the figures were distorted by Zeneca's purchase of the Astra group. Whatever the ability of existing industry to cope at around 60p to the euro, that still leaves the question of where future investment will go.

THE PERSISTENCE OF OLD PROBLEMS

The paradox is that the increases in flexibility and efficiency wrought by the Thatcher reforms, the power of the City of London, the global reach of the best British companies, and the technology of some industry leaders may be obscuring the persistence of old British problems. These can be summed up as poor productivity, low levels of innovation and enterprise, and, especially, continuing weaknesses in the education and training systems. New Labour is still able to blame these problems on its long-serving predecessors, and is willing to highlight them, although there must be a limit to how long they can get away with that.

There were considerable improvements in productivity under the Tories. Output per head rose almost 4% a year in the 1979-90 period; the first time it had reached continental levels since the 1960s. This was not enough, however, to close the gap. A 1999 report from the Department of Trade and Industry shows British productivity, measured by GDP per hour worked, lagging behind France by 26%. French productivity seems to be growing rapidly again with the introduction of the 35-hour week. The contrast is between French unemployment at 10.4% on an OECD basis in early 2000, compared with a UK figure of 5.9%, so not everyone may favour the French methods of improving productivity. Measured by output per person employed, the USA is the world leader. On this measure, the UK is even further behind, with the British worker contributing a third less output than his US counterpart. Although the number of British scientific papers published, relative to population, almost equals the United States figure, the UK's registration of patents remains one of the lowest in the industrialised countries, and commercial spending on R&D has consistently been one of the lowest. Government spending on research is also low. It is much the same complaint as in 1900. New Labour has identified these as key policy issues. It has a long-term target to get the proportion of 30 year olds with a third-level qualification from 36% of the population to 50%. Strategies in primary schools, along with life-long learning policies are designed to reduce the seven million people reckoned to lack basic literacy and numeracy. This will be a difficult task, and the results may take decades to show through. Stable macroeconomic conditions and changes in capital taxation may produce quicker results in innovation, especially if the underlying structure of manufacturing has indeed improved. The independence of the Bank of England and the present commitment to fiscal discipline should ensure more stability, but perhaps at the price of an over-valued exchange rate.

BRITAIN'S RELATIVE PERFORMANCE

The key question as to whether British performance relative to Europe will be better in the future than in the past is, therefore, not easy to answer. The economy is undoubtedly more flexible, efficient and lower-cost than before the Thatcher era. But even if the UK's sustainable, non-inflationary growth rate has increased, has it increased enough to keep up with the eurozone? The issue is relative, not absolute, performance, which depends on the eurozone's long-term growth prospects. The Treasury has tentatively, if unofficially, raised the forecast for the UK's long-term sustainable growth rate to 2.5%. That looks comfortable beside the 1.4% annual growth achieved by Germany since 1992, and is in line with the eurozone average. But the difficult years after German unification and before the launch of the euro may not be a good guide to the future. Already, the strength of recovery in the eurozone indicates that there is potential for some years of strong, catch-up growth after the tight monetary policies which followed German re-unification and preceded the launch of the euro.

France is the case *par excellence*. The economy is estimated to have grown by around 4% in 1999, and may expand by 3% in 2000, with any error likely to be on the upside. Exports were up

4.4% in the third quarter of 1999, the strongest growth for a decade, reflecting the franc's favourable euro exchange rate and improvements in its main markets. Consumer confidence began growing in June 1999 and falling unemployment and low inflation should keep it buoyant. Even a mere cyclical upturn in Germany and Italy should be enough to restore growth in the core euro states to the 2.5-3% range, while bringing growth in the whole zone comfortably above 3%. Now there is evidence of restructuring in the continental economies which may increase their long-term growth potential.

Germany is the key. There is a belief that the government's 1999 corporate and income tax-cutting package marks a decisive break with the policies of the past. Germany also has one of the most deregulated electricity and telecommunications markets in Europe. There is a shift from the old relationship-based ownership models to more market-driven ones, symbolised by the hostile Vodafone take-over of Mannesmann. It may be significant that Germany's Neuer Markt has become the home of Europe's new breed of high-tech stocks, with a capitalisation of €60bn, and that London has failed to establish a similar presence.

There is clear potential for added economic growth were Germany to liberalise its services sector. Germany, France and others have huge scope to deregulate their labour markets. This is politically difficult but, as unemployment falls due to higher growth, it is not unreasonable to imagine that, since the need for reform is recognised, some change will take place, thereby accelerating the decline in unemployment. The "Polder Model" already shows that this can be done within a "European Model". Even if labour markets are not reformed - and the Lisbon summit was not too encouraging in this respect - it is easy to underestimate European potential. The French response to the 35-hour week is a case in point, with employers securing a temporary wage freeze and restructuring of working hours as part of the process. The impact can already be seen in a rise in productivity, already one of the highest in the world. In this, optimistic scenario for Europe, the euro should rise against sterling, easing the competitive pressures on the UK economy, but growth might again begin to lag behind that of the continent.

CONCLUSION

A Singular Economy
The British economy has undergone restructuring on the scale of a revolution in the past 20 years. This has made it more efficient and flexible, and raised the long-term growth rate and lowered the non-inflationary unemployment rate. Even these changes, however, are not enough to prevent sterling being an awkward fit for the euro, as the UK is for so much of the EU. At the same time, the past two years show that the alternative of non-membership is little better.

The differences are more fundamental than those which are often cited, such as high levels of home-ownership in the UK, which is financed by variable mortgage rates, making the economy more volatile in its response to interest rate changes. Rather, they lie in the importance of financial services and overseas assets and liabilities for the UK, combined with the traditional excess of domestic demand over supply, makes the UK economy inherently prone to volatility and inflation. The Bank of England's clear mandate to fight inflation has pushed sterling to levels which threaten what remains of manufacturing. The "British disease", evident since the beginning of the last century, has been ameliorated, but not yet cured. It can be cured only over the long-run, by improvements in British skills and productivity.

The burning question is whether, in the meantime, euro membership would help or hinder that process. There is a strong argument that it would not make matters any worse, and might make long-term restructuring easier. Inside EMU, the UK could well tend to have inflation higher than the eurozone average. But its trading firms might find this easier to deal with – since it would be transparent to them and their workers – than the alternative outside EMU of loss of competitiveness through an overvalued exchange rate. Membership would clarify the issues and the challenges, which a national currency and national monetary policy can obscure. It comes down to Geoffrey Owen's argument again, which says the UK has lost out by remaining aloof from EU developments, on the grounds that its singularities meant it was better to go it alone. The British economy is singular, compared with the eurozone, but it does not necessarily follow that, over the long run, it can do better outside. The implications for the zone of having this singular entity *inside* is a topic for another time.

1   O'Brien (1999).
2   Owen (1998).
3   OECD (1999).
4   Brittan (1995).
5   OECD (1988).
6   OECD Economic Survey on the UK, June 2000.
7   Quoted in *Financial Times*, 10 June 2000.
8   Salomon Smith Barney (2000).
9   Department of Trade and Industry (1999); Hutton (1994).

SECTION TWO

BLAIR'S BRITAIN

Section Two

England's Europe

BACKGROUND AND CONTEXT

Until the arrival of the Blair government, Britain had been an awkward partner in Europe. As far back as the Schuman Declaration, British political leaders had approached the integration process with a mixture of distrust, suspicion, disdain, and even hostility. It was only when the change in Britain's fortunes in the post-War period, and the realities of its diminished status in international politics and economics became understood and accepted by elements of the policy elite, that EEC membership was sought, belatedly and reluctantly. This pattern of behaviour was to be repeated in each of the subsequent grand phases of integration. The reluctance to participate, until forced to by circumstances, gave rise to what became known as the late-joiner syndrome.[1] Britain only entered each stage (with the exception of the Single Market) after it had already been established, and then tried to change it to meet its own requirements.

Consequently, Britain sought by times to rewrite the rules, as with the Community Budget, or tried to frustrate what others saw as a natural evolution, as with the Social Chapter and the extension of qualified majority voting. At other times, Britain stood against deepening integration and simply refused to participate in a grand project, as with the single currency or the Schengen Agreement, thus perpetuating the late-joiner syndrome. It is hardly surprising that, in the phrase coined by Stephen George, Britain came to be regarded as "an awkward partner"[2] in Europe. More accurately it could have been described as "the awkward partner", the one member state for which the flexibility clause in the Amsterdam Treaty was originally intended, with John Major's triumphant declaration of "game, set and match" still ringing in the ears of the other national leaders.

Throughout the half-century of integration which preceded the victory of New Labour, the old Labour Party, no less than the Conservatives, had contributed handsomely to British awkwardness. From Attlee onwards it had done so whenever in government (refusing, for example, to join the ERM in 1979) and in opposition had periodically proved hostile to the very concept of Europe, even to the point of advocating British withdrawal from the Community under the leadership of Michael Foot.[3] Before coming to power, Blair had promised to reverse Britain's European policy and to end its perennial awkwardness within Europe, although his party had opposed the Maastricht Treaty. In view of the consistency of Britain's past behaviour and Labour's previous hostility towards Europe the Blair government's commitment to a positive and proactive role in Europe is startling and raises issues which are both novel and arresting. The question here is whether New Labour is developing a coherent long-term vision of Britain in Europe that is broadly acceptable across the British political spectrum and, if so, whether it can deliver on what it promised in opposition. If it is engaged in shaping a new vision, and especially if there are real prospects of realising it, then the awkward partnership of the past would be fit for burial sometime in the future. The late-joiner syndrome would disappear and the implications for the speed and direction of European integration would be far-reaching.

It has to be said from the outset that, consistent with the analysis of the previous IEA study, Britain's problem with Europe is essentially an English one.[4] Neither the Scots nor the Welsh suffer from the identity crisis manifest in the tortured relationship of the English with their fellow Europeans. In that sense, this section is devoted almost exclusively to an English, rather than a British, European policy. The underlying theme is that it is England's Europe which is at issue, as it has been since the Coal and Steel Community was first mooted. The confusion between British and English, in which the two are generally taken to be synonymous (especially in continental Europe) or are used interchangeably, even by the more meticulous commentators, has obscured a central reality in analysing UK policy on Europe (to take a more neutral, and accurate, adjective). Now that Scotland and Wales have emerged, however hesitantly, from the shades of political invisibility, it is proper to identify the reality, and to name it for what it is: England has a problem with Europe, not Britain. England's concept of what Europe has been, is now and will be, is the *raison d'être* for the awkward partnership.

1   Gillespie, ed. (1996).
2   George (1994).
3   Halligan (1981).
4   Gillespie, ed. (1996).

CHAPTER SIX

Labour's Long March

Brendan Halligan

INTRODUCTION

The contract with the British people which Blair had unilaterally concluded prior to the last general election also included a new Labour policy on Europe. It would have been illogical for the brave departure contemplated by New Labour not to include a refashioned role for Britain in world affairs and, more particularly, within the region to which it belongs by way of geography, history, culture and economics. Furthermore, the genesis of New Labour had included a revision of Labour policy on Europe which ultimately became a revolution leading to the repudiation of Michael Foot's commitment to withdrawal. The rebranding of the Labour Party as "new", with its connotations of shedding baggage from the past and embracing the challenges of the future, needs no further elaboration, other than for an examination of the implications for its European policy.

THE NEW DISPENSATION

The new policy on Europe had been in gestation within the Labour Party for nearly a decade prior to the last general election. It was grounded on an analysis of the party's and country's best interests as an integral part of its grand design for a new Britain. The time taken to reverse the old policy indicates that it was no overnight conversion to the cause of Europe for mere party advantage. Admittedly, it was partly born out of Labour's general revulsion with Thatcherism and was accelerated by her increasing stridency on Europe, unwittingly made more attractive for Labour by her caricature of the then Community as creeping back-door socialism.[1] There were, however, more positive influences at work. The trade union movement had, for example, warmed to Delors' plans for a Social Europe and had greeted him at the Trades Union Congress's 1988 annual conference as a saviour from the excesses of the Conservative government's market ideology.[2] Within the party, the benefits of positive engagement in Europe became more attractive the longer it remained isolated from power at home. Sister parties in the EU added to the argument that there was no alternative to Europe, with the SPD playing a crucial but low-key role in the process of conversion. At the geo-political level, the end of the Cold War and the forces of globalisation added to the argument that a strategic reassessment of Britain's future was urgent.

The process of conversion, as it could be truly described given the fervour of the beliefs it initially had to confront in Old Labour, was started early in the Kinnock leadership and was greatly advanced by him by the time of his resignation. It was continued by John Smith and, prior to the last election, could be said to have been finally completed by Tony Blair, making it an essential part of New Labour's vision for Britain. By the 1994 European Parliament elections the party's attitude on Europe had been transformed; at the annual conference a year later party policy was settled as being pro-Europe, (although with certain stated reservations in view of the impending general election). The benefits of EU membership were extolled in some detail, contrasting sharply with the negative (or destructive) criticism during the Foot era.

Nevertheless, the pro-European policy was hedged around with many caveats, as on federalism and EMU membership. The case for Europe was presented in instrumental rather than inspirational terms, leading to suspicions that there were no essential policy differences on Europe between Labour and the Conservatives (other than on the Social Chapter).[3] The main difference was said to be one of tone. But in the run-up to the general election such circumspection could equally have been understood as no more than the prudence New Labour practised, for example, on tax and public expenditure. Outside the demands of domestic politics, corroboration for New Labour's conversion came from an external arena which, of its nature, was a rigorous testing ground for examining the credibility of Blair's policy departure on Europe when in opposition.

THE PES

As part of its preparation for government, New Labour had to establish its credentials as a co-operative rather than an awkward partner in a forum that was European rather than domestic: the Party of European Socialists (PES). This umbrella organisation of social democratic parties in the European Union constitutes a political group in the European Parliament and provides continuous liaison between the party organisations in each member state. It is also a forum for political debate and agreeing common policy positions, such as the Socialist manifesto for the European elections. Drafting statements and manifestos exposes differences not only on particular policy issues but also on the more philosophical questions concerning the future of Europe. Old Labour, for example, was noted inside the PES for its somewhat irritating insistence on excluding itself from common positions, not quite the comradely attitude expected from an internationalist party; it seldom, if ever, showed any appetite for the federalist rhetoric favoured by its continental counterparts.

Crucially, the PES enables party leaders to get to know each other in the privacy of their many encounters; it is difficult to deceive or be deceived at these intimate, informal gatherings. More than any other political arena, the PES is the place for Europe's social democrats to reach measured judgements on each other in terms of personality and policy, and for party leaders to network with their counterparts. The success of Blair's campaign in convincing the PES of his party's change of heart can be gauged from the fact that, despite the reservations on EMU, during the run-up to the 1997 election New Labour's policy statements on Europe were already being received enthusiastically by the other social democratic parties.[4] Indeed, such was the comradely attitude within the PES that Blair could use its structures to prepare himself, as well as potential cabinet members and advisers, for their future European responsibilities, with the discreet support of the other leaders. By the time the election campaign commenced, Blair had established his credentials as a "normal" European political leader in the forum which mattered more than any other for the conduct of European politics, the inner circle of his peers as party leaders. In addition, he had cultivated the leaders of various Christian Democratic parties and had gone some way towards convincing them of his intention to change Britain's European policy when in government.

NEW LABOUR, NEW GOVERNMENT

It has been widely commented that the Blair government hit the ground running on assuming office, and did so because of Labour's intense and unprecedented preparation for power. If New Labour came to power fully formed in terms of policy and personnel, then Europe was no exception. That was soon made clear during the closing stages of the Amsterdam IGC where the arrival of the new government was greeted with relief by other member states and many previous British objections to various Treaty amendments were immediately and ruthlessly cast overboard. Doug Henderson, the new Minister for Labour, made it clear on his first appearance at the IGC that the Blair government wished to make a fresh start to Britain's relations with Europe; the reaction of his fellow negotiators was that a deal on Treaty amendments had, at last, become possible.[5] This belief was reinforced by the Foreign Secretary, Robin Cook, announcing that the confrontational approach of the Major government was to be immediately replaced by one of constructive engagement. Indeed, he went so far as to state that Britain wished to become the third player in Europe.[6] The appearance of Blair at an informal European Council two weeks later added to this feeling that a new era had begun. The performance of Blair at his first formal European Council in Amsterdam, only seven weeks after taking office, was that of a confident insider who broadly shared the views of his other prime ministerial colleagues on strengthening Europe. This merely reflected the reality that as party leader he had already made himself an insider; now he was an insider who was also a Prime Minister.

The Amsterdam Council opened a new era for Britain's relationship with Europe. It marked the end of Britain as Europe's awkward partner. This was true for both substance and style. On substance, Britain agreed to all the treaty amendments (with the exception of the Schengen Agreement mentioned below) and would probably have countenanced a further extension of qualified majority voting had Chancellor Kohl not unexpectedly imposed his own limitations to this because of German domestic politics involving the competences of the Länder. This co-operative approach contrasted profoundly with that of Major at Maastricht, where Britain had opposed virtually all reform proposals. As for style, that integral part of New Labour's persona, Blair exuded good-will and bonhomie, at times playing the novel role, at least for a British Prime Minister, of a helpful and constructive conciliator. The psychological shift from a difficult outsider to a positive insider was accomplished in a matter of weeks of New Labour coming to power and added a historic dimension to Amsterdam going far beyond the Treaty changes agreed by the IGC. The transformation has since been accepted as a fact of Europe's political life to such an extent that it no longer attracts comment. Yet, it was a turning point in Britain's European policy. Whether it can be sustained indefinitely is a matter for further analysis.

But, at Amsterdam, one feature of British policy on Europe endured. The late-joiner syndrome once more manifested itself with the British opt-out on the incorporation of the Schengen Agreement into the Treaties, an opt-out with repercussions for Ireland which was forced to follow suit because of the British-Irish Common Travel Area.[7] In this instance, however, the reaction of other member states was to accept the difficulties which lay behind the new government's inability to sign-up to the Schengen Agreement rather than the customary exasperation at British bloody-mindedness in insisting on having its own way.

SAME OLD PROBLEMS

Nevertheless, the fact remains that, within weeks of taking office, the Blair government found itself excluded from two core areas of EU policy, just as the Major government would have been: the free movement of peoples throughout the Community and, more ominously for the future, membership of the single currency. The former, it could be said, did not really matter as a test of New Labour's European credentials since the traditional British preoccupation with maintaining border controls (against other Europeans) was regarded as part of the British mystique and as a psychological barrier which a new government could not immediately overcome – however well motivated towards its European partners. The easy acceptance of the Schengen opt-out was Blair's reward for not being John Major, a price readily paid by the other member states for having a co-operative Britain at the Council table. In any case, the removal of border controls was not a sensitive political issue at Amsterdam since the treaty amendments simply incorporated existing legal obligations between thirteen member states into the general body of the

Treaty. Neither did it attract much media attention so that the British opt-out was neither an embarrassment for the Union as a whole nor a Major-style victory for Britain. It was, of course, as significant an example of variable geometry as the British and Danish opt-outs on the single currency and Britain's earlier opt-out on the Social Chapter, yet it was not the stuff of crisis.

Confirmation of the new attitude towards Britain came in the IGC approach to the treaty amendments on flexibility, or enhanced cooperation. Originally intended to get around British intransigence on the further deepening of integration,[8] the fact that the speed of the convoy could not be determined by that of the slowest ship, as Kohl had once famously expressed it, flexibility was seen instead at Amsterdam as a means of managing diversity in an enlarged European Union, a precaution against potential dissident voices in Central and European Europe rather than a weapon to beat down the British.[9] It created, of course, the prospect of a "core Europe" within an enlarged Union and could be invoked against Britain if the need arose but, for the time being, this was not its purpose. In retrospect, this change of strategy on flexibility may well be regarded as Blair's greatest triumph in repositioning Britain within Europe. New Labour also meant a New Britain in a New Europe.

Despite this psychological victory, Old Labour lingered on in the form of the single currency. Here there could be no pretence about the nature of the British partnership, neither on the part of other member states, who regarded membership as the truest test of European bona fides, nor within the UK where public opinion remained deeply divided on membership, especially in a Conservative Party rent by a controversy that would only get worse when the trauma of electoral defeat subsided.

INTERNALISING EUROPE

Yet this characterisation of opposition to EMU being simply a relic of Old Labour is inaccurate. It would be fairer to say it was a legacy of Old England, as Chapter Eight will argue. The Labour Party itself had undergone a transformation of attitude on Europe which placed it in the main stream of the continent's social democratic parties but at odds with the majority of the electorate, including a sizeable chunk of its own support. Political parties do not normally take this sort of risk, especially when embarking on government. It is more unusual when the issue at stake is deeply controversial. To do so smacks of strong leadership. But the first three years of office suggests that however strong this leadership might be, it is not irrational; there is no point in being so far ahead of public opinion on the euro that electoral support is wantonly thrown away (the theme of the following chapter).

The limits of manoeuvre imposed by public opinion have been accepted but New Labour has, nonetheless, matured into a political party which instinctively sees itself as being pro-European. The long march had reached the point by the party's centenary in 2000 that its official magazine, *Inside Labour*, could credibly represent New Labour as *the* European party in Britain. The solemn commemoration of the party's foundation was used to affirm its belief that the national interest demanded Britain should be at the heart of Europe.[10] The Conservatives were presented as anti-national because they were anti-European. The internalisation of this message as part of its core values confirmed that the party, as opposed to most of its supporters, had finally resolved a key element of its own identity crisis.

It enabled Blair, writing the preface to the White Paper on the IGC and Enlargement barely three years after the general election, to declare that "unlike its predecessors this government is unwaveringly pro-European".[11] In the light of past controversies, the claim was remarkable for its self-confident tone and the fact that it was not disputed. It summarised the facts as they were three years after taking office. For the first time in recent British history one of the two main parties had unequivocally committed itself to being pro-European over the long term. For its part, the awkward partnership had been laid to rest, and in its stead a co-operative partner had emerged, untroubled by strategic internal party dispute – whatever about the tactics – and united in its determination that Britain would play a European role commensurate with its strengths and interests, the role that other Europeans had long awaited.[12]

FUTURE SCENARIOS

The repercussions within British domestic politics were predictable. The adversarial nature of the system makes each of the two main parties move in opposite directions on most policy issues – as Labour marched determinedly towards Europe the

Conservative marched away in a long bitter retreat.[13] That each wound up in a mirror-image of its position in 1973 was ironic; it was also a reminder of the inconsistency which is said to be inherent in British policy on Europe because of the inability of the political system to reach consensus on big issues, such as a durable settlement on that question.[14] Apart from war-time coalitions the polarisation of politics is an endemic and an unavoidable consequence of the electoral system.[15] The result is stalemate on long-term goals, given that each of the two main parties will periodically enter government, with the main task seen as undoing what its predecessor had achieved. In the light of the polarisation of policy on Europe, it too falls into the category of systemic stalemate, or failure. It prompts the question which is central to this analysis, whether Labour's long march has finally led Britain to a measured, grand European strategy analogous to other large member states or is periodically condemned to being the most awkward partner in Europe.

On the assumption that the New Labour project is sustained for at least two terms, it can be said that the Labour Party organisation will be free of major controversy over Europe and will remain committed to being pro-European in the same sense that applies to other social democratic parties in Europe. The Labour government will consequently be able to adopt a positive stance within the integration process although, for electoral reasons, will be constrained from participating as fully in all core EU competences as it would wish. But with the passage of time it could be expected that these restraints will weaken. That is a benign scenario for Europe.

This, however, is predicated on New Labour's electoral success over the long run. Were it, for example, to retain power but with a sharply depleted majority it is quite possible that internal factions would re-emerge from what many suspect to be no more than hibernation. In that case, the government's capacity to keep pace with a deepening integration would be suspect and the scenario most likely to apply would be that of the late joiner, possibly a very late joiner.

Should the New Labour project fail and the Conservative Party return to office, scenarios for the future would, of course, be dramatically changed because the Conservatives have embarked on their own long march; to the heart-land of England as some would say. The secular decline in their vote in Scotland and Wales has had the effect of making the Conservatives an English party in parliamentary terms, and to appear as the voice of a new English nationalism. Devolution in Scotland and Wales has re-inforced that trend as the local party organisations there re-invent themselves in order to survive. The upshot, if policy statements are taken as a dependable guide, has been a more virulent form of opposition to Europe than John Major experienced, the difference being that this time it is concentrated in the leadership. The Conservative Party orientation on Europe has become one of picking and choosing common policies under the label of "flexibility", which in this instance is the polar opposite of Joschka Fischer's *avant-garde*; it is conceived as a rear-guard. The most likely outcome of any such policy would be Britain becoming an EU outsider, since dining *à la carte* from the EU menu is anathema to those who view flexibility as the means of achieving ever-closer union.

FAULT-LINES IN NEW LABOUR

These scenarios are a reminder of the precariousness of Blair's achievements. There is a fault-line between the party's position on Europe and the attitude of the bulk of Labour support. It lies along the deep cleavage dividing those who look forward to the future and those who cling to the past, metaphors which might broadly explain the two cultures fighting for British identity. As ever, social realities are more complex than cryptic formulations, but as some commentators note,[16] playing the patriot game has become a feature of debate between the two main parties in which labels and symbols are used as short-hand for sharing or retaining sovereignty.

But the debate is not just between the parties; it is also within the parties and between them and their supporters. Within the parties it has become progressively more muted as anti-Europeans are marginalised in New Labour and pro-Europeans exiled in William Hague's Conservative Party. The more difficult and decisive debate is that between each party and its own "natural" support within the electorate.

The political reality for Blair is that he has not carried his party supporters with him on Europe to anything like the same extent as the activists. Prior to the general election of 1997, the electorate was not called upon by New Labour to be pro-European and the issue was carefully tucked away where it could do least, or no, damage. It was just as well. At that stage, the party's working class supporters overwhelmingly favoured the retention of sterling by a five-to-one majority. Middle class supporters were about evenly divided.[17] Taken as a whole, New Labour voters were strongly opposed to the euro and it made good electoral sense to keep Europe off the domestic agenda. In government, such subterfuge could hardly be continued.

The opinion polls indicate that potential Labour voters have not been converted to Europe any more than the rest of the electorate. This puts them at odds with Blair's stance on the most divisive issue in British politics and, if exploited by his Conservative opponents, could fracture the support base laboriously constructed by New Labour strategists. In electoral terms, this fault-line between the government's policy and the electorate's instincts could hardly be more threatening. On one estimate the government would need to change the minds of nearly five million voters in order to win a referendum on the euro.[18] Any attempt would inevitably provoke losses in overall party support and in a worse case scenario the defections could be substantial. It requires little insight to conclude that the Blair government began with a strategic dilemma of its own making; the policy which had won the election was directly at variance with that it wished to pursue in office. That it is the inevitable legacy of Labour's past hostility to Europe is but one more example of the damage serial inconsistency on Europe has inflicted on British politics.

CONCLUSION

The problem facing Blair as he embarked on his prime ministership was stark. The avowed objective of New Labour was to end the old awkward relationship with Europe and open a new era in which Britain would play a positive proactive role at the core of the integration process. History had, however, ordained that Britain was at least temporarily excluded from what other member states perceived to be that core – participation in the single currency; the immediate future offered little prospect of overcoming British prejudices against submerging sterling in a common European currency and sharing monetary sovereignty under the auspices of a European Central Bank. It would be a defensible hypothesis to argue that the Blair government had a strategy for resolving this dilemma, one which was discernible from the days of opposition. Equally, it could be argued that the traditional British policy of muddling through would continue. The following chapter looks at the Blair government's engagement with Europe to see if a strategy existed and, if so, how it was implemented.

---

1   Gowland and Turner (2000), p. 269.
2   Gowland and Turner (2000), p. 242.
3   Gillespie, ed. (1996).
4   Labour Party Manifesto (1996).
5   McDonagh (1998), pp 183-184.
6   *The Independent*, 6 May 1997.
7   Tonra, ed. (1997).
8   McDonagh (1998), p. 143.
9   Tonra, ed. (1997).
10   *Inside Labour*, February 2000.
11   White Paper, March 2000.
12   Young (1998), p. 515.
13   Major (1999), p. 358.
14   Young (1998).
15   Gray, *The Guardian*, 9 June 2000.
16   *Economist*, 1 April 2000.
17   Whitely (1999).
18   *ibid.*

CHAPTER SEVEN

The Postponed Question

Brendan Halligan

INTRODUCTION

During the Major years, the battle over Europe had inexorably crystallised around sterling. Joining the new single currency fashioned at Maastricht had become a surrogate for the battle of Britain in Europe. For the opponents of membership, to concede monetary union was to accept all that allegedly flowed from it, the progressive dilution of sovereignty and the eventual, indeed inevitable, creation of political union, usually labelled a "European superstate". For its proponents, membership would ensure Britain's proper place in Europe as well as bringing tangible economic benefits. The intensity and passion of the debate, especially within the Conservative Party[1] was unmatched elsewhere in Europe, with the possible exception of Denmark. For many it was the last stand in defence of British independence, identity, or, even, its way of life.

Yet the battle raged on throughout the Major years, and, if anything, became more intense. Attempts to confine the debate to economic arguments failed and were exposed for what they were: secondary concerns in a larger dispute. The real *causus belli* was political; it was not the euro as such, but Europe itself. Resistance to the euro was identified as springing from a source deeper than the mere economic and said by one commentator[2] to originate in a detestation of "every small shift to further integration, never mind the euro which is a massive one". The division lay between those who could not "find even a single good thing to say about the European Union" and those who could.

From the tone of the euro debate there could be little doubt that the divisions ran so deep as to be virtually irreconcilable; the polls indicated that as many as 40 per cent of the electorate believed Britain had not benefited from EU membership with only 30 per cent believing it had.[3]

This chapter takes the euro as a surrogate for the British debate on Europe and explores the strategy of the Blair government for dealing with the legacy of Major's opt-out at Maastricht (the heart of his "game, set and match" verdict on that IGC). It emerges as one of containing the issue rather than confronting it head on. Not unexpectedly, the strategy created problems of its own and may ultimately prove to have been self-defeating. Yet when launched, it had a defensible rationale and, consequently, is the appropriate starting point for the analysis.

THE POSTPONED QUESTION

Some member states, it is said,[4] enter the integration process with deep reservations about its ultimate goal. Economic necessity or political imperatives may have compelled the state to seek membership, but the electorate would prefer they had not, and wish that integration could be frozen at the point of entry. But integration, as its history has proven, has an in-built momentum and while it may stall for prolonged periods, it cannot be halted indefinitely. Sooner or later, it will reach the stage where any fundamental reservation will be put to the test. This is the postponed question about Europe; for Britain it is the euro.

Until the postponed question is answered, goes the argument, the member state remains outside the "coalition of the willing" prepared to travel as long as it takes on what Andrew Schonfield accurately, if poetically, described as the "journey to an unknown destination".[5]

One thing can be said with certainty about this destination: it will involve a more substantial sharing of sovereignty than that required at any point of entry or conceded in subsequent treaty amendments. But what cannot be foreseen is how it is to be exercised and what the full repercussions will be for the classical prerogatives of the nation state. In many senses the journey is an act of faith; it is understandable that it should be a profession that some member states are not yet prepared to make. For this reason the flexibility clause, referred to in the previous chapter, had been inserted in the Amsterdam Treaty and this is why the coalition of the willing want to have it made more flexible again.

On taking office the Blair government well realised that the decision on the euro was the defining moment for Britain's involvement in Europe. Its predecessors had postponed answering the question. For its part, New Labour had done likewise in opposition. Given sterling's former role as a reserve currency and Parliament's authority over the Bank of England it was inevitable that monetary sovereignty should prove more contentious for Britain than for other member states and become the litmus test for its commitment to Europe.

Sterling was unmatched as a symbol of national sovereignty and it mattered little that monetary sovereignty was more shadow than substance; what mattered was that sharing it would constitute a profound statement about Britain's future role, in the world as much as in Europe – upon which there was no settled opinion. Yet dealing with this discord was unavoidable for the new government and, in many ways, would be the definitive test of its ambitions to be at the core of Europe and of its claim that, unlike its predecessors, it would be unwaveringly pro-European.

SIDELINING THE EURO

One method of managing an apparently intractable dilemma is to buy time by re-formulating the problem and changing the questions to be answered. There is nothing particularly original about this approach but it had been pursued by New Labour when in opposition as part of its electoral strategy to neutralise contentious issues on which the Conservative government could make capital.

The policy statement adopted by the 1995 annual conference had jettisoned the old anti-European shibboleths but had set down preconditions for British membership of EMU relating to economic convergence and competitiveness, and making it conditional on "the consent of the British people". This was regarded at the time as a far from ringing endorsement of early British entry to EMU, although the commitment to a referendum was part of a broader strategy of resorting to the popular will on constitutional matters. Conveniently, it also left the Conservatives without a target to shoot at during the election campaign and, more critically, sanitised those anti-European elements of the media which wanted, on this occasion, to take a pro-Labour stance. The electoral strategists in New Labour had clearly determined that the media could have their EMU cake and eat it.

The first actions of the Blair government in relation to EMU indicated that strategy on the euro would be broadly consistent with the position adopted in opposition. Initially it required two strategic manoeuvres, one on the independence of the Bank of England and the other on the constitutionality of, and conditions for, British membership of the single currency.

In his opening weeks of office, the Chancellor of the Exchequer, Gordon Brown, gave the Bank of England authority to determine interest rates,[6] – previously the province of Chancellors who, when setting the prevailing rate were, not unnaturally, sometimes preoccupied as much with politics as with economics. This move had the effect of going some distance towards granting Britain's central bank the degree of independence laid down by the Maastricht Treaty as a precondition for EMU membership.

The Chancellor's initiative was itself a significant change to the British constitution since it ended the prerogative of the House of Commons to determine monetary as well as fiscal policy. It was not presented in these terms, of course, but rather as an essential component of New Labour's macro-economic policy designed to end the cycle of boom and bust. One effect of this would be to introduce a stability culture which, either by coincidence or design, was close to that of Germany and France (as well as most other EU member states, including Ireland). This sea-change in the culture of UK macro-economic policy held out the tantalising prospect of Britain moving towards the European model so firmly embedded in the Maastricht Treaty. It also offered the intriguing possibility of convergence over time towards the European business cycle.[7]

The medium-term significance of the move was that it created the potential for the alignment of UK interest rates towards the European norm, all other things being equal as economists would instantly add. In these terms, the new role for the Bank of England in determining interest rates in order to meet a low inflation target was additionally a means of meeting the Maastricht criteria by stealth, a tactic all the more ingenious for the lack of comment it attracted from those opposed to British membership of EMU. As events transpired, other things were not equal and the differential between UK and European interest rates remained, although it narrowed significantly throughout the first part of 2000.

PRAGMATISM OR PRINCIPLE?

The second manoeuvre related to the question of EMU membership itself. The Blair government bought time by declaring there was no constitutional impediment to British membership of EMU, an issue which had excited feverish speculation over the previous years, especially among the opponents of membership. That having been done, the focus was then put on the self-evident. It was said, as it had been in opposition, that there were economic obstacles to be overcome before membership could be contemplated and the Chancellor, in October 1997, set out five conditions which had to be met before the government would recommend membership of the euro to the British people.[8] These did no more than repeat, and amplify, the pre-conditions already laid down in party policy two years earlier. However, as noted later in Chapter Eleven, the conditions were sufficiently elastic to mean whatever they might be required to mean when it was deemed appropriate to make a decision. While dressed up as sensible and pragmatic economic benchmarks, primarily concerned with aligning business cycles and assessing the economic costs and benefits of membership, they were essentially a political tool for buying time, a sort of Augustinian economics of let us join, but not now. The tactic had worked well in opposition; it would serve just as well in government.

This particular initiative was intended to reformulate the questions to be answered. Instead of focusing on the principle of EMU membership, the British public was invited to debate the conditions in which it could be undertaken, a shift to the when and how of the euro rather than the why. This manoeuvre had two immediate positive side-effects for the Blair government during its first year in office. It forced the opponents of membership to state their opposition with greater force and clarity than might have been thought prudent, with some explicitly stating that Britain should never join and with the new Conservative leader, William Hague, committing himself to ruling out membership for the lifetime of two parliaments (ordinarily seven to eight years, but taken in this case to mean a decade or so). The suspicion grew that the Conservative Party favoured never joining the euro and that opposition to membership was a surrogate for opposition to Europe itself, which had begun to look like the start of a slippery slope to withdrawal.[9]

This made the position of the Blair government appear all the more reasonable at that time in the eyes of the other member states; it was generally accepted as credible and rational, the second positive side-effect of the policy. In effect, Britain became regarded as a "pre-in" rather than as an "out", a psychological shift in keeping with the atmosphere generated at Amsterdam. This, in turn, allowed Blair to remain for the time being at the core of Europe on the grounds that his government wished in principle to join EMU but for the moment could not do so for reasons which were comprehensible to other EU political leaders, all of whom recognised a political time- bomb when they saw one.

The Chancellor's statement spelled out the government's dilemma. On the one hand, it was the first British government to declare itself for the principle of monetary union. On the other, it ruled out British participation for the lifetime of the Parliament, thus pushing the referendum into the expected second term of office. The underlying cause was not spelled out, however: the problem with membership was not economic, but political.[10] The polls clearly showed a substantial majority against EMU and there was no guarantee that party unity could be sustained in the heat of a referendum campaign. Were divisions to emerge they might prove difficult to heal before the general election and New Labour would have unnecessarily damaged one of its greatest assets: discipline under fire. There was no need to explain these calculations to other EU party leaders and governments; they understood that Blair could not risk a split over Europe, such as had plagued Labour in the past and had devastated the Conservatives.[11]

Yet, even in the early stages in the government's life, there were those who argued that the tactic of buying time was a mistake on at least two grounds: ardent opponents would refuse to comply with the new conditions for debate; and, given the immense popularity and goodwill which marked his first years in office, Blair could personally have led such a campaign for British membership to success. This latter argument has to be evaluated in the light of three points. Firstly, the ambition to win a second term of office, which meant avoiding unnecessary political risks. Secondly, the constitutional and broader reform of Britain, which took precedence over European affairs. Thirdly, British hostility to the euro, which is a surrogate for British antipathy to Europe itself. It is not at all clear that Blair could have overcome this visceral opposition, notwithstanding the level of support for his government then indicated by the polls. It was deemed prudent not to try. Prudence is, after all, a distinguishing characteristic of the Blair style, an adherent surely of the Irish saying *is fearr rith maith ná droch sheasamh*, a good run is better than a bad stand.

STRATEGIC RISKS

A third strategic manoeuvre was executed more than a year later, in early 1999. The strategy of sidelining the euro to the greatest extent possible was advanced to the stage where it could be compressed into a short political slogan, one so full of common sense that the Major government had also previously employed it. In a House of Commons statement, made by Blair as Prime Minister rather than by Gordon Brown as Chancellor, the British people were asked to prepare for the euro before being asked to decide.[12] This "prepare and decide" slogan neatly encapsulated the government's strategy of reformulating the question of membership as one of pragmatism rather than principle. It had the added advantage that preparations would necessarily take time and the decision to join could justifiably be postponed until the conditions had been met. No doubt, the expectation was that public opinion would suspend judgement in the interim and that at an opportune moment it could be galvanised into support, especially if a pro-EMU campaign were lead personally by the Prime Minister.

The more obvious danger in this strategy was the volatility of public opinion, and so it proved. Instead of remaining frozen in time just waiting to be thawed out, public opinion moved continuously in one direction, so that by mid-2000 there was a two-to- one majority against joining the euro. Indeed, at that stage one third of the electorate actually favoured leaving the Union.[13] Furthermore, as the option of holding a referendum in the life-time of the parliament had disappeared, this meant the first term of office was to be primarily concerned with buying time on Europe, even at the sacrifice of losing support for the euro (and, arguably, EU membership itself). It would also suggest that a longer-term strategy was in play, one predicated on Monnet's dictum that the only way to deal with British exceptionalism on Europe was to confront it with facts which were so unambiguous that they automatically dictated the action to be followed. By 2002, the euro would be a fact in so far as the circulation of notes and coins would be a more tangible proof of its existence than the financial products already traded through the London markets.

A further calculation would be that when the notes and coins were circulated, Britain might be the only member state not participating in the euro. That element of the strategy was undone by the Danish referendum result in September 2000, a further example of the dangers inherent in buying time and leaving onself exposed to events. Another consideration would be enlargement of the Union which by then would be raising the possibility, if not probability, of some new member states, such as Estonia, automatically joining the euro shortly afterwards as part of the *acquis*. In those circumstances, the exceptionalism of Britain would be even more pronounced, dramatically so, were it to remain outside the single currency. The facts, as Monnet might have remarked, would at that stage be overwhelming and would have to be addressed eventually by Britain entering the euro, late as usual but nonetheless welcome for all that. The wisdom of allowing the inevitable to happen, and of acting as the midwife of history only when the baby was ready to be born, would appear to have been too tempting.

Nevertheless, since no strategy is without its risks, non-participation in the euro for a protracted period would cruelly expose Britain once again as the awkward man of Europe and run counter to Blair's ambition of Britain becoming a core member state. The exposure would be all the more visible as the eurozone constructed a governance system to manage the world's second largest currency. The differentiation between the ECOFIN Council and Euro 12 (the finance and economics ministers of the eurozone) in terms of their policy remit will doubtless become blurred over time; ultimately ECOFIN could fade away as a forum for real decision-making and be reduced to a rubber stamp endorsing what had been previoulsy agreed by Euro 12 . Were that to happen the prospect of a British Chancellor waiting alone in the ante-room of Euro 12 until called to join the same ministers now constituted as ECOFIN would be at odds with the strategy of being at the core, but an inevitable penalty for the late-joiner syndrome. Blair himself had a foretaste of things to come when presiding over the European Council which inaugurated the euro. He was described as an umpire, not a player.

Another risk associated with the strategy is the sterling/euro exchange rate. It is widely accepted in retrospect that the rate at which Britain entered the ERM was too high, and that the timing was all wrong. It is instructive to recall that, whereas sterling shadowed the deutschmark at around DM3.00 under Nigel Lawson, the exchange rate in early 2000 averaged DM3.25, a rate then regarded by many as uncompetitive for British manufacturing. In view of the Bank of England's mandate to deliver a low-inflation regime, the interest-rate weapon was no longer available for managing the exchange rate and, leaving aside economic arguments about its effectiveness for that purpose, it followed that the markets were left free to determine the exchange rate; or, to put it less contentiously, the Bank of England had no overt role in exchange-rate policy.

This created a tension between maintaining low inflation and massaging the exchange rate downwards to a level that would be compatible with long-term competitiveness inside a monetary union. Advocates of entry, say in 2002 when the notes and coins are put in circulation, argued that sterling should have been put on a path below the DM3.00 range by the beginning of 2000 since the Maastricht criterion of two years' exchange-rate stability prior to entry to Stage Three of EMU might be rigorously applied from the moment Britain decided it should join. That, at least, was the opinion of ECB President, Wim Duisenberg.[14] From this perspective, it had become too late to achieve membership in 2002 at a rate generally conceived as competitive. But, to complicate matters, sterling later began to depreciate and moved gradually towards a rate that could be regarded as competitive. This simply reinforced the belief that economics was not the best foundation for the debate.

DANGER AHEAD

Uncertainty over the behaviour of the sterling exchange rate could none the less emerge as the Achilles heel of the "prepare and decide" strategy. It is difficult to see how the interest/exchange rates dilemma can be consciously overcome in view of the policy paradigm imposed on the Bank of England. It could transpire that if sterling strengthened unduly then fear of being permanently locked in at an uncompetitive exchange rate would cause some proponents of membership to side on pragmatic grounds with those who oppose it on principle. For Blair, such a coalition would be a nightmare scenario, and would undo an otherwise carefully constructed strategy. On the other hand, remaining passive in the face of exchange-rate movements gives the impression that no long-term strategy has been developed for euro membership and that things are being made up on an *ad hoc* basis by the government. This would be the view of those who grew impatient at what they believed to be a lack of decisive political leadership. At the beginning of 2000, for example, the new Director General of the CBI said his organisation would no longer campaign for membership until the government gave unequivocal leadership on the issue.[15] Although the statement was subsequently retracted, it was regarded at the time as a significant setback for Blair and taken by some government critics as part of the cost of a buying-time strategy. Indeed, it led to charges that the government's policy was "decisively indecisive" and that its approach to an early entry in the next parliament was both irresponsible and dangerous.[16] For its part, the government stuck to what the Foreign Secretary called a very bold policy of leadership. By mid-2000 the volume of criticism had grown louder, yet few offered a credible way out of the morass.[17]

There were two other approaches to dealing with uncertainty. Perhaps, after all, the exchange rate was not so uncompetitive at the level prevailing in the first half of 2000 because reforms had made the British economy one of the most competitive in the world. On that basis, the entry-rate could be almost anything dictated by the markets without imposing undue strain on competitiveness. It cannot be said that this view commanded universal support in the wake of some high-profile plant closures and in mid-2000 the air was thick with argument that the strong pound was killing British industry. An alternative approach would be for the government to end the uncertainty by declaring an entry-rate before or during the referendum so that "the British people" would know what they were voting on. Aside from the political benefits of defusing fears about competitiveness, presuming the stated rate (or range) was pitched low enough, stating a rate beforehand would have the more fundamental benefit of introducing legal certainty into the people's decision, a consideration of some importance given that amendments to the unwritten constitution of the UK would be the substantive question for resolution.

But this approach would not be as simple as it might seem at first. Unlike the UK's ill-fated entry into the ERM neither the timing nor entry-rate would be matters for the UK alone to decide. Because of the Maastricht Treaty provisions on EMU, both would have to be decided jointly by the eurozone member states and the

UK.[18] While this procedure would necessarily introduce complications (almost too awful to contemplate), it is argued in Chapter Eleven that a joint EU/UK statement on the rate would be accepted by the markets as a *fait accompli* and that there would be no re-run of "Black Wednesday". Furthermore, it has been suggested that entry into the euro could be effected immediately after the referendum, thus obviating the necessity for the two-year waiting period to demonstrate stability in the £/euro exchange rate (as the Maastricht Treaty would require on a strict interpretation).

It goes without saying that there are many imponderables in such a scenario, too many for comfort. The electorate, the markets, the ECB and the members of the eurozone would each have a separate role to play. All these ducks would have to be put in a rather complicated row for the strategy to work, but with skilful management it might be pulled off. This approach would have the great merit of not forcing the Blair government or the Bank of England to do the impossible i.e. to manage the exchange rate downwards while simultaneously pursuing a low-inflation policy. And if this is the real explanation for what lay behind the "wait and see" strategy on the euro then concerns about getting the entry-rate right were redundant, since it can be made to be "right" by fiat.

This cursory sketching of the uncertainties surrounding the Chancellor's "convergence criteria" highlights the complexity of devising and orchestrating an optimum entry strategy for the UK. For all that, UK government strategists may be more sanguine about the future than suspected. For example, prior to the advent of the euro, Irish analysts were greatly preoccupied with the implications of a weak sterling and the resulting threat to Irish competitiveness. But this chapter has focused on the opposite – a phenomenally strong sterling. Concerns over a strong sterling may, perhaps, be misplaced and the exchange rate may weaken as a result of a shift in market sentiment or because of a dollar depreciation. A British government covering all options might be forgiven for regarding the early years of the euro as atypical and for presuming that there is a good possibility the markets will correct themselves in time, leaving sterling at its equilibrium level, somewhat below DM 3.00. Were that to happen competitiveness would simply take care of itself. The other criteria would be quickly disposed of and the issue put to the people.

THE END OF ECONOMICS

At one stage during the Blair government's tenure, the above arguments dominated the debate but they began to give way to the political as the government ran into difficulties with the electorate and the media. The authority of the government was weakened by a series of set-backs that are analysed in Section One of this volume and it lost control of the euro debate which could no longer be contained within a macro-economic strait-jacket. At first, differences between ministers on the advisability of letting the exchange rate ride so high became public, adding to the government's loss of authority. Then, the Conservative Party grew more vocal in its opposition to the euro, encouraged by a recovery in the polls, gains in the local elections (May 2000), the dramatic loss in New Labour's popular support after the petrol crisis in September 2000, and greater unity in the shadow cabinet.

These developments, in particular a more critical media, let the political genie out of the bottle and the economic case for or against the euro sank into second place. The argument became, in the words of the commentator quoted earlier, "more real".[19] In short, it had become political. The choice was being debated as one "about the existential future of the offshore island, between geography and history".

CONCLUSION

On this analysis, the Blair government's strategy of keeping the euro debate within the confines of economics had failed. The prepare-and-decide strategy had initially bought time for Britain with its EU partners and so provided space for the internal reform programme to proceed unimpeded by otherwise unavoidable controversy over Europe. But it could not be sustained for ever without drawing attention to the contradiction of Britain wanting to be at the core of the Union but refusing to do so. Neither could it prevent the real issue from becoming progressively more visible; the future of Britain in Europe. Consequently, euro membership will not be decided earlier than 2002 and winning public support will be fraught with difficulties: the exchange rate, competitiveness, synchronisation of business cycles, the inherent opposition of the media and, above all, Britain's loveless affair with Europe.

For the duration of Blair's first term of office the most visible consequence of Britain's problems with Europe will be the continuation of the late-joiner syndrome in respect of EMU. The strategy for ending it is based on the proposition that there will be a second term in which another Blair government can turn public opinion and secure support for membership. This is a high-risk stance since it assumes that a second term can be won and also that public opinion on the issue can then be reversed. Neither can be guaranteed. Were either assumption to fail, Britain would be kept outside EMU for a decade or more. A referendum defeat would be rightly seen in the rest of the Union as a decisive rejection of EMU and Britain would revert from a "pre-in" to an "out". The late-joiner syndrome would give way to the outsider scenario that is discussed in Chapter Thirteen.

A change of government would put euro membership on hold for the lifetime of the next parliament and would have somewhat the same effect as a referendum defeat – Britain "out" of EMU and outside the EU core. The role of an outsider would be all the more marked in a Union undertaking institutional reforms in response to enlargement and, possibly, engaging in the use of flexibility so that an *avant-garde* could lay the foundations for deeper integration. In such circumstances, the postponed question discussed at the opening of this chapter would have been answered in the negative. By its own choice, Britain would be outside the European core and largely irrelevant in shaping the Union's future.

These considerations demonstrate how critical it is for the Blair government to win on two fronts to realise the ambition of Britain remaining at the European core. Like the recipe for Mrs Beaton's hare soup, which first requires that the hare be caught, New Labour has to win a second term, and that will be largely determined on the success of domestic policies. Then it has to win the referendum on the euro, and that will be determined predominately by its success in changing British attitudes on Europe. As the next chapter argues, its greatest challenge was to change, not British, but English, attitudes. It is the English who have to answer the postponed question.

---

1   Major (1998), pp 84, 342, 584.
2   Young (2000b).
3   *The Economist*, 21 July 2000.

4   Fallessen (1993).
5   Schonfield (1972).
6   Brown (1997).
7   OECD (2000).
8   HM Treasury (1997). The five economic tests are: (i) Are business cycles and economic structures compatible so that we and others could live comfortably with euro interest rates on a permanent basis? (ii) If problems emerge is there sufficient flexibility to deal with them? (iii) Would joining EMU create better conditions for firms making long-term decisions to invest in Britain? (iv) What impact would entry into EMU have on the competitive position of Britain's financial services industry, particularly the City's wholesale markets? (v) Will joining EMU promote higher growth, stability, and a lasting increase in jobs?
9   *Financial Times*, 19 June 2000.
10   Gamble and Kelly (2000), p. 19.
11   Gamble and Kelly (2000), p. 20
12   Blair (1999).
13   *Financial Times*, 6 June 2000.
14   Duisenberg (1999).
15   Brown, Crooks and Martin (2000).
16   Wolf (2000).
17   *Financial Times*, 6 June 2000; 19 June 2000.
18   Barret (1995).
19   Young (2000b).

CHAPTER EIGHT

England's Europe

Brendan Halligan

INTRODUCTION

The tumult over Britain's membership of the euro is a reminder of an underlying social and political phenomenon with which the Blair government had to contend on taking office: Britain is uncomfortable in its European skin. The main argument of this chapter is that Blair is actively attempting to make the British public psychologically more comfortable with the concept of Europe. For the duration, no decisions will be made by his government which would disturb this process of adjustment – hence putting the euro on an elastically long finger, protecting the London euro-bond market and opposing tax harmonisation. All these are negative tactics, of course, and do not add up to a positive strategy on Europe. But, the argument would go on, a positive strategy has been put in place to move Britain closer to Europe and, simultaneously, to move Europe closer to Britain. While reshaping Britain, Blair is also shaping a new Europe, one consistent with the British psyche and sense of identity. But it is not Britain which is the focus of Blair's European strategy, it is England.

ENGLAND AND EUROPE

The previous study argued that Britain was suffering from a crisis of state and political identity. Among its many ramifications was the unravelling of British identity into its component parts, from which it had been originally constructed to create what Linda Colley has called "an artificial identity".[1] Fundamental to the endurance of that identity had been the equation of Englishness with Britishness. Indeed, being British and English had become synonymous; the synonym did not apply either to the Scots or Welsh, who both managed in varying degrees to create a multiple identity based on their own region and the island as a whole. In contrast, the English had a uni-polar identity which subsumed the entire island into their region. One survey indicated that three-quarters of the English saw themselves as equally or more British than English.[2] But forces, which were analysed in Chapter Four, have conspired to loosen the Scottish and Welsh ties to Britain. In order to save the Union it became imperative to devolve power to Edinburgh and Cardiff, thus draining sovereignty away from the centre as one part of the solution to Britain's dual sovereignty problem. Consequently, Englishness has been progressively beached as the tide of Britishness recedes, and debate as to what it means to be English, as distinct from British, has slowly but persistently taken on a new significance.

If nations are imagined communities then the debate is a good example of how one community, the British, is being deconstructed and another, the English, assembled in its stead. The significance of this process is that it enables the use of English cultural phenomena in the interpretation of British policy in European and international affairs. This is of particular relevance in examining the British preference for intergovernmentalism in Europe rather than the forms of supra-nationalism on which the Community method is founded. It is one thing to comment that the British have consistently opted for intergovernmentalism, thus placing themselves at odds with much of the thrust of the integration process, quite another to ask why; in other words, the analytical challenge is to try to get to the root of the awkward partnership which Blair set out to end. In this regard, the debate on the nature of Englishness can be a valuable tool; the novelty of the current bout of soul-searching lies in its intensity and pervasiveness – proof that it reflects a deep-rooted social reality justifying the use of the term "crisis" to describe it.

The importance of the debate springs from its conscious differentiation between English and British. It exposes with greater clarity those characteristics by which the English define themselves or, (to accommodate those not yet convinced that the process has reached such a point) by which they might ultimately define themselves. This process of inner reflection has been said to signify "the death of Britain".[3] If Britain is dead, or dying, then its component parts step out of its shade to remind us they were always there and who they really are.

So far as it has gone the debate has yielded (or, perhaps, simply reconfirmed) a number of clues which go some way towards explaining the root causes of the lack of enthusiasm for "Europe", which are generally attributed to Britain as a whole. Gaitskell in his party's rejection of the EEC referred to "a thousand years of history", a phrase which made sense to his Labour Party audience. It played to feelings of pride in a unique historical experience in a way that was immediately understood.[4] Despite the passage of years, and the intervening changes wryly noted by some commentators,[5] the many layers of meaning encapsulated in Gaitskell's phrase still ring true in England.[6] They connote a sense of superiority, preclude an emotional empathy with other Europeans and indicate there was no need to become embroiled in a partnership with other European states. Evidence to the contrary has consequently lacked emotional appeal and, even when overwhelming, was disputed; where accepted, it was admitted only with reluctance. There has been little enthusiasm for taking part in Europe, it being seen as a penance rather than a blessing. The heart and the head were, and are, at loggerheads.

There is no belief in Europe because there is nothing to believe in. Instead of being an ideal, as for other Europeans, it is merely a mechanism; worse still, it is a source of trouble inspired by foreigners who need careful watching (so that their plots are exposed and their radicalism curbed). Centuries of keeping other europeans at bay and a belief in the superiority of British institutions have left their mark. It is a "them and us"[7] attitude, based on the belief that the British path of political development ws radically different from, and superior to, that of its Continental neighbours.[8]

Blair, himself, provided one of the best commentaries on this attitude towards Europe (when speaking in Warsaw in October 2000), although he understandably referred to Britain rather than England. "A proud and independent island race" had found the reasons for Europe "always less than absolutely compelling". The result had been a half-century of gross miscalculation characterised by hesitation, alienation and incomprehension, but with occasional bursts of enlightened brilliance which only served to underline the frustration of Britain's partners with what was the norm. The three adjectives used to describe the British (taken in the chapter as a synonym for the English) conform with other analysis: pride, independence and separateness. To them Blair added two other distinguishing characteristics shaping the psyche: victors in the Second World War and the main European ally of the United States. All in all, this self-image concocted from Britain's past is heady stuff and explains the late-joiner syndrome which Blair defined as a choice between catching up or staying out.

The historical exceptionalism of England has also been recognised in academic analysis[9] as the cause of its problems with Europe, sometimes with the focus being placed on the traditional animosity with France, this being used to explain why Delors became a hate figure in some sections of public opinion and the media (especially the *Sun* newspaper). This emphasis on ancient and modern rivalries with other European states is too pervasive for it to be dismissed as amateur psychology. As one study put it, prejudice as well as rational calculation of national self-interest, play a part in shaping attitudes and policies.[10]

Other member states suffer from this psychosis as well: Denmark and Sweden both have postponed questions about their membership, while Greece only finally decided on its European vocation under the Simitis government. Some others were lucky enough to escape deep soul searching since either history or geography left them no choice other than Europe. And others again who have entered wholeheartedly into the process of sharing sovereignty still have a postponed question about future integration, Ireland and Finland being the most obvious examples in respect of security and defence. The English exceptionalism may, therefore, be a matter of degree. Their problem is that Britain is too large for it to go unnoticed by the rest of the Union. Also, some features of that same exceptionalism (its uninterrupted history of parliamentary democracy to take one example) persuaded many that Britain was essential as a core state if Europe were to reflect the best of its diverse traditions. So Britain could hardly avoid standing out as an odd man in a crowd of enthusiastic Europeans. The difficulty was in understanding why the British were reluctant Europeans. Separating out the English from the British may perhaps help towards a general understanding of the reasons underlying the awkward partnership and induce a greater degree of patience as the Blair government tries to disentangle itself from the meshes of history – England's history that is.

LOSING AN EMPIRE, FINDING A ROLE

If a (glorious) imperial past has led the English to an ingrained belief that sovereignty need not be shared this could explain why finding a new role in place of a lost empire is so slow and painful. It could also explain the psychological barriers to engagement in partnership with other peoples on the basis of formal equality. Any co-operative venture, such as the European Union, demands a certain submergence of self and that sacrifice can be more easily made by those peoples who have good reason to make it. National sovereignty, it might be said, is only given up or shared when there is a manifest necessity to do so. Perhaps this explains why it was easier for the vanquished than for the victors to pool sovereignty after the second World War in the new Europe. It was relatively easy, too, for small nations with few illusions about the real substance of their sovereignty.

What comes through from the English debate is that the necessity for Europe is weakly felt. Classically expressed, the goal of uniting the peoples of Europe finds little resonance in the English mind. Some commentators have lamented the absence of inspiration in the long tortured debate about Europe; but that is surely understandable in terms of the temperament the English believe themselves to possess and is at variance with their own sense of destiny.

The obverse of all that is admirable in Englishness is the innate sense of superiority and separateness, to which some commentators admit. Held unquestioningly, it can lead to an antipathy to sharing sovereignty with other states on grounds of equality, particularly if it involves encroaching on the supremacy of parliament. Taken to an extreme, the concept of sharing sovereignty (except with the US) becomes anathema, a point that Monnet well realised in debating the creation of the Coal and Steel Community with the Labour government of the day.[11]

The argument here is that the British problem with Europe is an English one. It is neither Scottish nor Welsh. But England bulks so large in Britain, and the two are so often taken as synonymous, that confusion between them is inevitable. Yet it is England's self-image which explains the awkward-partner and the late-joiner syndromes with as much precision as reflections on social phenomena can allow. It explains, above all, the British preference for intergovernmentalism in Europe and the aversion to integration or shared sovereignty. If this be so, then in order for

Britain to become a core country in the Union, Blair must alter English self-beliefs, and align them to a Europe which itself is adapted to English sensitivities. In political terms, this means that Europe must be as much intergovernmental as it is integrated. Ideally, the two should be in equilibrium. Meanwhile, Europe should refrain from appearing or aspiring to become a superstate and Britain should dribble out sovereignty only as necessity demands. Just as on the euro, time has to be bought so both sets of change can be seen to be taking place.

BLAIR'S STRATEGY

Achieving this complex objective of creating an "England's Europe" (and, for the other member states, a Europe's England) would require Blair to take on a leadership role in the Union, for himself and for Britain. At a minimum, it would demand action on three fronts: becoming the *primus inter pares* or at least an equal player in the European Council; assuming the mantle of Europe's leading social democrat and statesman; and binding other member states to Britain in a web of bi-lateral relationships. All three achievements could then be fused into the common purpose of leveraging influence in the European Council (and within any IGC it might summon) in order to reshape the Union into something the English could live with, and other Europeans find acceptable. The difficulty with this approach is time. The pressures for a hard-core Europe will grow stronger as enlargement looms nearer. Nevertheless, this three-pronged approach seems to be the best explanation of what is being attempted.

At state level, the role of *primus inter pares* in the European Council has been filled jointly by Germany and France, a relationship solidified over time by the Franco-German alliance in a structured framework.[12] At the level of political personalities, German and French leaders invariably occupy the role of Europe's de facto leadership. The joint letter of the German Chancellor and the French President to other participants prior to each European Council, for example, became an accepted feature of Europe's political life and gave guidance and direction to the meetings, which were generally followed by the other heads of state and government without too much dissent.

The Kohl-Mitterrand axis was the last great example of this joint leadership, fuelled in large measure by the personal chemistry between them. But the arrival of Blair in the European Council virtually coincided with the defeat of Kohl and the death of Mitterrand. Initially, Kohl's departure left a vacuum in German and European politics which his successor, Gerhard Schroeder, seemed incapable of filling. Simultaneously, France entered another period of cohabitation following the Gaullist general election defeat. Despite the fact that Schroeder and the French Prime Minister, Lionel Jospin, both came from the PES camp, the Franco-German alliance entered one of its rockiest phases just as Blair entered the European Council. The circumstances could hardly have been more propitious for a new British leader to try and reconfigure Europe's collective leadership.

Up to the end of 1999, Blair's political stardom allowed him to play a prominent role in the European Council. Indeed, circumstances conspired to add to his opportunities. At the end of 1999, Schroeder lay within a hair's breadth of a collapse of authority in Germany and Europe, while the Chirac-Jospin partnership proved lack-lustre. At that point, the dominance of the Franco-German leadership was being matched for the first time by that from another member state and it was reasonable to forecast that a second term of office would make Britain part of Europe's leadership and elevate Blair as its leading politician.

Events, as one of his predecessors might have remarked, intervened. Kohl's sudden fall from grace at the end of 1999 rescued Schroeder. His stature was transformed, helped additionally by a general recognition that the German economy was beginning to recover. In France, cohabitation began to work more smoothly and France recovered its élan. In the meanwhile, the working relationships within the Franco-German alliance were restored to something akin to their former warmth with a noticeably improved rapport between Schroeder and Jospin. Despite coming from a small member state, the Dutch Prime Minister, Wim Kok, also began to play a respected and influential role in the Council. Overnight, as it were, Blair's candidacy for Europe's number-one leader became less promising than it had been. By the third anniversary of coming to power, his image had been dented by a series of domestic setbacks, which fed back negatively into the European arena.

These events confirm that politics is a game of snakes and ladders and that predictions are notoriously at the mercy of events. Nevertheless, it can be argued that by mid-2000 Blair had, at least, established Britain as part of the leading triumvirate in Europe and put himself at its head along with Schroeder, Jospin and Chirac. The significance of such an achievement requires qualification. The Franco-German leadership of the Union rests on more than their national economic or political weight. Neither is it dependent on the personalities who happen to be in power. The joint leadership is based on a long established alliance which has become highly structured over time, prevents another member state from assuming *the* leadership role in Europe and limits any such ambitions. At best, another large member state could be admitted to a triumvirate, but no more. That said, the challenge of breaking into Franco-German alliance puts a premium on Britain using every available element of influence within the European Council so as to become an integral part of Europe's collective leadership.

THE THIRD WAY

That consideration introduces the question of vision, a trait not normally associated with the English style and leads back to the PES. Here, the attractions of the Third Way were obvious. Its intellectual force lay in its marriage of the market economy and the welfare state and in its political appeal in the electoral success of New Labour. The Third Way contrasted with the confused ideology of the SPD and the old orthodoxies of the Parti Socialiste to such an extent that Schroeder was initially forced to ape Blair, and Jospin thrown back in defence of traditional certainties (as at the PES party leaders' conference in Malmo in 1997). New Labour's programme seemed more in tune with European values than those of other social democrats, especially in its acceptance of market disciplines and its abandonment of dogma. It had an honesty of purpose that bespoke courage and a new vocabulary allowing social democrats to address issues as electorates saw them, rather than twisting reality to formulae devoid of meaning.

The importance of the PES in this ideological debate is that the member parties are "natural" parties of government; for example social democrats were in office in the majority of member states in 2000, and in the remainder they could credibly aspire to power. This feature makes the PES a natural testing ground for leaders and for ideas, a sort of antechamber to the councils of the Union. To a lesser extent, the same is true of the European People's Party (PPE), consisting of the Christian Democratic parties; but the greater political cohesion and wider geographical spread of the PES means that it provides unequalled opportunities to shape policy, exert political influence and create personal networks across the Union – and is likely to do so even more after enlargement.

Being neither German nor French, and unable to use an established network on which to build a European career, Blair can by way of compensation, employ a winning ideological formula. His main competitor is the statism of French socialism, which can be dismissed as a peculiarity of the French, rather than a model for other socialists. The Scandinavian model, which might have provided competition, is largely discredited in a world devoted to deregulation and supply-side economics. Schroeder has not yet framed a coherent policy framework, veering between the new way (*die neue mitte*) and the old ways of the SPD. In the ideological debate within Europe's social democratic camp, the agenda was largely set by New Labour and Blair had succeeded in making the British variant of "socialism" a serious contender for the vision of society Europeans should be offered by social democrats. Since this vision is so personally identified with Blair he is himself an integral part of the struggle for leadership. Should it be won by New Labour, Blair would be recognised as Europe's leading social democratic theorist. Were he to prove its most successful practitioner it could not but fail to rub off in the European Council and the second element of the strategy would be in place.

HUBS, SPOKES AND BICYCLE WHEELS

The third element of the strategy is the shaping of Europe. It has to be Europe which corresponds with English nationalism and consequently implies limitations on integrationist orthodoxies, especially federalism. While the success of this element is greatly dependent on Blair himself in terms of the personal authority he can command in the European Council, it is insufficient in itself; structures are required to give effect to vision, as Blair's management of the Labour Party testifies. There his list of achievements is impressive. He reformed the party organisation, rewrote its constitution, developed new policies, tamed a fractious membership, planned the general election campaign and ran it under his supervision. Blair's personal stamp was impressed on

New Labour to such an extent that he personifies the party, as did Mrs. Thatcher the Conservatives. As Prime Minister, this singular managerial style has been maintained. Were it to be applied to European politics then a similar systemisation of approach could be expected. The first years of office confirm that it has.

The metaphor of the bicycle wheel is apt as an explanation of Blair's European strategy, since integration has often been described in terms of the bicycle. In this case, Britain is the hub, bilateral projects with other member states the spokes, and a new vision of Europe the rim. As said previously, the Blair government had to base its statecraft strategy on the reality that Britain lacked an established network within the European Union, a consequence of the awkward partnership; neither could it draw on a pre-existing alliance, like France or Germany, A structure had to be created *de novo* but its ultimate effectiveness would depend on the strength of bilateral projects and the credibility of the vision on offer.

The pattern of Blair's diplomacy within the Union implies the conscious development of projects tailor-made to the joint interests of Britain and other member states, which in some cases are government to government and in others party to party. An early but high-profile example was the Anglo-French initiative on European defence expressed in the Saint Malo declaration. With Germany, it began with a joint-party project on developing the policy content of the Third Way. Surprisingly, perhaps, there has been a commonality of view with the Spanish conservative government on labour-market policy.[13] Ireland provided a particular but ready-made project on Northern Ireland. With the Portuguese Presidency it was the information society. By that point, the strategy had become the subject of comment in the media and was readily admitted in diplomatic circles. One analysis claimed that it was to help Britain set agendas and win arguments by cultivating tactical alliances with the "minnow states" of a Europe no longer in the grip of a dominant Franco-German axis.[14] The list of minnows included Portugal, Belgium, the Netherlands, Ireland, Sweden and Denmark, suggesting a greater degree of diplomatic activism than might have been suspected. The range of issues was no less impressive and encompassed the information society, active welfare policies, the Third Way and the reform of the EU. When added to those already constructed with the larger fish in the EU pool, they covered most of the points on the Union's agenda.

This broad-brush resumé confirms that the Blair government has been assiduously pursuing a grand strategy since it took office: choose issues with the potential to determine the Union's future agenda and identify the member state best suited for a particular project. The purpose of each bilateral project is to cement personal and governmental relations across other member states and, at the same time, influence what the Union does in practice. This would reflect the belief that the Union is as much defined by what it does as by the Treaties and that legal forms will follow substantive policies.

While it is true that British diplomacy has in the past engaged in analogous activities, the present strategy is far more ambitious in scale than anything previously attempted, and contrasts sharply with Rifkind's ad-hoc approach in the dying days of the Major government. The contrast was particularly evident, for example, at the Lisbon Council in March 2000 which was specifically focused on creating "the most competitive and dynamic knowledge-based economy in the world". The Blair government had placed great store on this project, believing that it would confirm the argument that Europe was moving closer to Britain in terms of economic objectives and social goals and, more generally, that the Third Way would triumph as the basis for the European model in the information age. In the event, that expectation was fulfilled. Beforehand, Britain worked assiduously in developing a series of joint papers with other member states, at which it was by far the most active member state, to the point where it attracted attention. The exercise suggests that the "spokes strategy" has a second dimension. It can also be successfully deployed in a specific policy area since there was general agreement that Britain had greatly influenced the Lisbon Council's conclusions and wrong footed those who opposed the Third Way, such as France.

This success need not be exaggerated, since most of what was agreed at Lisbon made good sense and might always have been adopted. But it was a straw in the wind, a reminder that a new-style diplomacy was at work, and that it was successful in putting its own gloss on a new mission for Europe. The ultimate test of success will, however, be determined in the upper reaches of political debate on the Union to be created in the light of enlargement. It also suggested a far better working relationship between the Prime Minister, the Chancellor and the Foreign Secretary than the media believed. The Chancellor had to carry the can on the euro while the Foreign Secretary notched up an impressive list of European achievements, including the overall management of the British Presidency in the first part of 1998.[15] Despite the potential for misrepresentation of their respective roles (seen by some as the reverse of their attitudes in opposition) the Chancellor and Foreign Secretary combined with the Prime Minister to provide a consistent and coherent sense of direction to Britain's new policy of positively shaping the EU agenda. Success was built on teamwork, with clear lines of responsibility for each of the triumvirate.

For Blair's overall strategy to succeed it must be one with which the English can live and which can simultaneously satisfy other Europeans. To meet what could, on the basis of previous experience, be regarded as mutually exclusive objectives, the new Europe must allow Britain to remain a core member state, despite its non-participation in the euro. At the same time it must eschew the path of the federalism classically associated with the founding fathers. In simplistic terms, the Union ahead should be both integrationist and intergovernmental, and the two should be in balance. Put another way, it demands a second core to the European Union which is essentially intergovernmental and to which Britain can adhere because it appeals to the national character; perforce it must make sense to the other member states as a logical extension of the European ambition and be as significant as the creation of the EMU.

THE SECOND CORE

This marriage of objectives could be achieved by making security a core EU competence. Since the Maastricht Treaty, the Union has been engaged in security or soft defence – the sort of activities inscribed in the Petersberg Tasks but which can be extended, as in the Kosovo intervention, to include peace enforcement. Kosovo raised concerns over stability in Europe's own "near abroad" and the need for structured responses was set out in the December 1999 Helsinki Council Conclusions, notably the ambition to create a rapid reaction force. In that context, European security provided a ready-made opportunity to shift the focus of attention from the First to the Second Pillar.

Blair systematically focused the security debate on Europe's capability to respond rapidly to crises requiring military intervention; in other words, on practical problems to be solved should the Union be intent on securing its external borders. Capability-building brought the rationalisation of the European arms industry into sharper focus and gave it the practical edge it might otherwise have lacked. Parallel with this debate on external security, defence doctrines are being, or have already been, re-evaluated in most member states, especially in those states belonging to NATO, to take account of post-Cold War conditions; all this creates a state of flux in which initiatives on security policy have a higher than normal chance of success. It is clear from Kosovo that the pre-conditions exist for formulating a new security doctrine for the Union in which it accepts responsibility for maintaining stability in its border regions and for acting on humanitarian grounds to restore peace in adjacent areas affected by ethnic conflict.

The Helsinki Council decisions to establish the rapid reaction force and create security structures are evidence of the speed with which a new European security order is being constructed. It is not yet clear how the conditions for external involvement will be defined in military or political terms, how the geographic reach of the doctrine is to be identified or how mandates are to be reinterpreted. A European security doctrine has yet to be formulated, and the complex series of interrelationships between the EU, WEU and NATO also have to be re-ordered to take account of US sensitivities, the needs of EU applicant states and non-EU members of NATO and the particular concerns of Russia. Chapter Ten identifies the Union's relationship with the US as most problematic in so far as NATO is essentially a US-led alliance which, until now, has resided amicably alongside the EU because of the clear-cut division of responsibilities between the two; the one a civil and the other a military power. As the Union encroaches across a hitherto rigid divide, ironically at US prompting, concerns have been expressed in the US that its defence hegemony is under threat. A contrary view has also emerged, of course, that the Europeans should be left to defend themselves, and to pay for the privilege.

In countering perceived threats to the Atlantic alliance, Blair is better positioned than any EU leader to work out a new *modus vivendi* between Europe and the United States. The special relationship between Britain and the US, sometimes the object of doubt, has been nurtured by Blair for a variety of reasons (not least on Northern Ireland) and in mid-2000 was possibly at its warmest since Kennedy and Macmillan. This was due in no small part to the personal empathy between Blair and Clinton but was also attributed to Britain's role in providing political leadership and military resources in Kosovo. The appointment of George Robertson as NATO General Secretary symbolised the warmth of the Anglo-American relationship and positioned Britain at the core of NATO, while Chris Patten's appointment at the hub of the Commission's foreign policy added to Britain's value as an European interlocutor.

Future European security policy will necessarily be dependent on American goodwill if it is to have effect; it will lead to a new form of partnership between the EU and US distinct from, but nonetheless interdependent with, the American role in Europe via NATO. The potential for mismanaging these parallel partnerships is obvious and the need for structured dialogue is accepted lest the Atlantic alliance be undermined. In this new context, the necessity for an acceptable interlocutor is imperative and Blair would be the natural choice as Europe's special partner with the US and as the leader of its evolving security policy. Were this to transpire then the past weakness of Britain being perceived by other Europeans as the American Trojan Horse would be transformed into a strength. Britain would become indispensable for reconciling European defence under American protection with European security under the EU; the synergy between the two would centrally depend on Britain's renowned diplomatic skills.

Putting security at the core of the Union has numerous attractions as a strategy for Blair. Firstly, European security does not have to be invented as a major EU policy issue since it is already evolving into a core competence. Secondly, it would rank in importance with the European Community as a pillar of the Union. Thirdly, it allows Britain to play to its strengths in diplomacy and military affairs. Fourthly, it creates a new arena for European cooperation, in which Britain is perceived as a leader. Lastly, it must perforce be intergovernmental, thereby falling outside the Community's institutional architecture and so avoiding the odium of deepening integration. Taken in the round, this second core would satisfy all the requirements of moving Europe close to England.

Corroboration for this viewpoint is evident in academic circles, for example. The historian and commentator, Timothy Garton Ash, believed that Europe had set itself the wrong priority in the early 1990s by opting for EMU rather than enlargement and, more particularly, the security of the Balkans. The EU was said to have fiddled in Maastricht while Sarajevo began to burn.[16] Even if EMU were to be right in principle and feasible in practice it was nonetheless the wrong way to go. In any event, it might actually fail (a recurring British theme) and that made it important to have some other big undertaking where the EU could succeed: enlargement, foreign and security policy – and a common defence force.[17] This analysis encapsulated the rationale for the second core and indicated that it strongly resonated with those deep psychological prejudices which Blair had to satisfy were he to succeed in his end goal of an England's Europe.

CONCLUSION

A Union with two cores of equal weight would add up to a vision of Europe which would satisfy many basic requirements of Britain's European policy. It would correspond to the English self-image of Britain being a world player singularly endowed with diplomatic skills and military prowess. It would create an alternative but intergovernmentalist core for the Union which would be credible to other Europeans since it would meet a real and common need. By creating the second core in the form of, say, a European Security Community, Blair would reshape the European Union and turn it decisively away from the more traditional goal of a unitary governance system, sometimes described as a federation. Here then, the bicycle wheel would be complete. With Britain at the hub of a new security order, and with various member states allied to it through the spokes of mutually beneficial projects (or interests), the over-arching rim could be constructed and eventually welded in position. To follow the bicycle analogy still further, the European Union would then be the bike, with one wheel built around the European Community and the other around a European Security Community.

To achieve this goal of a dual-core Union, time is no less necessary than with the euro. The bilateral projects will take time to mature. A new US administration will have to be courted and won. The other member states will need to absorb the implications of the Petersberg Tasks and the lessons of Kosovo. In short, the classical progress of European integration based on the iterative refinement of policies and processes will have to unfold at its own pace. This does no more than underline the commonplace observation that within any grand strategy there is always a tension between time and the desired goals.

If the goal were attainable then Blair could argue that Britain was truly at the core of Europe, that this Europe had put a boundary around integration and had struck out in a new direction. The journey to the unknown destination could credibly be presented as one towards a Union of nation states rather than a Union which subsumed them into a federation. The English instinct for retaining the forms of sovereignty would be satisfied. In time, fears about any further loss could be quietened and membership of the euro would follow as a matter of course and good common sense. This would be the most benign of scenarios. But future uncertainties require the consideration of alternatives, including the possibility that English nationalism can not be so easily tamed. The awkward partner could still be lurking around the corner.

1   Colley (1994).
2   Davies, Peter (1999).
3   Marr (2000).
4   Young (1999).
5   Paxman (1999).
6   John Lloyd, *Financial Times*, 19 December 1996.
7   *ibid.*
8   Bogdanor (1998).
9   Gowland and Turner (2000), pp 141-151.
10   Gowland and Turner, p. 142.
11   Duchêne (1994).
12   IEA (1996).
13   Blair and Aznar (2000).
14   Black (2000).
15   Cook (1997).
16   Garton Ash (1999).
17   *ibid.*

CHAPTER NINE

The Return of the Prodigals

Brendan Halligan

INTRODUCTION

In February 2000, speaking in Gent[1], not too far from Bruges, Blair could describe the change in Britain's relations with Europe since he had come to power as "fundamental". He believed the awkward partnership was no more and had been replaced by a new strategic orientation. Britain was playing its full part in Europe as a positive committed partner. In fact, its destiny was to be a leading partner in Europe. Why this change of heart? What were the reasons for moving from confrontation to cooperation? What had led Blair to state that, unlike its predecessors, his government was "unwaveringly pro-European"?[2] The answer given was that constructive membership of the European Union is in Britain's fundamental national interest. Since so many in Britain still hold a diametrically opposite view, the change of heart has all to do with how the national interest is perceived.

For New Labour, the conventional justifications for "ever closer union" came to be accepted in more or less the same manner as in other member states: peace, democracy, economic success, market access and interdependency. Enlargement added its own special flavour in terms of a more stable, peaceful and prosperous Europe which would entrench stability, free markets and democracy right across "our continent", as Blair described it. It would also bring Britain "huge" new economic opportunities through easier access to important new markets and adding also to the flow of foreign inward investment (over £150bn) because Britain's membership of the Union provided direct access to the world's largest market.

NEW BRITON, NEW EUROPEAN

These sorts of arguments are common currency in other member states and in themselves do not explain the change of heart, or why Blair has gone so far as to describe his government as unwaveringly pro-European. The explanation offered is all the more credible because it is so self-evident: Blair sees Britain as European. No longer is Britain taken as a world power, either as a partner with the United States in a global alliance or as the head of an international Commonwealth of states bound together by distinctive ties and shared interests. Instead, Britain is primarily regarded as an integral part of the European continent to which its interests are indissolubly linked. In this resolution of the identity crisis, British identity is defined as also being European, and Britain's national interests flow naturally from that re-definition.

Two forces have driven New Labour towards this conclusion, or are advanced as sufficient cause for the identification of Britain as a European state. The first is globalisation, with which Blair is particularly exercised. He believes globalisation has already made the old economic order redundant. The best means of taking advantage of the global economy, and occasionally seeking refuge from its negative implications, is to position Britain at the heart of a strong regional economy. Globalisation demands modernisation and an emphasis on education, re-skilling and entrepreneurship. These have become familiar themes with which he addresses the need for Britain to modernise in order to meet the global challenge, and his preoccupation with globalisation and modernisation is clear.[3]

The second is enlargement. Blair has gone beyond the inevitability of the process to work out scenarios for the new Europe. It would be unthinkable in his view for Britain not to be proactively at the heart of a Union encompassing 550 million people and binding some 30 interdependent states. Enlargement presents economic opportunities, but these can only be fully exploited if Britain is unequivocally a full member of the EU. Enlargement also substantiates the need to construct a new European security order and it is in Britain's self-interest to shape it. Moreover, it provides an unrivalled opportunity for Britain to play a leading European role in a vital common task. Lastly, enlargement necessitates institutional reform, which Blair described as absolutely momentous;[4] here again positive British engagement in determining the reforms can only be in its national interest.

This new mission for Britain in Europe has been pushed at the Labour Party membership and British people(s) with a fervour which, if it does not yet match the evangelism of Mrs Thatcher, seems set to match it eventually. Yet, a note of caution is necessary. New Labour's conversion to an unwavering pro-European stance has been put in its broad socio-political context and analysed in Chapter Two. The English element of British public opinion remains determinedly suspicious of things European, such as the euro, and a significant minority is hostile to the very idea of membership. As Chapters Three and Eight indicated, the print media play a crucial role in shaping opinion on Europe either, as Blair described it, by being essentially hostile to the European Union or else supine in the face of that hostility.[5] Indeed, the general tenor of commentary from those elements of the media which might have been expected to be broadly favourable to Europe has been supine at best. It has echoed the hostility of the Murdoch/Black press. Blair's reaction has been to become openly critical of the media, as he did after the Helsinki Council and during the Gent speech.

THE ROLE OF THE PRINT MEDIA

Whether the print media's hostility on Europe can be countered is open to question. It seems improbable that the Murdoch/Black chains will adopt the objective approach for which Blair pleads, and unlikely that other print media will counterbalance their anti-Europe bias. Negative reporting of Europe is crucial in terms of its cumulative impact on public opinion regarding euro membership. Chapter Seven argued that the euro had been sidelined to give priority to domestic reform, even at the cost of putting a question-mark against Blair's representation of Britain as a positive partner in Europe. But membership, having been accepted in principle, would ultimately be sought when the domestic reforms had been bedded down. Public opinion would then be galvanised in support by a combination of Blair's charismatic leadership and the weight of economic realities. That strategy has been put in doubt by the print media. Also, by caution and delay on Blair's part.

The media impact, too, on Blair's ambition to create what has been described in the previous chapter as England's Europe, or what Hugo Young called Blair's "opportunity to reposition the national mind".[6] Objectively, the emergence of a second EU core centered around security and defence should lead to a Europe compatible with English public opinion. Politically, it may have little chance. The media will not easily or readily mediate a complex political process. Neither will they report fully on Blair's determination to minimise further integration in the Community pillar and maximise intergovernmentalism in Pillar Two. The sense of what is happening in Europe at the behest of Britain will hardly be conveyed to the British public in a consistent, comprehensible and comprehensive manner. On the contrary, the media may continue to give vent to the xenophobic fury[7] they normally unleash at times of unavoidable disputes and the neurotic suspicion the people had long been taught to apply to everything coming out of Brussels[8] may well be fed with even greater assiduity. How Blair overcomes that threat would be one of the more fascinating features of a second term of office, were it to be secured.

Yet, the dilemma will have to be resolved if the awkward partnership is not to re-appear. Britain's problem with Europe is essentially an English one. Whether the print media are the cause or the effect of English antipathy towards Europe is immaterial. Until such time as the process of circular causation is broken there is little chance of public opinion being conditioned as Blair would wish, and the goal of an England's Europe may consequently prove too elusive.

Here, there is a hint of the tragic. John Major's government, particularly through Douglas Hurd when Foreign Secretary, had argued that Europe was moving in the direction of Britain, meaning that integration had run its course and that intergovernmentalism, admittedly in an enhanced form, would become the new predominant form of inter-state collaboration in Europe. Although few listened to what was regarded as a self-serving delusion, it had the seeds of a truth.

The future grand projects for the EU, internal and external security, are inherently biased in the intergovernmental direction; the longer they mature the more they will define the European Union as a hybrid of shared sovereignty and collective action, rather than the federation which a Union could be taken to imply. Blair could argue convincingly that the force of history is behind the sort of Europe with which England could be comfortable. If only it were allowed to unfold then Europe and England might wake up some day and, to their common astonishment, recognise each other as soul-mates.

The process of awakening has already begun. The Foreign Policy Centre dismissed the concept of the EU as a state in the course of construction and repackaged it as a network in which the member states both co-operated and competed and in which power was shared and dispersed around many centres. "Network Europe" was presented as a decentralised system of governance where power was shared horizontally between member states, European institutions and non-state actors, rather than vertically within a state.[9] This analytical insight had the great merit of reflecting reality. On that basis it was being argued that the EU taking shape in the 21st century was "closer to what successive British governments have been seeking than we might ever have imagined".[10] The British approach, politically and economically, was the one which increasingly prevailed in the EU and inter-governmentalism had become its operating principle.[11] What lay ahead was a Europe in which the British could feel comfortable. These voices may be the precursor of what in time will become a chorus. If so, the tone of the debate about Europe will be significantly changed.

VISION OR DREAM?

Meanwhile, Blair is continuing his project of reshaping Europe so that at the opportune time there is something tangible and reassuring to demonstrate to English public opinion about the future of the EU, something that will put the spectre of a European superstate to rest. In Gent, Blair went so far as to spell out a vision, although self-consciously admitting it was not part of the British style, for a people too pragmatic to believe in visions (the masking of English as British was again evident). The vision was remarkable only for what it did not say, there being no reference to deeper integration or stronger institutions at the expense of national sovereignty. The White Paper on "Reform for Enlargement", published in the same month, reiterated the same modest, pragmatic vision of nation states working together in their own and their common interests. It specifically ruled out the extension of qualified majority voting to treaty changes and accession (as would all other member states) and insisted on retaining unanimity for voting on taxation, border controls, social security, defence and "own resources"; it confirmed the proposition that Blair's vision for Europe is more intergovernmentalist than had been intended by the architects of the Treaties, and feared by the bulk of English public opinion.

Blair's vision of Europe was further refined in his Warsaw speech (6 October 2000); indeed by that stage embarrassment at offering a vision had given way to self-confidence in outlining the sort of European Union to be expected after enlargement. Two models were briskly dismissed: those of a free-trade area similar to NAFTA and a classical federation. The first did not remotely answer the modern demands people placed on Europe. The second also failed the test of the people because they would not willingly give up their individual nationhoods. Instead, a third way was posited – a unique combination of the intergovernmental and the supranational. This model had the enviable strength of corresponding with what already existed, in contrast to those based on theorising about the future. Moreover, although this was not said, it conformed with the Community method of incremental deepening on the basis of necessity.

This third-way model for an enlarged Union was to be solidly based on free, independent sovereign states and its legitimacy would rest on their national institutions. It followed naturally that the overrriding authority in the Union should be the European Council; it should set the agenda. The role of the Commission, previously unaddressed, reflected an uneasy compromise between supranationalism and intergovernmentalism. On the one hand, it would be independent and strong, and would retain its right of initiative in order to protect small member states and overcome sectional interests. On the other hand, it would simply propose the Union's agenda to the European Council to debate, modify and endorse, thus implying a political subservience to the European Council at odds with the institutional architecture laid down by the treaties. Were this to be the case, as would seem inevitable, then the shift to intergovernmentalism would be decisive. It would become a permanent feature, and the defining characteristic of the Union. By way of corroboration, Blair added that representatives of national parliaments should constitute a second chamber in the European Parliament charged with ensuring democratic oversight at a European level of the division of competences between the member states and the Union, as well as of the common foreign and security policy. Finally, lest there be any doubt about the thrust of this model, Blair ruled out a single binding document laying down a European constitution and, as an alternative, offered a British-style "constitution" consisting of a mix of treaties, laws and precedents, thereby reflecting the common law preference for diversity, flexibility and, some might say, creative ambiguity.

Blair's thinking on the future European Union had, therefore, been unveiled in stages during his term of office and what might have been inferred from the earlier interventions had become explicit by the time of the Warsaw speech. The tone could hardly be faulted: it was pro-European. The logic was impeccable – if the starting premises were accepted. The approach was holistic; all items on the EU agenda were covered. The time-span was long term; the challenge of governing an enlarged Union was met head on. And the end goal was unmistakable in its simplicity: federation was out and the nation state was in. The future governance system was clear; the European Council would be in charge with the Commission relegated to a supporting role.

If the dichotomy between a free-trade area and a classic federation were to be accepted as the only basis for debate then the Blair vision came across as an attractive escape route for those hostile to supranationalism. But elsewhere within Europe some took a different point of departure. For the Belgian Prime Minister, Guy Verhofstadt, intergovernmentalism was only an intermediary stage in the integration process, a means to a supranational end and not an end in itself. Fischer's speech was, *inter alia*, an attempt to grapple with the political consequences of economic and monetary union which, consistent with much German thinking on the matter, led inexorably to political union. These and other contemporaneous contributions to the debate on Europe's future reflected as philosophy conflicting with that of Blair; reduced to its starkest, the choice on offer was between intergovernmentalism and supranationalism. In practice, each would incorporate elements of the other but their centre of gravity would be profoundly different.

The debate about the finality of Europe has no more than begun and, as President Chirac suggested in the Reichstag (27 June 2000), will probably only commence properly after Nice and then continue into the IGC intended to deal with the fundamental reforms made necessary by enlargement. Blair starts into this debate with a number of advantages. He was early into the field with offering reflections on the future Europe. He has successively refined his ideas and won allies for his cause as diverse as Spain and Sweden. He bases his proposals on what actually exists, always an attractive proposition for politicians facing uncertainty, and they come across as reasonable and persuasive. Given New Labour's political and diplomatic activism as a party and government they stand a good chance of being accepted and, in the run-up to the General Election, Blair could credibly argue that for the first time in the short history of the EU a British government was in the vanguard of those framing the future. Moreover, he could argue that his government's views were consistent with the needs of Europe's citizens, their determination to retain their own identities and national institutions and, more importantly, the psyche of his own electorate. England's Europe, it could be said, is being fashioned. The problem, as always, is time.

The more protracted the debate in Britain on the euro the greater is the possibility of disenchantment in other member states at its failure to join the current core. This would also be to the detriment of Blair's ambition for Britain to be among Europe's leaders. On the one hand, the eurozone participants might ultimately regard British non-participation as irrelevant, an attitude which has surfaced from time to time, and this too would have the effect of diminishing Britain's capacity for leadership. On the other, the task of creating a second EU core around security and defence may so dominate the European agenda that Britain's leading role will compensate for its failure to join the euro. Neither scenario can be advanced with any confidence but the second-core concept indicates that security will be as important to Britain in terms of its European vocation as the euro was to Germany and France in the 1990s. It has something of the same capacity to transform relations between the member states and a similar potential to confer political leadership on its leading advocates. Whether it turns out to be a vision or a dream depends on developments in Britain itself and in the Union now facing enlargement.

THE RETURN OF THE PRODIGAL

But by far the biggest transforming influence in the Union is enlargement. The nearer it comes, the greater the necessity to act. Conventionally, action is described in terms of reforming the institutions, as the Amsterdam IGC attempted, but increasingly is being discussed in a broader dimension which could endanger the Blair project. Flexibility, or enhanced cooperation, has reappeared on the agenda. The argument is that the Amsterdam Treaty is too rigid in the way in which flexibility can be invoked, since it effectively gives a national veto over the use of enhanced cooperation. Chapter Six recalled that it was originally intended to deal with Britain's awkward partnership and that its recycling as an instrument to deal with more diverse interests in an enlarged Union was arguably Blair's greatest triumph at Amsterdam. But something has changed for a number of reasons. In some minds, it is an absurdity to pretend that institutions designed for six member states, however reformed, can function effectively for 26, or more. It is not just a matter of increased numbers adversely affecting the capacity to act but the broadening of the field of action and the consequent need for coherence in global affairs. Flexibility is seen as a logical response to the inevitable. It is also presented as a necessity to allow an *avant-garde* to construct a federation. The dreaded "f" word has reappeared, with flexibility as its new companion. Political union is once more being presented as "the last brick in the building of European integration"[9], hardly what Blair would like to hear. Like a prodigal son, federalism has returned home to Europe.

Moreover, as Joschka Fischer emphasised, "the completion of political integration will depend decisively on France and Germany" since every previous stage of integration depended essentially on the alliance of Franco-German interests. This theme was repeated by President Chirac speaking before the Reichstag. The reassertion of Franco-German leadership on this most fundamental of questions relating to Europe has the potential to change both the context and the content of the future debate on the Union, to the double jeopardy of the Blair project. Furthermore, Fischer's scenario whereby the Eurozone will constitute the *avant-garde* leading the way towards political union would throw Britain's inability (or refusal) to join the euro into new relief. It would be saying that Britain was not ready for political union, and might never be. Those in Britain who contend that monetary union is but a surrogate for political union would be confirmed in their belief, if Fischer proves to be right. Membership of the euro is, indeed, the postponed question.

Against this background, the late-joiner syndrome evidenced by staying outside the euro could gather force as an analysis of Britain's long-term perspective in Europe. It is conceivable that the awkward partner will reappear were Britain to block amendment to the Amsterdam flexibility clauses at the IGC. It has become the "big idea" for the conference, not just because the other issues are smaller but because it genuinely is a large question; while it may be of symbolic rather than real value in the immediate future, it is the symbolism itself which has become important politically. A more operational flexibility signals a determination to sustain a principled and pragmatic momentum towards the finality of political union. For Britain to block it would signal the opposite and that it had become awkward once more, despite all the protestations to the contrary. The Blair government has stated it is not opposed to flexibility or groups of member states going forward together. But it is opposed to a hard core from which other member states are excluded. That is to beg the question. Flexibility is being advanced as a means of dealing with member states which wish to exclude themselves from further integration. The euro is currently its most graphic example, and Euro 12 an example of a hard core from which three member states have voluntarily excluded themselves. There is, then, a logical contradiction between being in favour of flexibility but against a hard core which will have to be resolved by Britain lest it be perceived as reverting to the awkwardness of the past.

RETURN OF ANOTHER PRODIGAL

Something else may also be at work in some European minds: the spectre of another Conservative government. Were Blair to fail to win a second term then its Conservative successor would bring Britain's European policy back to the days of Mrs Thatcher, without the countervailing influence of a pro-European element in the cabinet or the party at large. Under William Hague, the Conservatives have moved away from John Major's balance of opposites[10] and have given full rein to a strident Euroscepticism, a euphemism for refusing to share sovereignty any further than where it suits. Ironically, this policy stance is centered around a preference for flexibility, which, in turn, is taken to mean the right to pick and choose from the menu of new competences as Britain prefers. If followed by all other member states this policy of opportunism would lead to the creation of a mosaic Europe in which unicity was shattered. For that reason, the reaction of other member states is more likely to be that proposed by Fischer; an *avant-garde* would move ahead smartly, with Britain effectively left as an outsider.

The return of the Conservatives to office was considered improbable in the two years following their 1997 election débâcle. The probability of the Blair government serving two terms in office was regarded as high and this perception coloured much of the analysis on Britain's future European policy. By autumn 2000, such high expectations were modified in the light of a series of setbacks to the Blair government and the recovery of the Conservative opposition in the opinion polls. Those cut off on the continent might be forgiven for believing that their indulgence of Britain at Amsterdam was premature. While Labour may have been the prodigal returning to Brussels it could be the Conservatives who will return as the prodigal to Downing Street. In that case, flexibility would resume its original guise as a means of side-lining Britain. The precaution of making it more easily invoked in anticipation of a possible Conservative return to office would take on greater urgency at IGC 2000.

These concerns about the outcome of the next general election reflect the doubts expressed about the Third Way in Chapters Two and Three. Its Achilles' heel was always going to be its capacity to deliver and so meet expectations heightened to a fervour by New Labour's rhetoric in opposition. State and market reform, even when popular consent is required, lie largely within the power of government to initiate and then implement. Societal reform is quite another matter – a government may decree change but not be able to enforce it. Health, education, social security, transport and crime are as central to the Third Way as lower taxes, flexible labour markets and vigorous SMEs; but they are of a different order in terms of delivery by government. Unfortunately, for politicians in power, these tend to be the issues on which they are judged and electorates have a notoriously shorter time frame in which results are expected.

CONCLUSION

"Blair's Britain" can be said to rest on the pillars of state, market and societal reform. The first leads to a new constitutional order satisfying the competing needs of identities differentiated by nationality or region, the second to a more vigorous entrepreneurial culture and the third to a society which reconciles class and other divisions on the basis of *communitarian* values, thereby releasing the potential for growth and prosperity. Taken in conjunction with other indispensable policies, such as sound macro-economic management, they constitute the domestic reform programme, or what has been described as "Blair's Britain". Its success stands in doubt.

The effect of political vulnerability at home will be greater caution on Europe. The argument that European policy is greatly dependent on the success of domestic reforms takes on added force in the run-up to an election, especially when European policy issues are themselves the stuff of domestic debate. It was never going to be the case that Europe could only be tackled when the reform of Britain had been completed. That would be far too simplistic a conclusion and, in any event, does not correspond with the facts of what the Blair government attempted up to mid-term. Rather, the argument has been that Britain cannot answer the postponed question about Europe – does it embrace or reject the finality of the concept – until it answers the question about itself; what is to be the configuration of state, market and society? The problems encountered on the Third Way simply confirm that obstacles on the road to Brussels cannot be overcome until after the next election.

"Blair's Britain" and "England's Europe" are thus inextricably interwoven. Each represents a different facet of the challenge Britain has faced since victory in the second World War: how to win the peace. For many, the peace was lost in terms of the economy,[11] for others in term of society, and, for some, in terms of protecting the union. But for a number, however small, it was lost in Europe[12]; for them, at least, that was the decisive failure. It is not too far from the mark to suggest that Blair sees the past half-century in the same light and that for him the transformation he seeks is, at once, that of a Britain at ease with itself and of a Europe in which is can finally repose. The verdict on this composite ambition must be a peculiarly Scottish one: not proven. For other Europeans, their sentence is to await another jury on "Blair's Britain" and "England's Europe".

---

1   Blair (2000).
2   White Paper (2000).
3   *ibid.*
4   *ibid.*
5   Blair (2000).
6   Young (1998), p. 514.
7   Gowland and Turner (2000), p. 142.

8   Young (1998), p. 514.
9   Fischer (2000).
10   Major (1999).
11   Corelli Barnett (1995).
12   Denman (1998); Given (1999).

CHAPTER TEN

Defence and Security

Ronan Fanning

Along with serial inconsistency, (the) discrepancy
between deeds and words is the political style
that infuses, time and again, the history of
Britain-in-Europe. Fatally aberrant, often
counter-productive, these are practices the
political nation has regularly adopted as its only
way of coping with the project that dominates its
existence.[1]

What Hugo Young wrote in 1998 of Blair's "sinuous duplicities"
on Europe - of how, "in his early days, Blair treated Europe as a
subject about which it was dangerous to tell the truth: risky ... to
decide and stake out a position on what the truth really was ...
reluctant in the beginning, whatever he actually believed, to
address the fact that being pro-European might require a
commitment to look Euro-scepticism square in the face and stare
it down"[2] remains at the heart of a consideration of the British
defence and security initiative in 2000.

Yet, if the Labour Party's 1999 European election débâcle
reinforced Blair's temperamental disinclination to stake out a
position on Europe which might prove electorally
disadvantageous, there are signs that he has recovered his nerve
with the advent of the new millennium; that "he remains as
dogged in his strategic determination as ever", that he may indeed
prove to be "more interested in changing the country irreversibly
than he is in marginal seats".[3]

For there is no doubting the driving force of Blair's obsession
with the theme of nations needing "to have a sense of their place
in the world". He sees Britain "not as a super power but as a

pivotal power, as a power that is at the crux of the alliances and international politics which shape the world and its future" and he stresses its formidable network of international contacts. "Our extraordinarily close relations with nations in every part of the globe through the Commonwealth. Our membership of the UN Security Council, of NATO and of the G8. The close relationship forged through two world wars and the Cold War with the USA. And our crucial membership of the European Union. We are at the pivot of all these inter-connecting alliances and groupings.... The key for Britain is that we build and shape alliances to give us strength and influence to advance our own national interests...not just for Britain but for the world."[4]

More than any of his predecessors in 10 Downing Street, Blair wants Britain to assume a major role in Europe "by playing our part fully. Half-hearted partners are rarely leading partners." He has set himself "a bold aim: that over the next few years Britain resolves once and for all, its ambivalence towards Europe"[5]. He insists that the consummation of his European vision remains "a central ambition for the New Labour government". No other British Prime Minister has possessed the self-confidence to acclaim the European Union as "one of the outstanding political achievements of the twentieth century" or to laud the EU in such startlingly un-British language as a "project (that) has succeeded brilliantly" or to denounce "Britain's hesitation over Europe (as) one of my country's greatest miscalculations of the post-war years...For the first time in our history, we were content to stand aside from a major development on the continent."[6]

Blair's ambition to become the pre-eminent leader in the EU assumes a special significance because of his remarkable predominance over his Cabinet colleagues. One shrewd observer of the Whitehall scene, Peter Hennessy, has observed that "there are only two words that matter in government: 'Tony wants'. ... The Prime Minister's influence over policy is far greater than that in any previous administration, Labour or Conservative."[7] Blair's controlling influence over foreign and defence policy was initially compounded by his Foreign Secretary's relative lack of interest in Europe; despite Robin Cook's undoubted intellectual strengths, he did not at first immerse himself in the cut and thrust of intergovernmental politics in Brussels. Although Cook's Tokyo speech of 6 September 1999 highlighting the advantages of the euro - remarkably, his first major speech on the euro since the 1997 election - heralded a belated determination to reassert himself in the arena of European policy, it was Downing Street rather than the Foreign Office which carved out the new departure in European policy and it was Blair's direction to the Cabinet Office Secretariat and Policy Unit to drive European policy which gave birth to the Saint Malo initiative.

As long as Britain remained outside EMU, a prime minister ambitious to become a leader in Europe needed to identify an alternative policy area in which Britain might take a major initiative. Defence and security is a policy area, moreover, where the British (like the French) enjoyed a comparative advantage and where there was a widely recognised need for reform. Britain's Strategic Defence Review, for example, is seen as a demonstration of how military reform can be "genuinely foreign policy-led, and not simply an excuse for cost cutting". It has been an inspiration that others are following, and the success of the Strategic Defence Review "can do much to reassure our North American allies about Europe's willingness to create efficient and flexible armed forces".[8] Defence and security thus offer opportunities to lead the EU in a direction Britain accepts or, better still, that Britain wants - an ambition obviously more achievable in respect of defence than in respect of EMU.

The British acceptance of the European Union's commitment to the principle of "the eventual framing of a common defence policy, which might in time lead to a common defence" was first embodied in the Maastricht Treaty of 1991. But, during the negotiation of the 1997 Amsterdam Treaty, the British opposed Franco-German pressure to chart a course which would eventually lead to the WEU merging with the EU because of their perennial fear "that any attempt to boost Europe's defence identity, either through a stronger WEU or the EU itself, could impair NATO's military effectiveness, or needlessly duplicate its functions, or annoy the Americans and so hasten their departure from Europe". The AmsterdamTreaty did nothing to clarify the WEU's role or to mollify the French, who remained "semi-detached from NATO". Blair first identified the opportunities offered by this situation in the spring of 1998 when he began to talk of Britain taking a lead on European defence. He may have realised that, if the British could appear to be better Europeans in this area, they might win considerable credit with their partners; and that in the strange world of EU politics, it is possible to buy goodwill by making concessions that are more symbolic than substantial.

The game plan, as here delineated by Charles Grant of the

Centre for European Reform, was to strengthen European defence and to woo the French without putting American noses too far out of joint.[9] The origins of Saint Malo, insist the French, may be found in the creation of the "Franco-German Brigade" and the idea of a Eurocorps in which Belgium, Luxembourg and Spain would also participate. Saint Malo, seen in this light, is not so much Blair's initiative as a product of Blair's response to persistent invitations from Paris and Bonn to join the Eurocorps. The joint declaration on European defence issued after the Anglo-French summit at Saint Malo on 3-4 December 1998 gave concrete expression to such aspirations. It aimed "at making a reality of the Treaty of Amsterdam" and, in particular, at achieving "full and rapid implementation of the Amsterdam provisions on CFSP"; this included "the progressive framing of a common defence policy in the framework of CFSP". The European Union, it was also declared at Saint Malo, "must have the capacity for autonomous action, backed up by credible military force, the means to decide to use them and a readiness to do so, in order to respond to international crises". But that aspiration went hand in hand with a reaffirmation of the WEU's and NATO's "collective defence commitments to which member states subscribe". But the meat of the Saint Malo declaration is in its third article, which provides that in order for the European Union to take decisions and approve military action where the Alliance as a whole is not engaged, the Union must be given appropriate structures and a capacity for analysis of situations, sources of intelligence and a capability for relevant strategic planning, without unnecessary duplication, taking account of the existing assets of the WEU and the evolution of its relations with the EU. In this regard, the European Union will also need to have recourse to suitable military means (European capabilities predesignated within NATO's European pillar or national or multinational European means outside the NATO framework).

Blair interpreted Saint Malo as the "first step to defining the new approach. We decided that we should go beyond the Berlin arrangements agreed by NATO in 1996 to give Europe a genuine capacity to act, and act quickly, in cases where the Alliance as a whole is not militarily engaged. In any particular crisis, the European Union will develop a comprehensive policy."[10] George Robertson, then Secretary of State for Defence, echoed the Prime Minister at the same conference next day when he described the government's "ultimate aim" as "not so much a European Security

and Defence *identity* but something altogether more ambitious –
namely a European Defence *capability*. Our objective has been
quite simple. We want to strengthen the ability of the EU to
pursue foreign policy objectives." Kosovo, the argument runs,
should have removed any doubts about the "need to see how we
can co-operate better, complement each other's capability, have
the full range of defence options open to us".[11] The Chancellor of
the Exchequer subsequently joined the chorus when he argued
that the more influence Britain has in Bonn and Paris, the more
influence she will have in Washington; that the Atlantic Alliance is
not "in contradiction" with Britain's European commitments; that
"British interests are best served by being strong in Europe"; "that
there are no grounds for believing that to be pro-British it is
necessary to be anti-European. Indeed, history suggests that far
from being isolationist Britain has always thrived when it is
outward looking and internationalist."[12]

It is not that Blair "has chosen the Europeans over the
Americans. He simply thinks that no such choice needs to be
made."[13] Kosovo, moreover, reinforced the conviction in
Whitehall that its Washington flank is secure and it is assumed the
Clinton administration and, indeed, most moderate Republicans,
want the United States to have a friend at the heart of Europe and
that Blair is their favourite candidate for that role – more so than
ever with the mounting political disarray in Germany. "America
wants Britain to be a strong ally in a strong Europe. The stronger
we are in Europe, the stronger our American relationship."[14]

The prevailing wisdom in the Foreign Office is that the
symbolic significance of the Saint Malo declaration is that it is the
first time Britain has ever taken an initiative in a key area of
European policy. Blair claims that Saint Malo demonstrates that
"Britain can be positive in Europe". Nor does he fear that it will
end either in the British nightmares of a rupture with the United
States or of the British Army coming under the control of the
European Commission. The French, so this British interpretation
assumes, have accepted Blair's bona fides because British
negotiators gave way gracefully when differences arose on the
wording of the Saint Malo communiqué even if they "still cannot
quite believe" that it means Blair has "put aside anything that put
the slightest question mark over US military leadership. But
nowhere else does he have a better chance to show that Britain is
a beneficiary of, rather than a hostage to, European
cooperation."[15]

Blair's high-profile and high-risk strategy during the war[16] paid off. "Britain's self-image as a military power" has been enhanced and the Kosovo experience will undoubtedly contribute to the enormously important and "positive historical traditions of Britain's armed forces, reinforced by the view that disarmament and appeasement before World War II nearly brought disaster". Yet, taken together, the Saint Malo Declaration and Kosovo also give new and more sophisticated expression to Britain's traditional quest for a role "as a privileged interlocutor between continental Europe and the USA, thereby 'holding the balance' between the two and avoided being dominated as it might be by either in isolation". Indeed a cynic might suggest that the covert purpose of Saint Malo was to obviate what Dr Philip Sabin, in what now reads as a remarkably prescient paper delivered to an IEA seminar some years ago, described as "the oft-touted need for Britain to come off the fence and make a definite choice between the USA and Europe, between NATO and the EU".[17]

In theory, the Americans support a European Security and Defense Identity (ESDI) because, as the Deputy Secretary of State, Strobe Talbott, told the London conference to celebrate NATO's 50th anniversary,[18] they, too, want "a capability within the Alliance whereby the European members can address and solve problems without always requiring US combat involvement. That's in everyone's interest." But Talbott also voiced American apprehensions about the "risks and costs" of ESDI and the need for transparency and consultation. He warned that, "if ESDI is misconceived, misunderstood or mishandled, it could create the impression – which could eventually lead to the reality – that a new, European-only alliance is being born out of the old, trans-Atlantic one" and that the ties binding American and European security could thereby be endangered". He also stressed American concerns that ESDI should not discriminate against the eight non-EU NATO-members, arguing that six of them were European states which, "by definition, are covered by the "E" in ESDI, and ... have a direct, proprietary and participatory stake in the enterprise as a whole". Although Talbott denied that "ESDI was fatally flawed" by his identification of "these two potential pitfalls", it is difficult to see how his insistence upon keeping ESDI "from going astray" by adhering to the "bottom lines and red lines" delineated by the North Atlantic Council in Berlin in June 1996 can be reconciled with Saint Malo.

In practice, American support for ESDI rests on the perception that the "E" in ESDI stands not for the European Union but for Europe-in-NATO. Blair's contribution to the same conference, which put the Saint Malo declaration in the context of going beyond NATO's 1996 Berlin arrangements only in order "to give Europe a genuine capacity to act ... quickly in cases where the Alliance as whole is not militarily engaged", seemed rooted in the same perception. Although he envisaged the European Union developing "a comprehensive policy" in a crisis, he insisted that deployment of forces must remain a matter for individual governments and he specifically ruled out any role for the European Parliament, the European Commission or the Court of Justice. "To retain US engagement in Europe" is what propels Blair's quest for greater European self-reliance in defence and his sensitivity to American concerns likewise found expression in his insisting that the non-EU members of NATO should "be able to play a full role in European operations, without reserve".[19]

The linkage between Blair's European policy and his policy of strengthening the Anglo-American alliance found explicit expression in his Chicago speech in April 1999:

> For far too long British ambivalence to Europe has made us irrelevant in Europe, and consequently of less importance to the United States. We have finally done away with the false proposition that we must choose between two diverging paths – the transatlantic relationship or Europe. For the first time in the last three decades we have a government that is both pro-Europe and pro-American. I firmly believe that it is in Britain's interest, but it is also in the interests of the US and of Europe.[20]

The Washington meeting of the North Atlantic Council duly reaffirmed NATO's "commitment to building the ESDI *within* the Alliance" (author's italics). But while it welcomed the impetus given to a common European defence and security identity by the Saint Malo Declaration and acknowledged the EU's resolve to take autonomous "decisions and approve military action where the Alliance as a whole is not involved", it also attached "the utmost importance to ensuring the fullest possible involvement of non-EU European Allies in EU-led crisis operations".[21] The EU's role in developing the concept of ESDI was likewise diminished in NATO's new Strategic Concept which describes the process as requiring "close cooperation between NATO, the WEU and, *if and when appropriate*, the European Union" (author's italics).[22] NATO's Secretary General, Dr Javier Solana, was even more dismissive; he made no mention whatever of the EU and bluntly stressed that "the European Security and Defence Initiative will be rooted in the Alliance. It will strengthen the transatlantic relationship."[23]

Blair spelt out the message that "common defence and the transatlantic link will of course remain the bedrock of the Alliance" to the House of Commons; that the Saint Malo initiative "will strengthen NATO and will ... strengthen the essential transatlantic link". But NATO's readiness, "as the EU defines its defence arrangements", to make NATO assets "available for EU-led crisis management operations", remained subject to the approval of the North Atlantic Council; yet again he "emphasised the importance of fully involving those allies who are not members of the EU in this process".[24]

The European Council meeting at Cologne proclaimed "a decisive step forward" along the path charted at Saint Malo with the announcement of the intention "to give the European Union the necessary means and capabilities to assume its responsibilities regarding a common European policy on security and defence". It declared that the EU "must have the capacity for autonomous action, backed up by credible military forces, the means to decide to use them, and a readiness to do so, in order to respond to international crises without prejudice to actions by NATO". But here, too, the appetite for autonomy was qualified by an anxiety not to offend NATO by developing "an effective EU-crisis management in which NATO members, as well as neutral and non-allied members of the EU can participate fully and on an equal footing in the EU operations" and putting arrangements in place that allowed the participation of "non-EU European allies and partners".[25] Again, it was Strobe Talbott who voiced American anxieties when he noted that the Cologne communiqué "could be read to imply that Europe's default position would be to act outside the Alliance whenever possible, rather than through the Alliance".[26]

Yet the improbability of EU aspirations towards an autonomous defence and security policy taking a course independent of NATO was reinforced at Cologne by the nomination of Dr Javier Solana, then NATO's Secretary General, to the post of "Mr CFSP". In one breath the French welcomed "this right choice" and claimed that "Europe now has a public figure endowed with all the political authority required to embody the common foreign policy"; in the next they demanded that "Europeans must henceforth opt resolutely for an autonomous defence capability". The ambiguity was fudged with the pious formula that "the issue of the linkage between this European defence effort and NATO's should also be tackled with realism and simplicity and without any dogmatism".[27]

The appointment of Blair's Defence Secretary, George Robertson, as NATO's Secretary General was devised as a safeguard against the divergence of European and American security interests - it was because of British commitment to NATO, boasted Robin Cook in the House of Commons, "that we were able to secure the appointment of one of our own colleagues Lord Robertson, as the head of NATO".[28] Robertson's unswerving insistence that "NATO is and must remain the cornerstone of our security and defence policy" is music to American ears.[29]

Helsinki put flesh on the bones of Saint Malo: the communiqué of 11 December 1999, underlining the European Council's "determination to develop an autonomous capacity to take decisions and, where NATO as whole is not engaged, to launch and conduct EU-led military operations in response to international crises", marked a further step in enshrining the Blairite vision at the heart of CFSP in the shape of what has since been known as EDSP (the European Strategic and Defence Policy). The Council agreed, in particular, on

- cooperating voluntarily in EU-led operations, member states must be able by 2003, to deploy within 60 days and sustain for at least one year military forces of up to 50,000-60,000 persons capable of the full range of Petersberg tasks;

- new political and military bodies and structures will be established within the Council to enable the Union to ensure the necessary political guidance and strategic direction to such operations, while respecting the single institutional framework;

- modalities will be developed for full consultation, cooperation and transparency between the EU and NATO, taking into account the needs of all EU member states;

- appropriate arrangements will be defined that would allow, while respecting the Union's decision-making autonomy, non-EU European NATO members and other interested states to contribute to EU military crisis management.

- a non-military crisis management mechanism will be established to co-ordinate and make more effective the various civilian means and resources, in parallel with the military ones, at the disposal of the Union and the member states.[30]

Blair envisions Britain shaping EDSP so as to strengthen the transatlantic bond "by making NATO a more balanced partnership, and by giving Europeans the capacity to act whenever the United States, for its own reasons, decides not to be involved. Only then will Europe pull its weight in world security and share more of the burden with the United States." "We are listened to more closely in Washington if we are leading in Europe. And we have more weight in Europe if we are listened to in Washington. My vision for Britain is as a bridge between the EU and the USA. ... The EU and the US standing together, coming closer, is the single most important priority for the new international order for reasons of economic development and for reasons of global security."[31]

The new-found European readiness to improve their defence capabilities for the EU when they had not been ready to do so for NATO undoubtedly bruised American feelings. Nevertheless, the prevailing opinion in the Pentagon is that the United States will be "a strong and avid supporter of ESDP" if it develops along the lines agreed at Washington and Helsinki. Nor should such support be interpreted as a pulling away from Europe; rather is it a recognition that a stronger Europe (in regard to the Petersberg tasks) ultimately means a stronger NATO. But the Americans are suspicious that EU rhetoric on ESDP is outrunning the reality and there is scepticism, especially in Congress, about European arguments that higher defence expenditure is not necessary and that it is simply a matter of reallocation of existing resources. There is scepticism, in particular, about whether EU states, at a time when they are still cutting their defence budgets, are willing to pay for creating their own military assets. For while the Americans acknowledge that it would be nonsense for the EU to seek to duplicate everything NATO does and they assume that they will continue to provide intelligence and a lot of command and control expertise, they also assume that the new ESDP force must provide its own lift assets.[32]

But what if American and European (and, in particular, French) interests *do* diverge? Even the most ardent proponents of the Blairite strategy of using defence as the issue to put Britain at the heart of the European Union acknowledge that "mutual paranoia between France and the US may yet thwart the European (defence) initiative. Many French policy-makers are convinced that the US will work hard to block it, while many Americans believe that France's real agenda is to weaken NATO."[33] The lessons of the Suez crisis of 1956, as one senior American source recently reminded me, have not been forgotten: never since then have the British engaged in military operations without first informing the Americans; never since then have the French trusted the Americans. The most acute American apprehension is that the French will push for structures "permitting an EU caucus to emerge within NATO. They fear that the process of developing a consensus will shift from NATO to the EU, and that the Europeans will then present the US, Canada, Norway and Turkey with a common position that is not open to negotiation."[34] They remain suspicious, in other words, that the French are manoeuvring to arrive at a situation where decision-making on defence policy will become bottom-up, in the sense that the EU will take decisions on defence without any American input and they regard the French route as the surest way to provoke Congress to opt for American disengagement from Europe. They interpret the Saint Malo declaration, which was provocative not least because it took the American foreign policy-making establishment by surprise, as a classic example of the French trading on Blair's desire to be at the heart of Europe by nudging him towards bottom-up decision making. "Having a voice at the table is the link", according to one American official; "if the US does not have a voice in making the political decisions that drives CFSP, then the link is broken".[35] If, on the other hand, the Americans do have a voice in making the political decisions that drive CFSP, then CFSP can scarcely be described as an autonomous European policy with all the consequences that entails for the neo-Gaullist aspirations of the French.

The NATO decision-making process has been traditionally characterised by a much greater emphasis on consensus-building than has been the case within the European Union. On security issues, moreover, you only have the option of your assets and 75 per cent of the military assets available to European forces are

American. The Kosovo bombing campaign spelt out the lesson with brutal directness: of the 1,850 targets selected in the course of the campaign all but one were selected by the Americans and only two countries other than the US (Britain and Germany) had aircraft capable of defence suppression. Without American assets, moreover, any European defence force would have major weaknesses of reconnaissance and intelligence gathering.[36]

But the French insist that the capacity to run autonomous military missions provided for in the Saint Malo declaration includes intelligence and the intelligence-gathering dimension of the special relationship between London and Washington (which includes spying on other EU states) may threaten Blair's European ambitions. Hence the claim of one French official "that Britain will not be able to play a leading role in the EU unless they jettison their special intelligence links to the US: Britain must choose Europe or betray it". And it is not just the French "but many of Britain's partners (who) regard that special relationship as yet another indication, alongside the opt-out from the eurozone, that Britain is less than fully committed to the EU".[37] Although such gestures as the £5bn British package of defence equipment orders - in particular the preference for European Meteor air-to-air missiles over the American alternative - are designed to soothe such apprehensions, the prospect of American deployment of a National Missile Defence system also threatens to drive a wedge between the British and the French.[38]

That the IEA's 1996 analysis, *Britain's European Question: the Issues for Ireland* did not anticipate that defence might become a substitute for EMU in a British attempt to position itself at the centre of Europe is but one measure of how dramatically the war in Kosovo changed international perspectives. The "Summing-Up and Conclusions" in the 1996 volume made no mention, for instance, of security or defence among the key factors "shaping and reshaping British and Irish relations and their joint prospects in Europe, both in the near and long term". There was, however, a chapter on "Britain and Europe: Integrated Security or the Rebalancing of Power?" in which Patrick Keatinge warned perspicaiously against our being "surprised ... if the "great power" mind-set is alive and well in the British debate in security". He also observed how "France - hitherto the eternal rival - now assumed the role of (Britain's) preferred partner at the hard end of the security policy spectrum" and cautioned that it was "clear that even if the United Kingdom wishes to cut a dash on defence it will be far from *communautaire* in its approach".[39]

When the French President and British Prime Minister reviewed progress when they met at King Hussein's funeral, Blair stressed the necessity of keeping the Americans on board; "that's your job", replied President Chirac. And so it is, but the exchange begs a larger question: on board for what? For American doubts remain and, despite Strobe Talbott's unambiguous support for the *concept* of ESDI, his two key questions on the *reality* of ESDI remain unanswered.

> First, will it work? Will it be able to do what it's supposed to do? Secondly, will it help keep the Alliance together and that means the whole Alliance, European and non-European, EU and non-EU? We would not want to see an ESDI that comes into being first within NATO but then grows out of NATO and finally grows away from NATO, since that would lead to an ESDI that initially duplicates NATO but could eventually compete with NATO.[40]

Raymond Seitz, former American Ambassador to the Court of St James, put the same point more waspishly when he admitted that "the United States has always worried that a wholly European defence system, if it ever came to pass, would operate with all the streamline efficiency of the Common Agricultural Policy....And America has always recognised that the more united Europe is the less influential Washington will be."[41] Recent proposals to offer NATO permanent seats or observer status on the European Military Committee of military representatives of the EU's member states in an attempt to assuage American fears prompts the sardonic suspicion that the proposals only amount to "a pretty good job of dividing the baby, with half on one side, half on the other, and no one particularly happy".[42] Nor do the pronouncements of General Klaus Naumann, the former chairman of NATO's military committee, that the Helsinki proposals for a Rapid Reaction Force could take ten years to implement and are already three years behind schedule inspire confidence.[43]

Yet the seductive power of the European Security Defence Initiative as "an example of Britain shaping the agenda of Europe"[44] endures, notwithstanding the Foreign Secretary's admission of Helsinki's limitations: "An initiative aimed at improving Europe's capacity for crisis management, for humanitarian intervention, for peace-keeping tasks. It is not about territorial defence, which remains the job of NATO."[45] Such protestations reflect the perennial British determination never to have to choose between Europe and America. But what if events were to make such a choice unavoidable? There are no greater grounds in the present than there have been in the past for believing that Britain would choose to offend her American allies in order to avoid offending her EU partners. Which is why one must at least doubt whether defence and security policy can in fact serve as the vehicle for Blair's European ambitions. It may be that, in the last analysis, the opportunity offered by the defence dimension to move Britain to the heart of Europe will prove illusory. If what we are witnessing is no more than an exercise in buying goodwill by making concessions that are more symbolic than substantial, then sooner or later Britain's European partners will discover that the symbols have no substance.

Kosovo may have borne brief witness to what Blair could do to restore Britain's influence in Europe, but it is doubtful if defence cooperation alone can give Britain the role Blair covets "in shaping Europe's destiny if it stands aside from EMU".[46] A realist interpretation rather suggests that, while "it is true that he craves acceptance as a good European, his Saint Malo initiative was in part a way to keep his EU partners sweet while going slow on the euro…. The war went well for Mr Blair, but it is a bit early to derive a moral from it."[47] If there are no more Kosovos, the fading glamour of Blair's success as a war leader may tarnish as economic imperatives reassert themselves as political priorities. In which case, the focus on defence as Britain's way forward in Europe may prove a delusion and the Prime Minister will have to look elsewhere for an engine to drive his European enterprise.

What, finally, of the implications for Ireland? For as long as the developments flowing from the Cologne and Helsinki conclusions "are to be framed on the basis of the Amsterdam Treaty and are focused on the Petersberg Tasks", Irish ministers and officials will doubtless echo Ahern's satisfaction "with the current emphasis on military and non-military crisis management and the development of the Union's decision-making structures and capabilities in this regard". But he has put on record that he sees no necessity or justification for the introduction of an Article V mutual defence clause into the EU which would turn it into a military alliance largely duplicating NATO, and which would completely prejudice the strategic character of Ireland's security and defence policy notwithstanding the Amsterdam and Maastricht treaties.

> I want to state as plainly as I can that there is no mandate at Union level for the introduction of Union-wide mutual defence commitments, of the type included in Article V of the WEU Treaty which would inevitably draw in the nuclear first-strike policy. At a domestic level, I do not believe that the Irish public is prepared to agree to any such developments, nor will I be advocating the same. This is a matter which our Partners should bear in mind in the context of any proposals to widen the IGC Agenda. It is not a road which the Irish people are prepared to travel.[48]

As the next general election looms larger on the horizon, ministerial anxiety about the hazards of circumnavigating the sacred cow of Irish neutrality still slumbering on that road will increase. Not for nothing did the recent White Paper on Defence evade all discussion of providing the capacity for Irish participation in the Rapid Reaction Force. But the implications for Ireland of the new structures triggered by the Helsinki conclusions cannot be ignored: a Political and Security Committee (PSC), composed of ambassadors and senior officials from the foreign ministries of the member states, will direct ESDP; a new Military Committee (composed of the chiefs of the national defence forces or their representatives) will offer specialised advice to the PSC; and a Military Staff Committee (composed of senior military officials) will provide operational expertise on ESDP and will also have a planning and co-ordination function. The participation of Irish ambassadors, officers and officials on these committees will, for the first time, put Ireland at the centre of European security architecture.

Javier Solana's reassurances when he visited Dublin that "ESDP is not about collective defence" and that the EU "has no ambition to take over or duplicate the work of NATO" came as sweet music to the ears of Irish officialdom; the EU, he also insisted, "is not in the business of creating a European army".[49] While there are those who may find this reluctance to ascribe the title of army to a force of 60,000 men somewhat disingenuous, if this distinction between a standing army such as NATO and a voluntary Rapid Reaction Force can be maintained, it will ease the task of the Irish government when they have to decide upon the conditions which will govern any Irish participation in EU crisis management operations.

1   Young (1998), p. 170.
2   Young (1998), pp 483-4.
3   Marr (2000).
4   Blair (1999h).
5   Blair (1999d).
6   Blair (2000).
7   Sylvester (1999).
8   Solana (1999).
9   Grant (1998), pp 44-47.
10   Blair (1999a).
11   Blair (1999d).
12   Brown (1999).
13   David (1999), p. 15.
14   Blair (2000).
15   Stevens (1999).
16   FitzGerald (1999).
17   Sabin (1996), pp 158-60.
18   Talbott (1999).
19   Blair (1999a).
20   Blair (1999b).
21   North Atlantic Council (1999), paragraphs 5, 9a and 9d.
22   North Atlantic Council (1999), paragraph 30.
23   Solana (1999a).
24   Blair (1999a).
25   European Council (1999), Annex III.
26   Talbott (1999a).
27   Moscovici (1999).
28   1 Dec. 1999.
29   Robertson (1999).
30   European Council (1999a), paragraphs 25-29; see also Annex IV for the Presidency Reports to the Helsinki European Council on "Strengthening the Common European Policy on Security and Defence" and on "Non-Military Crisis Management of the European Union".
31   Blair (1999h).
32   Bronson (200); Krusell (2000).
33   Grant (1999).
34   Schake, Bloch-Lainé and Grant (1999), p. 34.
35   Briefing at NATO headquarters, 1 July 1999.

36 Briefing by a senior NATO official, 1 July 1999.
37 Grant (2000), pp 21-25.
38 Nicoll and Grant, *Financial Times*, 17 May and 24 June 2000.
39 Gillespie (ed.) (1996), pp 144, 146, 151, 172.
40 Talbott (1999a).
41 Seitz (1998), pp 333-34.
42 Castle (2000).
43 *Daily Telegraph*, 30 March 2000.
44 House of Commons, 1 Dec. 1999.
45 Robin Cook's speech at Lisbon, 6 Jan. 2000.
46 Stevens (1999a).
47 David (1999), p. 16.
48 Ahern (2000).
49 Solana (2000).

SECTION THREE

BRITAIN AND IRELAND

Section Three

Britain and Ireland

BACKGROUND AND CONTEXT

During the second half of the twentieth century the historic relationship between Britain and Ireland was fundamentally changed - for the better – by several developments.

The first of these was gradual recognition by Britain – after the negative impact of Irish wartime neutrality on British public opinion had subsided – that, far from ever posing a threat to Britain, an independent Ireland has a vital interest in British security. Secondly, after the last War the emergence of atomic weapons altered the geo-political balance, making British strategic control of part of Ireland superfluous – a development which was greatly reinforced by the end of the Cold War.

Although differences about the means of restoring peace and stability in Northern Ireland were often sources of tension between Irish and British governments, the fundamental common purpose of the two governments in relation to this issue came in the 1980s and 1990s to create an atmosphere of close cooperation between them. This eventually led to the emergence of what it is hoped may be a permanent solution to this long-running problem. New institutional structures within Northern Ireland are now paralleled by a north/south institutional structure, and by institutions linking the Irish State and Northern Ireland with British central and regional governments.

Irish membership of the EU ended its unhealthy economic dependence on Britain, and helped to eliminate the inferiority/superiority complex that had previously distorted the attitudes of the two peoples towards each other. Moreover, although there have often been deep British-Irish policy differences on issues such as agriculture and structural funds, nevertheless within the councils of the EU, British and Irish ministers established personal relationships of a kind that had not previously been possible.

British unwillingness to accept free movement of people within the Community has, however, created a problem for Ireland; because of the common travel area within the archipelago, this has prevented Ireland from joining the Schengen Area. Moreover, British non-membership of EMU creates some problems for an Irish economy firmly situated within that monetary union, and makes more difficult the development of economic and social relationships between Northern Ireland and the Irish State. However, earlier fears that a weak sterling could give Britain an unfair competitive edge in trade with Ireland now seem unlikely to be realised at any stage.

Recent proposals that greater use be made of flexibility within the Union so as to enable a core group of member states to move towards further integration raise the possibility that, if Britain does not join EMU fairly soon, Ireland, with its commitment to integration, could find itself faced with the emergence of further undesirable divisions between it and the United Kingdom, including Northern Ireland.

In such circumstances the future could see fresh tensions developing between, on the one hand, Ireland's interest in full participation in an integrated Europe and, on the other hand, its interest in a closer relationship with a Northern Ireland that remains part of a United Kingdom opposed to further European integration.

However, if Britain joins EMU and thereafter seeks to participate positively in the future leadership of the Community, that could pose a risk of the emergence of a *directoire* of major EU states - a development that would not be in the interest of smaller countries such as Ireland. Difficult choices could lie ahead for future Irish governments.

CHAPTER ELEVEN

Sterling and the Euro

Lochlann Quinn

INTRODUCTION

There can be little doubt that Labour, under Blair, wishes to join the euro and that the decision to join will be political not economic. Prior to the introduction of the euro, there was little widespread demand from European business and industry and even less arguments in its favour from economists. This was, at all times, a political concept which, its protagonists believed, would help to integrate the European Union further. That is not to say that no economic arguments were put forward as to its benefits – quite the contrary. The elimination of the costs associated with currency exchange, the degree of stability it would bring to cross-border trade within the EU, the prospect of DM-type interest rates applicable throughout the EU were all cited as benefits, and in large measure were valid arguments. But these economic arguments were always secondary. EMU was a venture conceived at the highest political levels and then pronounced to be a good thing. The arguments as to its fundamental merit were rarely aired – it was a matter of belief. Those who believed in a closer Union supported it and vice versa. All the Irish political parties supported the concept of a single currency long before any analysis of the economic impact had been carried out. In the run-up to the referendum on the Maastricht Treaty there was relatively little debate on the full implications of Ireland's membership of the single currency – and little discussion, at the time, in most of the media. The debate in Ireland only really got off the ground among economic policy-makers after the decision had been taken by the people.

In the UK, the issue of whether to join the single currency has been under debate for some considerable time. Whereas the Conservative Party is split (although the majority appears to be against) the Labour Party has constructed a policy which appears to have secured general acceptance within its ranks. This policy is based on what can be referred to as the Five Tests which, if they are met, will allow Britain to join the euro. The basic tenet of the five tests is a convergence of the UK's economy with the euro economic cycle that would do no damage in the process. In this respect, the New Labour government's policy is, of course, similar in its essentials to that of its predecessor, although John Major had to contend with a large vocal segment of his party who were violently anti-euro, whereas if such a constituency exists in New Labour it remains remarkably silent.

In the UK the debate on, or analysis of, whether convergence is taking place – or will take place – will be essentially a side show. If convergence needs to be demonstrated it will be, for Gordon Brown's five tests can easily yield to a "yes" or "no" answer depending on the response required. A referendum on whether the UK should join EMU and adopt the euro is unlikely to be held unless there is a reasonable expectation that it can be won. Opinion is divided on whether it can. One side of the argument is that if Blair's government fully commits itself then it can win, but it will require New Labour to nail its colours to the euro mast, and by extension to the Union as a whole. The alternative view is that in the absence of a strong belief that victory is possible, Blair may not, in the end, make the commitment for fear of losing.

The primary factor in deciding whether to hold a referendum is likely to be the result of the next general election. And there can be little doubt that the euro will be an issue in the campaign because Hague will make it so. (And if Hague loses he will presumably, in time-honoured fashion, step aside, or be pushed). The key factor will be the size of the Conservative Party defeat and how it is interpreted, and following on from that who will succeed Hague and what will his or her attitude be?

The election result and the campaign will provide a lot of clues but their implications for holding a referendum may not be all that clear. Should a referendum take place it will be decided on the economic argument since it seems unlikely that the segment of the population who currently base their opinion on the political argument – "greater integration with Europe is necessary" or "we have gone far enough" –is unlikely to change its mind.

This sort of debate has been carried on in the UK now for some considerable time, the issues have been well thrashed out, and it is hard to see new compelling arguments being developed that could effect a change in attitude. However, as neither the pro nor anti-European factions constitute a majority of the electorate, the middle ground or those politically agnostic on the issue of Europe will swing – and here the economic argument will be the key determinant.

COMPARATIVE UK PERFORMANCE

Short-range economic forecasting is quite hazardous – and medium- to long-term forecasting (say five to ten years) is almost meaningless. In any event, for the purposes of this chapter (and for most other purposes too) the absolute performance of the economy is not that relevant; what will matter is the comparative performance, more specifically the comparative performance against the major, more mature, EU member states – in essence Germany, France, and Italy. The relative performance of the UK economy vis-à-vis these three economies is, for most people, the meaningful measure of performance. In that regard, it is interesting to note that for a long period when the UK economy under-performed against Germany, France and Italy (and hence was deemed to be "failing") it actually outperformed the US economy (see Appendix A).

So what are the prospects for the British economy compared to the other major EU economies? Starting with inflation – although that is only one factor – the view of the markets is that the outlook is good (see Appendix B). Long-term sterling bonds no longer carry a devaluation premium although this analysis may be slightly distorted by the fact that the shortage of government debt available to institutions has driven up the price. Gordon Brown's decision to cede independence to the Bank of England has given enormous assurance to the markets. The view now generally held is that the inflationary outlook in the UK is no different from that likely to apply within the eurozone as a whole. If this is correct, the historic relative decline of sterling vis-à-vis the DM (now euro) may well be over.

Regarding the prospects for the UK's economic growth – especially compared with Germany, France and Italy – the increasing globalisation of the major economies suggests that growth rates now are more likely to converge than they would have done, say, 30 to 40 years ago. Germany will continue to have difficulties because of the economic burden of subsidising the former East Germany, and Italy will take some time to learn to live within the disciplines of the euro. The French economy, on the other hand, has adapted well. As for the UK, it has some advantages over these three economies since its manufacturing base is smaller and consequently its service sector is larger. Parts of the EU manufacturing base are under threat from low-cost countries in Asia and Eastern Europe and the UK looks a little less vulnerable in this regard. The UK's lower tax environment and more flexible labour markets, combined with the fact that its unfunded pension obligations are considerably less than those of the other three economies, are all strong points in its favour. Clearly the British economy suffers from structural disadvantages (its education system for one) but, overall, it is difficult to see why over the next decade it should under-perform the big three economies. Hence, the most likely economic scenario at the time of the referendum is that of a UK economy performing as well as those of the big three, with a similar inflation rate and a currency that is holding its value vis-à-vis the euro. Up to mid-2000 the euro declined significantly but this trend may be reversed, in part, over the next few years.

The anti-case in the referendum campaign will be: "Five years outside the euro have not affected us in any adverse fashion: why do we need to join?" Consequently, it is difficult to be confident that a referendum on whether to join EMU can be won against the background of a successful UK economic performance. Curiously enough, Gordon Brown's decision to grant independence to the Bank of England may well have made it much more difficult for New Labour to win such a referendum.

DOES IT MATTER?

From an Irish point of view, UK membership of EMU would be a much tidier outcome. It would eliminate exchange movements related to trade with our single largest customer for both exports and imports. However, at this juncture, it may well be realistic for Irish policy-makers to assume that Britain may not join the euro within the next decade. As the title of this book is *Blair's Britain, England's Europe – A View from Ireland*, it is worthwhile to ask the question: Does this matter?

In the chapter on EMU in *Britain's European Question: the Issues for Ireland*, concerns were then expressed about Ireland joining

EMU on the assumption that initially the only participating member states were likely to be the DM block (Germany, the Netherlands, Austria, Belgium and Luxembourg) and France. At that time there was some doubt about whether Italy, Spain and Portugal would qualify. Consequently, much of Irish indigenous industry would be in great difficulty if the euro became a strong currency (following the historic model of the DM) and sterling, together with the other member states' currencies, continued a historic trend of weakening against the DM (now the euro). This was graphically illustrated during the currency crisis in 1992-3 when the Irish pound rose above stg£1.10 and Ireland was forced to devalue within the EMS.

Subsequently the euro turned out to have a far wider membership than was anticipated in some quarters. But the change in the UK's monetary governance itself has been of much greater significance. Gordon Brown's decision to give independence to the Bank of England has altered the economic landscape and the persistent weakening of sterling may well be a thing of the past; as has been said, that is certainly the view of the financial markets where long-term sterling bonds no longer carry an anticipated devaluation premium. Irish indigenous industry tends to do well when the Irish pound is at a discount to sterling; it is interesting to note that ever since the link with sterling was severed in 1979 the Irish pound has traded below parity with sterling except for a few brief intervening periods. The Irish economy has, over the past decade, become increasingly competitive. Low wage settlements, static or declining prices for electricity, telecommunications, air travel etc., and reduced corporate and personal tax rates have all combined to support the growth of the indigenous economy. Since the launch of the euro, the Irish pound:sterling exchange rate has settled below 85p (and below 80p in mid-2000) and many Irish businesses have reaped a bonus since many would trade profitably at rates from 95p to parity.

The changes in the Irish economy over the past decade, and particularly over the past five years, have been of such a magnitude that the indigenous manufacturing sector, although important, is no longer as significant as it was. Their biggest threat is, in effect, the success of the national economy; the fear is that with labour shortages the cost of employment will rise in real terms and erode profitability in what are low-profit industries. However, as long as employment is reallocated to industries better capable of absorbing increased costs this would cause no real loss to the economy. The growth of (largely US-owned) hi-tech industries in Ireland continues to be strong and their labour costs, or production costs, are usually insignificant relative to their technological superiority. The behaviour of sterling (up or down) vis-à-vis the euro or the US$ is not of great relevance to this segment.

If the UK does not join the euro the Irish pound (now euro) will remain at a discount to sterling over the short-term. This is for two reasons:

- the Bank of England will succeed in managing the inflation rate and co-ordinating it (unless it is subject to very unusual shocks) with inflation rates in the eurozone and the US.

- UK interest rates will not fall to the level of existing euro rates because of the impact that would have on UK house prices and subsequent inflation. UK policy-makers are all too aware of those problems. If these beliefs are proved correct then, in practice, sterling bonds and deposits would carry a premium over euro rates and hence the value of sterling would generally be maintained.

In summary, it is difficult to foresee a situation in the near future where sterling will decline so as to be at a discount to the old Irish pound. British industry is managing, with some difficulty, to live with current exchange rates and, although they may ease and change, a decline of 20 per cent in the value of sterling seems unlikely. As a result of the dramatic changes in the composition of the Irish economy, and changing performance of the UK economy and the greater credibility of sterling, many of the earlier fears concerning Ireland's de-coupling from sterling have eased. The worst case scenario of the Irish pound (or euro equivalent) trading at a significant premium to sterling, looks increasingly unlikely. As said, it would be tidier for Ireland if the UK joined the euro. If it doesn't, it probably doesn't matter all that much. There is one, but very remote, possibility where sterling might suffer a massive decline in value vis-à-vis the euro. If the Conservatives were to win the next election (always possible), and they decided to terminate the new independent status of the Bank of England, then this almost certainly would be damaging for sterling. But this scenario is very remote.

IRISH INFLATION RESULTING FROM
STRONG STERLING

Now for the other side of the picture, if the UK stays outside EMU and remains "strong" in relation to the euro, this could cause problems for Irish inflation. There is much comment in the media on this issue, but most of it has been misguided.

Between 1 January 1999 and 31 March 2000 the Irish pound depreciated against sterling by 12% – and going back a year further the decline approximates to 17%. But over most of this period Irish inflation remained low and the principal reason was that UK manufacturers had to absorb the exchange impact. In modern competitive markets manufacturers of most of the products that feature in the price index do not get real price increases, indeed, in many cases real price declines are the norm. Considering the growth of the Irish economy over the past five years the low level of inflation up to Spring 2000 was surprising and the subsequent increase (part self-inflicted and partly as a result of dollar-related energy costs) relate very little to sterling. In any event, any such increases are of a one-off nature and should not reoccur unless sterling were to continue strengthening against the euro on a "permanent basis". Such a scenario is unlikely.

The impact on the Irish economy of a strong sterling (which may well have peaked) has been surprisingly benign and in any event its impact is of a once-off duration.

The likely Impact on FDI into the UK of a Strong Sterling
This is unlikely to be significant. In recent times the UK has been the largest recipient of foreign direct investment (FDI) into the EU. Although its share of FDI can and will vary (as it did in 1999) the UK has been, and will continue to be, an attractive place to invest. There are two principal reasons for this conclusion.

First of all, even with a weak euro, absolute wage costs in the UK are less than those in France, Germany or Italy. Secondly, an appreciating currency tends to hurt labour-intensive low-margin (or low-technology) industries and may hasten the demise of some (or many) of those industries. FDI tends to come from expanding profitable sectors. New investment tends to be capital intensive, hence raising productivity, with labour costs being of much less importance. For these two reasons, a "strong" sterling is unlikely to have a significant impact on FDI into the UK.

Sterling's Entry Rate

One further scenario should, however, be considered. If the Labour government fully commits itself to joining the euro and is confident that it can win a referendum then one of the key issues will be to determine the appropriate entry rate. This raises the question of whether that rate, which will be permanent, could be fixed at a discount to the Irish pound. It is difficult to believe that New Labour would embark on a referendum unless it had received a clear signal from its fellow EU members that its participation in the euro was welcome. It would be of equal importance to reach an understanding on sterling's rate of entry. It is inconceivable that the UK would hold a referendum, get an endorsement to enter the euro, and then not join because of failure to negotiate an acceptable entry rate. That would be a political fiasco. Negotiations on an acceptable entry rate would have to be concluded formally or informally prior to holding the referendum.

What would that rate be? Clearly, the existing euro members would not want a rate that gave the UK a "permanent" advantage and the UK, equally, would not want to join at a permanent disadvantage. Hence a rate that represents the average rate in effect over the past ten to fifteen years seems probable. This suggests a rate not far from 3DM to the pound sterling with the possibility of a small premium up to say 3.10. It is also inconceivable that a rate of entry would be agreed that would put the 'old' Irish pound at a premium to sterling as that would require a rate of as low as DM2.48. Finally, if the markets believed the referendum would be won announcing the target rate (or range of rates) in advance would rapidly bring the market rate towards the expected range.

CONCLUSION: THE IMPLICATIONS FOR IRELAND

If the UK does not join the single currency within the next decade it probably would not matter too much to the Irish economy. Sterling would almost certainly remain at a premium to the Irish pound or its equivalent euro. If it does join, it is difficult to see an entry rate that would put sterling at a discount to the 'old' Irish pound.

Appendix A

Annual Average Rate of Increase of GDP per Head 1951–95

	UK	*US*	*Germany*	*France*	*Italy*
1951-73	2.54	1.82	4.74	3.99	4.86
1973–79	1.50	1.06	2.49	2.32	3.23
1979–87	1.92	0.66	1.37	0.93	1.92
1987–92	0.49	1.49	2.33	2.45	2.15
1992–95	2.60	2.38	1.06	0.89	2.53

Source: OECD (1999).

This table evidences two interesting aspects of the post-war UK economy. Whilst under-performing the big three European economics over the total period, the period of principal under-performance takes place while the UK is outside the EU. Since entry there has been a change. Furthermore, throughout the post-war period the UK has performed better (for most of the periods detailed above) than the US.

Appendix B

Changes in Consumer Prices to 1998
1990 = 100

	%
Italy	38
Germany	24
UK	17
France	16
EU	27
USA	25

Source: OECD (1999).

CHAPTER TWELVE

Britain and Ireland

Garret FitzGerald

INTRODUCTION

During the second half of the twentieth century there were profound changes in the relationship between Britain and Ireland.

First of all, in the latter part of this period British strategic concerns about Ireland, which since at least the sixteenth century had dominated England's Irish policy, largely evaporated. In the course of the Second World War it had already become clear that, so far as conventional warfare was concerned, Northern Ireland could supply most of Britain's strategic requirements in relation to its western approaches. This had no doubt influenced the views of the British chiefs of staff in relation to the 1938 return of the naval facilities that had been retained by Britain under the Anglo-Irish Agreement of 1921.[1] And, especially after the German conquest of France had forced all Atlantic convoys to be routed around the northern coast of Ireland, these facilities would have been of only little extra value to Britain. While the availability to the RAF of airfields in the Irish state might have been of some assistance in the Battle of the Atlantic, the secret agreement to permit aircraft from Northern Ireland to secure direct access to the Atlantic by over-flying Irish territory met most British needs in this respect. These and many other facilities[2] accorded to Britain so secretly that they evoked no reactions either from Germany or from anglophobe elements within Ireland, made a positive contribution, the nature and extent of which were not revealed until decades later.

Nevertheless there was intense – and it must be said understandable – British irritation with the wartime neutrality of the Irish State, especially on the part of Winston Churchill, who never became reconciled to the Chamberlain government's 1938 decision to return to Irish control the facilities which Churchill had personally negotiated in 1921. British opinion could not be expected to understand the fear of democratic Irish politicians that participation on the Allied side might precipitate a recurrence of the civil war that had wracked the country in 1922 – a recurrence that would almost certainly have attracted German support for the republican side, with all the dangers for both Ireland and Britain which that would have entailed. (Because, for obvious reasons, this factor influencing support for Irish neutrality across the whole political spectrum, including strongly pro-Allied politicians, was never openly stated or recorded, it has, I believe, been seriously underestimated by historians).

However, to British policy-makers the alternative chosen by de Valera – to operate neutrality secretly in a manner extremely favourable to Britain – must have demonstrated that the Irish State recognised fully that its vital interests lay with the preservation of Britain's independence vis-à-vis threats from the continent.

The fact is that with the achievement of independence Britain's difficulties ceased to be perceived as Ireland's opportunity – as had understandably been the perception of advocates of Irish independence from the sixteenth century onwards. This radical shift in the Irish perception of the interests of an independent Ireland in relation to Britain had in fact been publicly declared by de Valera even before Irish independence had been achieved. In the alternative document that he proposed to the Anglo-Irish Treaty of 1921 during the Irish parliamentary debate on that Agreement he had incorporated a commitment never to allow any foreign power "to use (its soil and territorial waters) for any purpose hostile to Great Britain and the other associated states".[3] This principle remained thereafter a cornerstone of Irish foreign policy.

After the Second World War the emergence of atomic weapons created a totally new strategic reality. At the end of the 1980s the collapse of the Soviet Union and the end of the Cold War further transformed the geopolitical situation. Thus by the 1990s nothing effectively remained of the strategic considerations that for so many centuries had underlain – indeed governed – British policy in relation to Ireland. So far as Britain was concerned the way was thus opened for a new and much more relaxed and constructive relationship with its neighbouring island.

THE NORTHERN IRELAND PROBLEM

On the Irish side, however, for much of the post-independence period there had remained a significant source of Anglo-Irish tension – the retention under British sovereignty of the north-eastern corner of Ireland, and the failure of successive British Governments between 1922 and 1969 to safeguard the rights of the nationalist minority in Northern Ireland. In 1949 this political division of the island was in fact given by the Irish Government as the reason for Irish non-participation in the North Atlantic Alliance. In that same year, following Ireland's declaration of a Republic and final departure from the Commonwealth, a negatively-worded reformulation of British policy with respect to Northern Ireland's relationship with the Republic had provoked a vigorous bout of irredentism on the part of the whole range of Irish constitutional politicians. This hostile stance was actively sustained for a full decade thereafter.

At the end of the 1950s, however, a change of leadership in the governing nationalist Fianna Fáil Party, from Eamon de Valera to Seán Lemass, brought about a shift in Irish policy on this issue – one that seemed at the time to foreshadow a much improved north-south relationship. But, within a decade of this shift in Irish policy, the Unionist government's repressive reaction to the Northern Ireland civil rights campaign had led to the emergence of the Provisional IRA, and to lethal violence on an extensive scale, much of it sectarian in character.

In the short and medium run, this outbreak of violence in Northern Ireland created severe Anglo-Irish tensions, mainly because of divergent appreciations of how the resultant threat to the security of the two states could most effectively be addressed. Ultimately, however, the IRA violence came to have a positive rather than a negative effect on relations between the two states. For their common interest in restoring peace and stability in Northern Ireland, and, especially from 1993 onwards, a gradually developing British recognition of the merits of the Irish view as to how this might be achieved, led eventually to the emergence of a joint approach to the problem.

This development was facilitated by the fact that on the Irish side residual territorial irredentism had given way to a clear-sighted pursuit of what was necessarily an un-stated objective: securing the emergence of a stable, reformed, Northern Ireland polity remaining within the United Kingdom until and unless a majority of the people of the area decided to join the Irish State.

Such a Northern Ireland polity would have to be one that would secure widespread support of nationalist opinion – and that would first require a reversal of a drift towards Sinn Féin during the early 1980s, which, if it were not checked, might encourage the IRA not merely to continue, but perhaps even eventually to heighten, their campaign of violence. If, instead, nationalist electoral support for Sinn Féin could be reduced, then the political leadership of IRA/Sinn Féin might be induced to abandon violence with a view to recovering ground lost at the polls.

Without prejudice to successful containment of the IRA, the achievement of this objective required a marked lowering of the profile of the security forces in the nationalist areas of Northern Ireland, where the nature, scale, and character of their activities had been intensifying the sense of alienation of the minority. It also demanded the adoption of a more even-handed approach by the British government towards the two communities in the North.

A shift in British policy along these lines, urged by the Irish government, eventually evoked a response from Margaret Thatcher. Her signature of the 1985 Anglo-Irish Agreement – albeit reluctant and much later regretted – created the conditions that secured a drop of one-third in electoral support for Sinn Féin between 1985 and 1987, and the gradual conversion of a majority of the IRA/Sinn Féin leadership to an abandonment of violence in favour of political action.

Evidence of its leaders' conversion to a primarily political agenda led in December 1993 to the adoption by the two governments of the Downing Street Declaration, which in turn produced the hoped-for cessation of IRA violence and, in 1998, the Belfast Agreement.

That Agreement, and the negotiations that preceded it, were products of extraordinarily close and intimate co-operation between the Irish and British Prime Ministers. The February 2000 unilateral British suspension of the institutions established under this Agreement, as a result of an inability on the part of IRA/Sinn Féin and the Ulster Unionist Party to agree on the issue of decommissioning of IRA arms, created temporary tensions between the two governments. But their co-operation nevertheless remained close, for these events had bound them together in a totally new co-operative relationship – and the disagreement related to means rather than to ends. In the event, through the joint efforts of the two governments, the institutions were in fact successfully restored three months later.

The emergence of the new co-operative British/Irish relationship that produced this outcome had been greatly helped by the appearance in the 1990s of a new generation of British political leaders. John Major and Tony Blair were free of the "hang-ups" about Ireland shared by many of their predecessors – who had been people of an age to have personal memories of, and perhaps to have retained at least subconscious resentment about, Irish war-time neutrality. On the Irish side this development was paralleled by the emergence after 1992 of non-anglophobic Taoisigh such as Albert Reynolds, John Bruton and Bertie Ahern.

The common purpose of the two governments throughout this process was the achievement of a settlement that would result in the elected representatives of the two Northern Ireland communities working together to govern a peaceful and stable Northern Ireland, closely linked economically to the Republic, but remaining politically a devolved entity within the United Kingdom until and unless a majority of its citizens decided otherwise.

The institutional structure designed to give effect to the new relationship was necessarily complex. It provided, first of all, for a new power-sharing governmental structure within Northern Ireland which was to include an Assembly, to be elected by the single transferable vote in multi-seat constituencies and a First Minister, Deputy First Minister, and ten-person Executive Committee, to be elected by the Assembly through the D'Hondt system of proportional representation.

Next, there was provision for a north-south Ministerial Council to supervise a dozen co-operative or implementation bodies that would undertake a range of economic and social functions on an all-Ireland basis. These arrangements had the dual purpose of providing a link with the Irish state that would satisfy Northern nationalist aspirations to an eventual north-south political relationship, and of securing practical co-operation in respect of matters that could more effectively be handled on an all-Ireland basis than separately in the two parts of the island.

This institutional architecture was completed by structures designed to foster co-operation between Ireland and Britain – including a British-Irish Intergovernmental Conference to promote bilateral co-operation and a British-Irish Council.

The Intergovernmental Conference has the particular task of dealing with non-devolved Northern Ireland matters. Through this body the Irish government may put forward views and proposals. The Conference is co-chaired by the Secretary of State for Northern Ireland and the Republic's Minister for Foreign Affairs. It subsumes similar bodies established in 1981 and again in 1985, but in this new format there is provision for the involvement of relevant members of the Northern Ireland Executive in its meetings, and it is serviced by a standing joint secretariat of officials dealing with non-devolved Northern Ireland matters.

The British-Irish Council, however, is a body within which both parts of Ireland will be linked to Scotland, Wales, the Isle of Man, Guernsey and Jersey, as well as to England – although because of the undeveloped state of devolution in that part of the United Kingdom, England will, for the time being at least, be represented by the British Government.

The impetus for this Council seems to have come from the Unionists, who appear to have seen it as some kind of counterbalance to the North-South Ministerial Conference. It is not clear, however, that either the Unionists who proposed it, or the British government which agreed to it, thought through the full implications of establishing a body of this kind at this formative stage of the United Kingdom devolution process.

It already seems clear that some politicians in Scotland and Wales see this Council as a forum through which their devolved assemblies and executives can perhaps exert pressure on the Westminster government, seeking to use the experience – and in particular the recent economic success – of the independent Irish state as a means of seeking for themselves greater freedom of action.

If that is in fact what happens, it may not suit the agenda either of the Unionists in Northern Ireland or of the UK government – although such a development could, perhaps, be welcome to the Northern Ireland nationalist parties. For its part the Irish government could find itself awkwardly placed in the event that elements of conflicts between Westminster and devolved administrations within the UK come up for discussion in this new forum. Certainly there will be considerable interest outside these islands in the working of this unique forum, which, for the first time in political history, brings together within a consultative body both the internal devolved components and the sovereign government of a large state and political representatives of a neighbouring state.

These various bodies were established in late 1999, after many delays deriving from the decommissioning blockage. And, after the February-May 2000 suspension, they were restored.

IRELAND AND BRITAIN IN THE EU CONTEXT

Two other quite different factors, unrelated to Northern Ireland, have also made substantial contributions to the new and healthier relationship between the two states.

First, as a result of Ireland's EU membership, the extreme and unhealthy economic dependence of Ireland on Britain disappeared. This is symbolised by the fact that, whereas as recently as twenty years ago, Ireland's currency was not merely linked to sterling but actually *was* sterling, from 1979 onwards Ireland was a member of the EMS with a separate currency, and, since January 1999, its currency has been the euro. And, second, since 1993 the Irish economy has grown several times faster than that of any other European state, to the point where the purchasing power of its per capita GNP is now quite close to, and rapidly gaining on, the UK level – from which as recently as 1986 it had fallen short by some 40 per cent.

At the time when the European Economic Community was established in 1957, the Irish state had reached a turning-point in its economic history. Futile attempts to achieve economic self-sufficiency had combined with the impact on Irish agriculture of Britain's intensified post-war "cheap food" policy to create a state of economic stagnation that contrasted glaringly with the rapid economic growth that had been occurring everywhere else in Europe throughout the post-war period. Between 1956 and 1959 these failed policies were, however, dramatically reversed, a process that culminated in a move towards Irish involvement in the newly established EEC.

In 1961 Ireland sought accession to the Community – a decision taken in the context of a simultaneous British application for membership. The extent of continued Irish economic dependence on Britain was seen at that time as precluding accession on any other basis. However, the subsequent delay in EEC acceptance of Britain's application, and thus of Irish entry, provided a prolonged breathing-space during which to prepare Ireland's small, highly-protected, and correspondingly weak, industrial sector for the freeing of trade. From 1966 onwards this process of preparation was accelerated as a result of the negotiation of an interim ten-year Anglo-Irish Free Trade Agreement.

Since 1958 foreign industrial investment had been encouraged – instead of, as had previously been the case, actively discouraged – and from 1960 onwards a growth rate of well over four per cent had been achieved. The maintenance of this growth rate after the slowing-down of economic growth in Europe and elsewhere following the 1973 oil crisis, enabled the Irish economy to start the process of catching up with the economies of Britain – and of the European mainland.

REORIENTATION OF THE IRISH ECONOMY

During the period of preparation for EEC accession, certain aspects of Ireland's likely future relationship with Britain in the context of Community membership began to become clear. First of all, throughout the whole of the post-war period it had been evident that the British economy had continued to lag behind that of continental Europe – a relative decline that had started towards the end of the nineteenth century, and had continued without remission during the intervening three-quarters of a century. While intensified competition within the EEC might be expected to have some stimulatory effects on British industrial performance, it was far from clear that even under these new conditions British growth rates would rise to continental levels. Thus the closer linkage of the Irish economy to that of the continent that was made possible by Irish accession was likely to prove very beneficial to Irish growth – if Ireland could succeed in reorienting its production significantly towards the continent.

This would be especially true of Irish agriculture, the potential of which had never been adequately realised because of the impact of Britain's cheap-food policy since the mid-nineteenth century in the only market effectively open to Irish farmers. At the same time, experience of attracting foreign industrial investment during the 1960s – at that time mainly from Britain and Germany – suggested that accession to the EEC might in time attract to English-speaking Ireland a substantial volume of investment by US industries seeking access to the dynamic continental market.

Everything thus pointed towards a major reorientation of the Irish economy towards the continent of Europe following eventual accession to the EEC. If, as was hoped, the dynamic created by new foreign investment in Ireland came to outweigh losses in protected industry, it was possible that the historic gap between British and Irish levels of prosperity might within a quarter of a century or so of EEC accession be bridged.

In the event this is what happened – despite the fact that from 1980 onwards the British economy improved its performance, growing at a rate similar to that of its continental neighbours, and, despite the unexpectedly large impact of declining emigration upon the Irish population, the growth of which until the mid-1980s diluted significantly the effect of increased output upon Irish per capita incomes.

Between 1972 – the eve of Irish and British entry to the Community – and 1999, the volume of Irish exports rose twenty-fold and the proportion going to the UK fell from 62% to 22%, while the proportion shipped to the thirteen continental countries, now members of the EU, more than doubled, rising from 19% to 44%. As regards imports, the proportion bought from Britain fell during this period from 52% to 32%.

BENEFICIAL EFFECTS OF EU MEMBERSHIP ON ANGLO-IRISH RELATIONS

The conscious reorientation of the Irish economy towards the European continent, together with active Irish participation in the institutions of the European Community, contributed to the process of easing bilateral tensions between Ireland and Britain. Part of the reason for this was that the substantial reduction of Irish economic dependence on Britain, together with successful Irish involvement in the institutional processes of the Community, contrasted sharply with evident British discomfort in its new European context. This contrast boosted Irish self-confidence and gradually eroded a national inferiority complex that had persisted long after the ending of the former colonial, or semi-colonial, relationship with Britain.

Moreover, the opportunities for informal Anglo-Irish contacts in the margins of meetings of the Council of Ministers in its various formations, and later in the European Council of Heads of State and Government, helped greatly to ease tensions arising from the Northern Ireland crisis, especially in the years from 1973 to 1982. And thereafter these informal contacts contributed significantly to the process through which the two states moved towards a common Northern Ireland policy.

IRISH AND BRITISH ECONOMIC INTERESTS IN THE EU DIVERGE

However, it had always been inevitable that British and Irish approaches to the evolution of the European Community would differ. First of all, in Ireland emotional attachment to recently acquired political sovereignty co-existed with a realisation that had grown during the decades since independence that, in relations between large and small states, sovereignty was of limited value to the latter – whereas it could be, and often was, employed by the former to exploit smaller neighbours. Thus, larger states could, and did, impose trade restrictions on the products of other states – including small neighbours, the limited size of whose domestic markets made it difficult for them to become competitive.

Again, in the case of Britain, it had been public policy from the mid-nineteenth century onwards to keep down labour costs artificially by pursuing a cheap-food policy – permitting the free import of basic foodstuffs from overseas. In this way Britain sought to retain the advantage in global trade that it had initially secured by having been at the forefront of the Industrial Revolution.

For all these reasons a small, and at the time largely agricultural, country such as Ireland, which had suffered severely from the pursuit of such policies by its larger European neighbours, had a powerful interest in maximising the sharing of sovereignty within a European Community so as to minimise the damage capable of being done to its interests through the exercise of sovereignty by the larger states.

Moreover, for smaller countries the exclusive right of legislative initiative of the independent European Commission offers powerful protection against possible exploitation by large countries. This key element of the Community's institutional structure has meant that the bigger states cannot push through Community legislation that might damage the interests of their smaller partners. And the qualified majority voting system also makes it more difficult for any individual large country to hold up progress towards a genuine common market – which proved an especially important factor in the creation of the Single European

Market, from which Ireland greatly benefited.

Finally, and more mundanely, during the early years of the Community the interests of some of the continental member states in protecting their farm sectors against world competition, together with Germany's need to maintain income levels in its high-cost agricultural sector, had combined to set EEC farm prices at very high levels – and the Common Agricultural Policy ensured that the surpluses thus created were supported by Community subsidies. To a depressed Irish farm sector, all this was welcome at the time of entry – although clearly such a system could not be indefinitely sustained. During the early decades of Irish membership, when agriculture was still contributing between 10% and 20% of national output, this system provided an important medium-term boost to the Irish economy.

In addition, Ireland was bound to benefit not only from financial flows to its farm sector but also, as one of the poorer countries in the EEC at the outset, from the structural funds. Indeed, because Ireland was the only member state to benefit significantly *both* from the CAP *and* from the structural funds, for many years after its accession EEC budgetary transfers represented a higher share of Irish GNP than was the case with any other member.

All these advantages of membership contrasted markedly with Britain's situation after accession. By virtue of its past imperial history and its traditional reluctance to become over-embroiled in European affairs outside the defence area, Britain was bound to be reluctant to share more sovereignty with its new European partners than was absolutely necessary. Even when, as in the case of the Single European Act, Britain's material interests lay with the introduction of qualified majority voting to overcome the objections of more protectionist states, its preoccupation with sovereignty initially prompted it to vote against the calling of the Intergovernmental Conference that was necessary in order to remove the veto in relation to these matters.

In sharp contrast to Ireland, Britain was bound to be a substantial net financial loser in relation to transfers arising from the Common Agricultural Policy – a negative factor which in the public mind in Britain has persistently offset the far more substantial, but less obvious, advantages of securing free access to continental markets.

During the 1990s the most striking European policy divergence between the two states was in relation to membership of the euro.

In 1979, fifty-seven years after independence, Ireland had finally broken away from sterling to join the EMS. Twenty years later it brought this policy to its logical conclusion by participating in the establishment of Economic and Monetary Union. There was some division of opinion on the issue in Ireland, as a number of economic experts feared that this would make the Irish economy dangerously vulnerable to competition from the UK if sterling lost value vis-à-vis the euro. But these fears largely evaporated as sterling rose sharply in value in the aftermath of the establishment of EMU.

There has remained, of course, the inconvenience of having two different, and at times wildly fluctuating, currencies on either side of the Irish border. But this has been seen as a regrettable, but hopefully temporary, consequence of Britain's hesitation about joining EMU.

Other fears that the booming Irish economy might suffer from overheating as a result of lower interest rates have remained, and, in the immediate aftermath of the creation of EMU, were even intensified as a result of the expansionist budgetary policy being pursued during this period by the Irish Government.

As the subject of Britain and the euro is discussed in more detail in another chapter, it is sufficient to say here that Ireland would certainly be much more comfortable with a Britain that had joined the EMU and that employed the same currency as Ireland. It can be seen, therefore, that some key British and Irish interests within the Community were always bound to differ sharply, at any rate so long as economic issues rather than political ones tended to dominate – as in fact turned out to be the case during the first two decades of British and Irish membership.

It is notable, however, that the pursuit of divergent economic interests by the two states created no substantial tensions between them. The truth is that no state, however large, expects another to support its economic interests when the interests of that state clearly lie elsewhere. True, there have been a couple of occasions when in the heat of the moment such a proposition was put to an Irish Minister by a British colleague who seemed momentarily to have forgotten that Ireland was no longer subordinate to Britain – but these rare lapses were received on the Irish side with amusement rather than irritation! [4]

SHIFT OF EU EMPHASIS TOWARDS POLITICAL ISSUES

However, when the issues at stake become political, the relationship between large and small states can become more difficult. When larger states disagree amongst themselves on political issues, each may expect – and even pressurise – smaller states to fall in behind it. Failure to respond to such pressures can evoke displeasure – with potentially damaging consequences when some other interest of the smaller state later comes to be at issue. During the first two decades of the two countries' membership there were few, if any, tensions of this kind between Ireland and Britain.[5] During that period Ireland shared, of course, the concerns of other continental member states that Britain become a more co-operative and engaged member of the Community. But so far as Ireland was concerned, this view could be and was usually capable of being expressed in positive terms that gave no offence; Britain could hardly resent, for instance, Irish expression of a hope that Britain would play a more active role in the Community, to balance the dominant positions of France and Germany.

CLOSER IRISH-BRITISH LINKS ON POLITICAL ISSUES?

However, this situation began to change somewhat in the 1990s partly because political issues started to loom larger within what had now become the European Union, and also, from 1993 onwards, as a side-effect of the increasingly close co-operation between Ireland and Britain in relation to Northern Ireland.

Among the political issues that have come to the fore in recent years has been the Schengen Agreement on free movement of persons. Although Ireland would have liked to have enjoyed free movement of persons with the continental EU countries as well as Britain, at the time when Britain was opting out of Schengen, Ireland's need to preserve the Anglo-Irish common travel area absolutely required it to join Britain in remaining outside this new arrangement. When Britain decided early in 1999 to adhere to aspects of Schengen other than frontier control and immigration, Ireland followed suit. Ireland would certainly wish that British policy were otherwise on this issue, but recognises that it will take time for Britain to overcome its hang-ups about free movement of European people – other than the Irish! – to its shores. [6]

More recently, even in relation to some economic issues,

Ireland and Britain have found their interests coinciding rather than, as they have so often in the past, diverging. An example of this is the pressure emanating from some continental EU countries to harmonise corporate tax rates as well as the tax base – a matter in respect of which Ireland and Britain, as countries which have low corporate tax rates, share a common interest.

Moreover, although Ireland and Britain have diametrically opposed views on the role of NATO (Britain being an enthusiastic member, whilst Ireland has remained reluctant to become involved in any kind of military alliance), it suited Ireland – at least until the end of 1998 when the British position on European defence changed dramatically – to have Britain stalling on this European defence issue. Britain's Saint Malo change of stance on European defence has, however, had the effect of bringing this issue forward, and this is a development which – even if, as seems likely, Ireland remains free of Article 5 NATO and WEU commitments – could pose some problems for Irish politicians in presenting Irish involvement in European security policy to public opinion, which remains suspicious of any external military involvement not firmly under UN auspices.

It may well be, however, that this Irish problem will before long be resolved by an arrangement under which European external defence is undertaken by NATO with its Article 5 mutual defence provision, while internal European security, involving the Petersberg tasks, is looked after by a separate European structure involving a Rapid Reaction Force with a capacity to use NATO assets. Such a structure, free of Article 5 obligations, would be one in which Ireland, together with other European neutrals, could comfortably participate. It is not clear whether, despite a likely Article 5 opt-out, a further Irish referendum may appear constitutionally necessary following the IGC in late 2000.

As a major European power, a Blairite Britain seeking to play a more active European role might see itself doing so primarily through the European Council, seeing this as the most effective strategic body through which to direct the EU's fortunes. It is thus conceivable that the generally more positive stance of the Blair government towards Europe could increase the danger of the eventual emergence of some kind of informal European Union *directoire* involving at least the three larger member states, and perhaps all of the Big Five. Clearly, that would not be in the interest of a small country such as Ireland.

Even if this danger does not materialise, there will be some fears that the elevation of the essentially intergovernmental defence and security aspect to a more important role might shift the balance of Community activity away from the traditional system that centres on the Commission's exclusive power of legislative initiative. However, these fears may prove unrealistic: it is difficult to see how the intergovernmental decision-making system with regard to security could at this late stage in the evolution of the European Union significantly erode or damage the Community's unique 50-year-old decision-making structure.

An impetus towards a modified institutional structure in which the role of the Commission could be devalued is more likely to come from German, and perhaps also French, pressure to avoid the danger of dilution of the Union's cohesion following extensive enlargement. This might be achieved by creating a new federal-type structure amongst a core of existing member states – a structure designed to enable Europe to play a stronger role in world affairs in the face of the growing dominance of the United States as the sole super-power. If such a core group of states were to emerge with a less balanced decision-making structure, this could pose problems for small states such as Ireland – and these problems would be intensified were Britain to remain outside such a core group. It seems unlikely, however, that Tony Blair would accept exclusion from such a core group of states; if he were successful in securing British participation in EMU after the next British general election, he would presumably aspire to an equal role for Britain with France and Germany in any new institutional arrangements developed within the Union.

POSSIBLE BRITISH PRESSURES FOR CLOSER IRISH-BRITISH CO-OPERATION WITHIN THE EU

In the period ahead, there may be some British pressure for Ireland to move closer to Britain in its European policy. The emphasis placed by Tony Blair on British-Irish common interests in the EU when he addressed the Dáil in November 1998 suggests that this may represent the Irish element of a British effort to develop more intense bilateral relations with each of Britain's EU partners. It may even be the case that some of our continental EU partners perceive such a shift in the emphasis of Irish policy towards a closer relationship with Britain as being already under way.

The alignment of Irish and British stances in relation to the harmonisation of corporate taxation, about which some high-tax continental EU countries feel strongly, and the presentation of a joint British-Irish paper at the March 2000 Lisbon European Council, may indeed already have given this impression.

Goodwill towards Ireland, on the part of countries such as Germany and France, which has already weakened somewhat as Ireland has moved towards greater prosperity, could be at risk in these circumstances. It could well be the case that, in the future, tensions between Ireland's relationship with Britain on the one hand and with Germany and France on the other, which have hitherto been largely absent, might become more of a problem for Irish diplomacy.

There must at least be a possibility that a future stronger pull towards Britain, with which successive Irish Governments have had to work closely in seeking to resolve the Northern Ireland crisis, could conflict with Ireland's need to enjoy a capacity for independent action in the European sphere. As we move into the new century, maintaining a balanced relationship simultaneously with all three of our major European partners may pose a challenge to Irish diplomatic ingenuity.

NOTES

1 Fisk (1983), pp 22-34.
2 Fanning (1983), pp 124-25.
3 Document No. 2 Par. 7.
4 FitzGerald (1991), pp 172-73.
5 Although see also FitzGerald (1991), p.161 (Hattersley) and p.596 (Thatcher).
6 But see Meehan (2000).

SYNTHESIS

CHAPTER THIRTEEN

Synthesis and Conclusions

*Gerard O'Neill**

THE NATIONAL INTEREST

Three objectives are central to the Irish national interest: peace in Northern Ireland, economic and social progress in the Republic and positive engagement in the European Union. The following synthesis and conclusions primarily relate to the achievement of these objectives but, where appropriate, conclusions are also drawn for the Union as a whole since its continued success is also clearly in the national interest.

As stated in Chapter One, Introduction, developments in Britain impinge directly on Ireland to a greater extent than developments in other member states of the European Union. Given that connection, it is necessary to identify future scenarios for Britain, to assess them individually in terms of probability and then to analyse their implications for Irish policy. This methodology broadly informed the previous IEA study, completed in 1996, and is continued here for the sake of consistency, as well as completeness.

OVERVIEW

It is clear that the Blair government has embarked on what it regards as a fundamental reform of Britain. Virtually all aspects of the state and society are being recast in order to overcome the long-term relative economic decline that was necessarily inherent

---

* This final chapter represents a consensus of the views of the authors of this study.

in the loss of empire in the first part of the twentieth century and the failure to compensate for that loss during most of the second. The over-riding objective is to modernise Britain so that it can be equipped to face into the 21st century with a renewed sense of self-confidence and a shared belief that progress can replace decline.

It is immediately obvious that this is an ambition on the grand scale. Indeed, in terms of scale, it is somewhat analogous to the programmes of renewal undertaken in France and Germany after the Second World War and will require roughly the same period of time to succeed. But it is also clear that it lacks two of the essential ingredients which, each in its own way, made French and German success possible: consensus in society on what needed to be done and an institutional infrastructure capable of delivering on objectives. The Third Way may indeed be the best path to a competitive economy and a just society; and devolution may be the surest way of accommodating national and regional identities so as to protect the integrity of the state. However, a broad consensus across British society about objectives and instruments has yet to be developed and may prove to be impossible to achieve. The necessary institutional infrastructure will take much time and effort to complete and, while the foundations have been laid, there is no guarantee that the process of state and societal reform can be brought to a successful conclusion.

These broad conclusions suggest that, despite the efforts of the Blair government to make its reform programme irreversible, great uncertainty still attaches to the future of Britain. Everything will depend on the length of time the current government stays in office and, presuming it were to be successful in securing re-election at least once, upon its long-term capacity to stick with strategies and policies despite periodic resistance. Consequently, it is only prudent to emphasise the uncertainty which characterises the future of Britain in the run-up to the next election.

This consideration makes it all the more necessary to identify those changes inaugurated by the Blair government which, with a reasonable degree of confidence, can be said to be irreversible. For a start, the reform of the state structure has gone beyond the point of no return. The partial devolution of power to Scotland and Wales is intended to preserve the United Kingdom as a composite state; while this strategy is completely at variance with that of the Major government and with the instincts of the Conservative Party under William Hague, it has bedded down to the point where it could hardly be undone without endangering the very Union the Conservative Party wishes to protect. From this it can be concluded that a form of quasi-federalism is here to stay and the exceptionalism of Northern Ireland within the United Kingdom as a region with devolved powers is a thing of the past.

In relation to macro-economic management it is reasonable to conclude that the stability culture introduced by New Labour will survive. The consequences of eroding the Bank of England's new independence, which is the lynch-pin of the system, would be so damaging that any future government will be deterred from weakening or ending it. The stability culture has, moreover, been reinforced by a medium-term framework which imposes discipline on the conduct of the public finances and has been underpinned by supply-side measures designed to enhance the competitiveness previously achieved by Conservative governments. As a result, it is difficult to foresee a reversion to the failed policies of the past. The cycle of boom and bust which singularly characterised the British economy has been broken. This is good news for the Irish and wider European economy.

These two initiatives, partial reform of the state and a macro-economic stability culture, stand out as the two achievements of the Blair government which will have a lasting impact on the governance of Britain.

Beyond that, it would be unwise to reach definitive conclusions at this point. The process of state reform is ongoing and is sensitively poised at a stage where it could either lead to an entirely new constitutional order or be frozen in its current unfinished form. The future surely turns on a small number of key issues: the electoral system; an English parliament and/or regional assemblies; the House of Lords; and the future role of parliament. Much will depend on how the crisis of political and state identity plays out, especially in England. All that can be said now is that such innovations await future parliaments.

Equally, it is too soon to pronounce on the reform of society. The Blair government started to make this point itself in mid-2000 as it began to condition the electorate for the next election. The task of rebuilding state institutions and reinforcing delivery systems is of a different dimension to that encountered in France and Germany after the War where the advantage of starting *de novo*, as it were, was exploited in creating new forms of governance. It is altogether more difficult to convince an established functioning democracy of the necessity for a root-and-branch reform. The institutional inertia encountered so far, in the health and education systems, for example, indicates that "modernisation" and "globalisation" are not yet accepted as arguments for a general call to action.

Finally, it is far too early to make a judgement on the permanence of the Blair government's European policy. The question of what role Britain is to play in Europe will remain unresolved until the issue of British identity – as distinct from English identity – is broadly settled. The outcome of the next election may give some indication of the mood of the electorate with regard to Europe but a subsequent referendum on the euro would be a truer test. Until then, it is impossible to arrive at any conclusion, however tentative, and the best that can be done is to develop scenarios.

These scenarios, which are set out below, are constructed on an entirely different basis to that employed in the previous study. In 1996, Britain under a Conservative government could justifiably be described as the awkward partner in Europe. Under New Labour, Britain has been transformed into its "polar opposite" – by becoming a positive, proactive member state with aspirations to play a leading role in the construction of an enlarged Union. This, too, is a major achievement of the Blair government – but it represents only a starting point for the scenarios. This is in no way to diminish or denigrate the significance of New Labour's accomplishments in the short space of three years; it is merely a recognition of the facts. It is quite possible that Britain's new European policy will be sustained over the long term, but it is also possible that it will be abandoned. The scenarios take both possibilities into account.

The following synthesis looks at the implications for Ireland of Britain under Blair in terms of Northern Ireland, the economy and Europe.

BRITAIN'S UNFINISHED CONSTITUTION

As anticipated in the previous IEA study, constitutional reform has occupied a central part of the agenda of the New Labour government. The radical changes already introduced herald a fundamental and far-reaching reshaping of the British state. But they represent work in progress, not a finished settlement. Crucial elements to be completed include electoral reform, freedom of information, democratisation of the House of Lords, and the installation of a parliament and/or regional assemblies in England.

Periods of transition are always difficult to manage, and the greatest difficulties for Labour's programme of constitutional change undoubtedly lie ahead. They involve change from a polity defined by an unwritten constitution, absolute parliamentary sovereignty, adversarialism and centralised power to one based on devolution of political authority, consensualism, coalitions and entrenchment of rights.

Moreover, it is too early to tell whether the reforms so far initiated – including the establishment of a Scottish Parliament and a Welsh Assembly – are truly "finished". With New Labour now the only "unionist" party in Britain (in the sense of having a strong political presence in Scotland, Wales and England – as well as its commitment to preserving the United Kingdom), conflict can be envisaged between that party's desire to remain in power with a strong majority at the level of central government and the need to grant an acceptable degree of autonomy to Edinburgh and Cardiff. Inevitably, tensions will arise and the manner in which they are managed will be decisive for the future configuration of the state. For this reason, the constitutional project is to be regarded as unfinished business.

Scotland holds the key to the future of the United Kingdom. The UK's very existence depends on a Scottish presence. Without Scotland, a successor state would have to be created around England and, while it would undoubtedly exercise considerable influence in European and in international affairs, that influence would be less than that of the United Kingdom as a whole. It is understandable, therefore, that the primary objective of devolution is to prevent a break-up of the British state and it can be expected that the constitutional project may be subject to modification over time in order to avoid such an outcome. This observation will hold true irrespective of which party is in power in London. The proven capacity of the British state to reinvent itself in the face of new challenges could prove to be its greatest strength.

Nevertheless, devolution could have a paradoxical effect on the internal stability of the United Kingdom; the more successful it is in solving the Scottish and Welsh questions the more it will require that the English question be resolved. Since identity, nationality, sovereignty and citizenship are the core of New Labour's programme of constitutional reform it is only natural that they should impact on English public opinion, by drawing attention, for example, to issues as diverse as a democratic deficit at national level and economic inequality at the regional level. What is perceived as preferential treatment for Scotland, Wales and Northern Ireland is leading to English demands for parity. Finding a role for England in a reformed United Kingdom is thus a major challenge. Getting it right would be good news for Britain, and good news for Europe.

NORTHERN IRELAND

Two main scenarios are possible in respect of Northern Ireland, and both are predicated on the outcome of the larger project to redesign the United Kingdom. Devolution could be extended to England by another Blair government and the United Kingdom could evolve over time into its own particular form of quasi-federalism, with national and regional identities being successfully accommodated by varying or asymmetric degrees of devolved power. In such circumstances, the United Kingdom would remain intact, and the rich diversity of its constitutional arrangements would provide a benign environment for a Northern Ireland seeking to develop firmly established, enduring institutions based on consent. British-Irish relations would be enhanced, making it more likely that peace would be maintained in Northern Ireland.

Alternatively, the British devolution project could run into difficulties. In that case, the future of the United Kingdom would be highly problematic and the outcome could conceivably range from the reconstitution of a unitary state to the dissolution of the Union. Intermediate possibilities could encompass the maintenance of the status quo in terms of devolution but with severe tension between London, on the one hand, and Edinburgh and Cardiff on the other. Much may depend on the political complexion of the governments in each capital. The implications for Northern Ireland would obviously depend on which scenario prevailed at any given moment, but self-evidently the context would be less positive than that created by a successfully functioning quasi-federation.

Here, again, Scotland is germane. The Scottish presence within the United Kingdom provides the Unionist community with a degree of psychological reassurance that often goes unrecognised. Were it to be ended, then Northern Ireland could be destabilised. There is no way of knowing how the Unionist community would react in such circumstances, nor is it possible to predict the response of the nationalist community. These uncertainties highlight the interdependence of devolution in the UK, peace in Northern Ireland and, indeed, economic progress on the whole island of Ireland. They reinforce the belief that devolution will in the event be successfully managed by London for reasons of *realpolitik*, aside from those based on democratic values. In that context, a much higher probability can be assigned to the scenario in which the Belfast Agreement succeeds than to those in which it could falter.

However, it is worth noting that Northern Ireland will continue to be seen as a separate issue from the rest of the programme of constitutional change in the UK. A successful outcome to the Belfast Agreement will – in the context of the wider British political agenda – take Northern Ireland off that same agenda: it may only "go back on" the agenda if the wider programme of constitutional change in Britain begins to experience profound difficulty. The British-Irish Council will provide a forum for further discussion of north-south and east-west relations for the archipelago. The potential inclusion of separate representation for England – or English regions – on the Council could add a novel dimension to its deliberations and even to its contribution to political and economic developments in both Britain and Ireland.

EURONOMICS

The economic outlook for Britain has become clearer since the previous study in 1996. The reforms introduced by Conservative governments increased productivity and have been strengthened by New Labour. The stability culture based on independence for the Bank of England and discipline in the public finances constitutes a new policy paradigm for macro-economic management. This combination suggests that the economy will continue to grow steadily at a low rate of inflation. This is the expectation of the markets in 2000 as evidenced by similar UK and EU yields on ten-year bonds.

As a result of these positive developments it can be taken that the five criteria laid down by the Chancellor, Gordon Brown, for British entry into the euro can be met on economic grounds, as the OECD report of mid-2000 confirmed. Of course, the decision to join the euro is a political one, and the real issue is how quickly after the next general election a referendum on joining the euro will be held.

As to the outcome, there can be little certainty. If taken at face value, the opinion polls, which consistently show a two-to-one majority against joining, would indicate an overwhelming rejection. But New Labour's working hypothesis is that a majority in favour of membership can be won after the next election. The reasons for this belief appear to be subjective, although they may be borne out by qualitative research. What can be said, however, is that this belief puts a strong premium on the leadership capacity of the next government, particularly on Tony Blair, and on the "innate good sense" of the electorate (who will be expected to place economic advantage over political reservations, to put the debate at its starkest). There is simply no way of knowing whether both suppositions will prove to be correct. Furthermore, they may not be put to the test. Should New Labour return with a seriously reduced majority or the Conservative Party win the election then the referendum could be indefinitely postponed – or held much later into the life of the new parliament. For those reasons, scenarios for Britain's future role in Europe have to be highly qualified.

BRITAIN IN EUROPE

The Blair government has set out a clear policy for Britain's future role in Europe. Simply put, Britain is to play the part it should, and could, always have played as a large member state. This represents a total rejection not only of Conservative policy in the Thatcher/Major era but also of Labour's past hostility to Europe. Unfortunately for Europe, and for Ireland, this policy need not represent a permanent change. It could be thrown off course by failure to join the euro or by the re-emergence of Euroscepticism in government under a Conservative administration. It follows that all of the scenarios identified in the previous study are still potentially valid and that none can be rejected as being outside the realm of the possible.

The underlying cause of this continuing uncertainty is not the euro as such, but British antipathy to Europe itself. Sentiment in Scotland and Wales is generally more pro-European than in England, notably in the South-east. Furthermore, Scotland and Wales already possess some of the attributes, and share some of the attitudes, of small member states and devolution can only accentuate these differences with England. It seems reasonable in this context to assert by way of a general proposition that Britain's problem with Europe is England. It is there that the identity crisis is at its strongest. That it is far from resolved is obvious enough from the current euro debate.

SCENARIOS

The conclusions to *Britain's European Question: the Issues for Ireland* outlined five broad scenarios which, from an Irish perspective, ranged from the malign to the benign in terms of being able to participate in the core of the European Union. What follows is an analysis of these same scenarios in the light of subsequent developments in Britain. They have been reordered slightly to correspond more closely with the logic of the possible relationship between Britain and Europe, starting with Britain being outside the Union and ending with Britain inside as a European leader.

The Outsider
Originally this scenario envisaged Britain remaining outside some core EU competences, as with the Social Chapter and the euro. This scenario best explained the consequences of the Major government's hostility to deepening the integration process. It has been totally rejected by the Blair government. But it has taken on a deeper meaning because of the flexibility issue and because of arguments inside the Conservative Party that Britain should actually withdraw from the Union. The outsider scenario would become relevant again if Britain failed to join the euro and if an *avant-garde* were formed by the eurozone. Over time Britain would then become a *de facto* outsider. It might even become a *de jure* outsider if Euroscepticism took possession of the Conservative Party in power.

The Opportunist
The second scenario – the opportunist – would account for a generalised pattern of behaviour on the part of Britain whereby, on the basis of self-interest, it chose or refused to join new EU competences as they arose. For this scenario to apply Britain would respect the *acquis communautaire* up to a certain point and thereafter be permitted by other member states to pick and choose as it wished from the menu of common policies and core

competences. In effect, this is what the Major government set out to do but other member states took the view that British derogations were temporary and would be ended in time; hence, the logic of such a strategy was never subjected to the ultimate test. The preference of the Conservative Party is for a form of flexibility which would permit the UK to opt out permanently from some competences, probably including the euro. Such behaviour could be characterised by other member states as opportunistic and would thus likely lead towards the outsider scenario because of their hostility to such behaviour.

The Late Joiner

The late-joiner scenario reflects Britain's persistent refusal to join European projects from the beginning and then being forced to do so later. This is the best long-term account of the British approach to Europe from Attlee to Major. It has been rejected by the Blair government in respect of future developments but has been forced upon it to some extent in relation to the legacy of the Major government concerning the euro and the Schengen Agreement. The late-joiner syndrome is characteristic of a negative approach to Europe which the Blair government has set out to end. The scenario could apply to a future Conservative government which shied away from the full consequences of the outsider or opportunist scenarios.

The Gambler

The gambler scenario was previously used to describe a strategy of Britain joining each new EU initiative and then gambling on changing it later to its own needs. This scenario applied to the Community Budget, the CAP and, to some extent, the Single Market (in respect of the free movement of people aspect of this market). The instinct of the Blair government is to opt into policies from the outset and the gambler approach might become its option so as subsequently to reshape a policy from the inside, rather than seeking a derogation to stay outside. This would have the prime disadvantage that when negatively pursued it degenerates into the awkward-partner syndrome. But if positively pursued it could be highly creative, as might be the case on security and defence. The Conservative Party is less likely to play the role of gambler, being ideologically predisposed against deepening integration.

The Leader

The leader scenario contemplated a Britain "fully committed to playing a leader's role in shaping the future of Europe". Under the Major government this was seen as the least likely scenario. But under the Blair government it has become a reality. Britain now shares a leadership role in most key areas affecting the evolution of integration and in actively trying to redefine the finality of the Union. The maintenance of this leadership role is, however, conditional on Britain joining the euro. More accurately, it can be said to depend on the success of the New Labour project and/or the return of the Conservative Party to the policy stance of the Heath government. Consequently, no certainty can be attached to the permanence of the leadership role adopted by the Blair government.

IMPLICATIONS FOR EUROPE

The implications for Europe of these base scenarios are analysed below and range from a multi-level Europe to one where the unicity of the Union is preserved and enlargement successfully managed. When viewed in the round, they indicate that Britain has an inordinate capacity to influence the future shape of the Union. This has more to do with the unpredictability of its stance on integration than with its absolute weight within the process. It could, for example, play a unifying role across Europe by helping to fashion a Union which all European states would wish, or feel themselves compelled, to join. Alternatively, it could play a destructive role (albeit unwittingly) by opting to stay outside the core Union and so offering other states a role model to follow. These possibilities reinforce the argument advanced in Chapter One, Introduction, that other member states have a self-interest in facilitating the resolution of Britain's identity crisis with Europe.

The revised scenarios are as follows:

The Outsider: Multi-level Europe

The outsider scenario implies the indefinite continuation of the European Economic Area with Britain rejoining some of the original members of EFTA in terms of their external association with the Union. It runs two risks. On the one hand, it could encourage other member states to follow suit. Alternatively, all other European states could join the Union and leave Britain outside in isolation. Neither would be benign scenarios for Europe. Indeed, were Britain to see itself heading for isolation then it could entertain thoughts of joining, say, NAFTA, as some Conservatives would prefer. In practice, this scenario would lead to a multi-level Europe, with different states associated with a core Union in a widely differing series of relationships. These relationships would be permanent in the sense that each would represent the full extent to which a country was prepared to share sovereignty.

The Opportunist: Mosaic Europe

The opportunist scenario raises the prospect of what the previous study dubbed a mosaic Europe. This would consist of a multi-tiered structure with different member states entitled to pick from a mosaic of policies in accordance with their individual preferences. The most likely reaction from the "coalition of the willing" would be to construct a core Europe, with other states becoming its satellites. The result would be a patchwork of different "Europes", each defined by a specific policy area in which a particular group of states elected to co-operate. The patchwork would give rise to institutional confusion and would probably prove unworkable in the long run.

The Late Joiner: Multi-speed Europe

The late-joiner scenario contains more familiar implications since it broadly corresponds with the past and current British experience in Europe. It involves a Europe of "concentric circles" with a group of the most willing and able comprising the *avant-garde* of integration and with the others free to join later by mutual agreement. For this scenario to work, the assumption is that all the rest would join in eventually; otherwise it would simply lead to a mosaic Europe. At present, it describes the British position relating to the eurozone and the Schengen Agreement and may in future become the optimal strategy for deepening integration within an enlarged Union. If the Blair government continues in office, Britain would not be an obstacle to this way forward. Under the Conservatives, Britain might well become the cause of some other member states invoking flexibility as the only practical way forward. The underlying assumption, however, would be a Europe in which all member states eventually arrived at the same destination but at different times.

The Gambler: Unstable Europe

The gambler scenario could create tension between Britain and its European partners. Its most disturbing implication is that Britain would retain its own singular view of what integration entails and would be willing on occasion to ambush other member states after they thought that some contentious issue had been finally settled. In an enlarged Union, the gambler syndrome could be highly disruptive, especially if the British example were followed by other member states. It would create instability in the system at a time when certainty over the *acquis* is of over-riding importance as a precondition for the success of the enlargement process. An unstable Europe subjected to recurring crises, à la Mrs Thatcher, would be highly undesirable.

The Leader: A Balanced Europe

The leadership scenario has implications for the rest of Europe which can be viewed either as positive or negative. As a leader, Britain brings a better balance to the grouping of large member states constituting the collective political leadership of the Union by partially moderating the dominance of the Franco-German alliance. It also imports important democratic values into the European governance system. These, and other factors, are beneficial to the future construction of Europe. But the Blair government has continued the intergovernmental instincts of Britain and is intent on a qualitative change in the integration process which ultimately could dilute the central role of the Community method. Moreover, if pushed to an extreme in an enlarged Union, British leadership could lead to a *directoire* consisting of France, Germany and Britain, with Italy, Spain and Poland aspiring to be part of it. The implications of this development for small member states would be disturbing.

On balance, however, a leadership role for Britain is positive for Europe as, with Britain at its heart, the diversity of European traditions and values would be more truly reflected in its institutions and decision-making. The awkward partnership would be ended and replaced by a proactive partner which brought a unique set of qualities to the task of constructing Europe. The outcome would be a Europe with the maximum potential to reconcile widening with deepening.

IMPLICATIONS FOR IRELAND

It has been taken as axiomatic throughout this study that Irish policy on Europe has been, and will remain, to stay at the core of the integration process. This strategy reflects the view that the Irish national interest is best served by participating as fully as possible in all Union competences and supporting the deepening of the integration process. In the previous study the scenarios then put forward for Britain's role in Europe were analysed for their compatibility with the central thrust of Ireland's European policy and in terms of their implications for British-Irish relations in respect of Northern Ireland. This methodology remains valid and is employed below in analysing the overall implications for Ireland of the scenarios developed both for Britain and for Europe.

The implications for Ireland of each of the revised scenarios are set out below:

The Outsider: Multi-level Europe

The outsider scenario, giving rise to a multi-level Europe, would be the most malign outcome for Ireland. It has the greatest potential to create friction between Irish and British interests on European matters and could also introduce complications in Northern Ireland, should the nationalist community baulk at virtual exclusion from the Union. In addition, a deterioration in competitiveness would remain a constant threat as, with Britain outside the euro, sterling could fluctuate over time. The interdependent relationship with Britain that has been built up in the multilateral context of the Union would be adversely affected, with a tendency for the relationship to drift back towards a bilateral one, in which the smaller partner is always at a disadvantage. The management of such a relationship could limit the freedom of Ireland to stay at the core of Europe. All in all, the implications of the outsider scenario strongly suggest that this scenario is the most malign for the Irish national interest.

The Opportunist: Mosaic Europe

The opportunist scenario leading to a mosaic Europe is less negative in its implications for Ireland, but would still be disturbing overall. At worst, Britain would freeze its involvement in the integration process at its current level and an *avant-garde* of some EU states would eventually go on to create something approximating to a federation. This scenario would leave Ireland outside the Schengen Agreement, for example, and expose the economy to the vagaries of the euro/sterling exchange rate. The problem of staying in the EU core would be magnified. In a fractured Europe, the pursuit of national interests would become far more complex than would otherwise be the case.

The Late Joiner: Multi-speed Europe

A multi-speed Europe involving Ireland travelling faster than Britain within the integration process has been the norm since both countries entered the EEC and its implications are well known. Generally speaking, they have been carefully managed by the two sides and there have been few negative effects on British-Irish relations, since they have been conducted in a multi-lateral context. From an Irish perspective, this scenario is relatively benign, although the euro/sterling relationship could cause competitiveness problems intermittently and could hamper cross-border economic developments.

The Gambler: Unstable Europe

Britain has been a gambler in the past in respect of key EU policies and the cause of tension with its partners. Paradoxically, this posture can work to the benefit of Ireland, when it acts as a mediator between Britain and the other states (for example, during the 1970s in relation to the Community Budget and direct elections to the European Parliament). It can also work the other way round, of course, the CAP being a case in point. These past experiences suggest that the implications of the scenario would depend on the actual cause of individual disputes as Britain tried to renegotiate part of the *acquis*.

The Leader: A Balanced Europe

In broad terms, a successful Union would be in Ireland's national interest, bringing greater economic opportunities in an enlarged Union founded on functioning democracies throughout Europe. It would provide space for Northern Ireland to work out its own destiny. But Britain as an EU leader would have some negative implications if it contributed to the creation of a *directoire* and by possibly making defence a core competence of a new form of Union in which the Community method was delegated to second place in preference to enhanced intergovernmentalism. All other small member states would, however, share the problem of how best to protect their national interests in such circumstances. The most benign interpretation of this scenario would be one in which Britain contributed positively to enlarging the Union in such a way that its current institutional balance was maintained and the role of small member states protected.

CONCLUSION

The election of New Labour in 1997 has opened up a series of possibilities for Britain which could transform its society and economy and settle its role in Europe. It is inevitable that in the early stages of any programme of fundamental reform the process should appear to be chaotic at times and the outcome uncertain. Neither should be allowed to detract from an understanding of the ultimate goals. This analysis has attempted to disentangle ambitions from the mass of everyday events and to analyse them for their long-term implications should they be fulfilled. In those terms, it can be concluded that Blair's Britain, as currently under construction, could go a long way towards resolving the identity issue identified in the previous study, and now generally accepted as a fact of British life. It would also permit the other dimension of the crisis to be resolved over time by securing a role for Britain in Europe consistent with its new-found identity. All this would imply a more positive and predictable environment for Britain's relationships with Europe in general and Ireland in particular.

But it has become apparent throughout this study that Blair's Britain faces formidable obstacles which could delay or even frustrate the reform programme's achievement. Indeed, the identity crisis may be about to enter a more dangerous phase with clashes over competing visions of Britain's internal governance and external relations growing stronger in the heat of a general election campaign and a subsequent referendum on the euro. In short, things may get worse before they get better. The analysis to date provides no dependable guidelines for anticipating the outcome.

The degree of uncertainty over Britain's future makes it all the more essential to develop a range of scenarios covering all the main probabilities and to identify their more important strategic implications. This concluding chapter has been one attempt in that direction. On some future occasion, the task may be less demanding and the results more definitive because of greater certainty on the part of the British peoples about their collective destiny.

References

Adams, Christopher (2000), "Treasury extends its influence by setting high targets", *Financial Times*, 19 July.

Ahern, Bertie (1998), "The Western Isles of Europe at the Millennium", The Lothian European Lecture, 29 October.

Ahern, Bertie (2000), "Ireland and the EU: Future Prospects", address to Institute of European Affairs, 21 March.

Ahmed, Kamal (2000), "The Blair Interview: 'I'll stop doing this job but I'll always be a father'" *The Observer*, 9 April.

Alibhai-Brown, Yasmin (2000), *Who do We Think We are? Imagining the New Britain*, London: Allen Lane, The Penguin Press.

Auer, Peter (1999), *Employment Revival in Europe*, International Labour Organisation.

Baker, David and Seawright, David (1998), *Britain For and Against Europe, British Politics and the Question of European Integration*, Oxford: Clarendon Press.

Baldwin, Tom (2000), "Kilfoyle accuses Chancellor of failing the poor", *The Times*, 28 March.

Baldwin, Tom (2000a), "Mandelson hints at deal on voting reform", *The Times*, 29 June.

Baldwin, Tom and Watson, Roland (2000), "Egos at the ready", *The Times*, 29 June.

Barnett, Anthony (1997), *This Time: Our Constitutional Revolution*, London: Vintage.

Barnett, Anthony (1999), "Corporate control", *Prospect*, 38, February, pp 24-29.

Barnett, Anthony (2000), "Parliament in Flux II: Busy Doing Nothing", *Times Literary Supplement*, 11 February.

Barnett, Anthony (2000a), "Corporate Populism and Partyless Democracy", *New Left Review* 3, second series, May/June, pp 80-90.

Barnett, Corelli (1995), *The Lost Victory, British Dreams, British Realities 1945-50*, London, Macmillan.

Barret, Gavin (1997), *EMU – The Third Stage, Treaty and Non-Treaty Basis of EMU*, Dublin: Institute of European Affairs.

Barry Jones, J. (1999), "The First Welsh National Assembly Election", *Government and Opposition*, 33 (2), (1999), pp 323-32.

Bell, Alex (2000), "Blair takes on Tories in attempt to raise Labour morale north of border", *The Irish Times*, 11 March.

Bell, Alex (2000a), "Scottish devolution tarnished by rising cost of building a chamber for the parliament", *The Irish Times,* 7 April

Bell, Alex (2000b), "Despite bad start, 62% of Scots think parliament should have more power", *The Irish Times*, 10 May.

Berrington, Hugh ed., (1998), *Britain in the Nineties, the Politics of Paradox*, special issue of *West European Politics*, 21 (1), January.

Blackburn, Robert and Plant, Raymond (eds) (1999), *Constitutional Reform: The Labour Government's Constitutional Reform Agenda*, London: Longman.

Black, Conrad (2000), submission to US International Trade Commission, reported in Fenton (2000).

Black, Ian (2000), "Blair courts the little guys of Europe", *The Guardian*, 22 June.

Black, Ian and White, Michael (2000), "Poverty pleas win Britain £3bn in EU aid", *The Guardian*, 27 June.

Blair, Tony (1995), address to Royal Institute of International Affairs, 5 April.

Blair, Tony (1996), 'Blair on the Constitution', *The Economist*, 14 September.

Blair, Tony (1997), speech at the Royal Ulster Agricultural Show, 16 May.

Blair, Tony (1997a), speech to Labour Party conference, 30 September.

Blair, Tony (1997b), speech to Lord Mayor's banquet, Guildhall, "The principles of a modern British foreign policy", 1 November.

Blair, Tony (1998) "A Modern Britain in a Modern Europe", speech in The Hague, 20 January, available in Tony Brown (ed), *European Document Series,* 20, Institute of European Affairs, Summer (1998), pp 6-12.

Blair, Tony (1998a), *The Third Way: New Politics for the New Century*, London: Fabian Society.

Blair, Tony (1998b), speech to French National Assembly on the Third Way, 24 March.

Blair, Tony (1998c), speech in Scotland, 12 November, reported in English (1999).

Blair, Tony (1998d), speech at Lord Mayor's banquet, 22 November.

Blair, Tony (1998e), speech to Oireachtas, *The Irish Times*, 27 November.

Blair, Tony (1999), National Changeover Plan statement, House of Commons, 23 February.

Blair, Tony (1999a), speech on "Nato, Europe, our future security", 8 March.

Blair, Tony (1999b), "Doctrine of the International Community" Chicago speech, 22 April.

Blair, Tony (1999c), statement to the House of Commons on the Nato summit in Washington, 26 April.

Blair, Tony (1999d), "The New Challenge for Europe", Aachen speech, 14 May.

Blair, Tony (1999e), speech to Labour Party conference, 30 September.

Blair, Tony (1999f), "Britain in Europe", London IMAX, 14 October.

Blair, Tony (1999g), Interview with *The Daily Telegraph*, 19 October, transcript available at http://www.number-10.gov.uk

Blair, Tony (1999h), speech at Lord Mayor's Banquet, 22 November.

Blair, Tony (2000), "Committed to Europe, Reforming Europe", speech at Gent, 23 February.

Blair, Tony (2000a), speech to Scottish Parliament, 9 March.

Blair, Tony (2000b), "Values not institutions make us British", speech to regional newspaper editors, 28 March.

Blair, Tony (2000c), interview with *The Observer*, 9 April.

Blair, Tony (2000d), speech to Labour Party Conference, 26 September.

Blair, Tony (2000e), speech to Warsaw Stock Exchange, 6 October.

Blair, Tony and Aznar, Jose-Maria (2000) "A Europe bolstered by a single currency", *Financial Times*. 13 June.

Blair, Tony and Persson, Göran (2000), "Reaching out to all of Europe", *Financial Times*, 21 September.

Blair, Tony and Schroder, Gerhard (1999), *Europe: The Third Way - die Neue Mitte*, London: Labour Party and SPD.

Bogdanor, Vernon (1999), "The British-Irish Council and Devolution", *Government and Opposition*, 33 (2), pp 287-298.

Bogdanor, Vernon (1999a), "Decentralisation or Disintegration?", *The Political Quarterly,* 70 (2), pp 185-194.

Bogdanor, Vernon (1999b), *Devolution in the United Kingdom*, Oxford: Oxford University Press.

Brittan, Samuel (1995), *Capitalism with a Human Face*, London: Edward Elgar.

Brittan, Samuel (2000), "Beware the politics of sterling", *Financial Times*, 13 April.

Brockliss, Laurence and Eastwood, David (eds) (1997), *A Union of Multiple Identities: The British Isles, c. 1750-c. 1850:* Manchester: Manchester University Press.

Bromley, Catherine and Curtice, John (1999), "Way out, bad news for Tony Blair: the public is not showing any sign of warming to the 'third way'", *The Guardian*, 29 November.

Bronson, Lisa (1999), briefing on "An American Perspective on Developments in European Security" by Deputy Assistant Secretary of Defense for European and Nato Affairs, Institute of European Affairs, Dublin, 10 March.

Brown, Alice (1999), "The New State of Scotland?" paper delivered to roundtable meeting, "Redefining relationships: North-South and East-West links in Ireland and Britain in the new Millennium", Department of Politics, UCD, 8 January.

Brown, Alice, McCrone, David and Paterson, Lindsay (1998), *Politics and Society in Scotland*, 2nd ed., London: Macmillan.

Brown, Colin (2000), "Blair assembles his battle fleet", *The Independent on Sunday*, 25 June.

Brown, Gordon, (1997), statement on Bank of England, *The Financial Times*, 7 May.

Brown, Gordon (1997a), Commons speech on EMU, 27 October, *Financial Times*, 28 October.

Brown, Gordon (1999), speech to TUC 'Unions and euro' conference, 13 May.

Brown, Gordon (2000), "This is the time to start building a Greater Britain", *The Times*, 10 January.

Brown, Kevin, Crooks, Ed and Martin, Peter (2000), "CBI to stop promoting UK's entry to euro-zone", *Financial Times*, 31 January.

Buller, Jim (2000), *National Statecraft and European Integration: The Conservative Government and the EU, 1979-97*, London: Continuum.

Buller, Jim (2000a), "Understanding Contemporary Conservative Euro-Scepticism: Statecraft and the Problem of Governing Autonomy", *The Political Quarterly*, 71 (3) July-September, pp 319-327.

Buckler, Steve and Dolowitz, David P. (2000), "New Labour's Ideology: A Reply to Michael Freeden", *The Political Quarterly*,

71 (1), January-March, pp 102-109.

Bulmer, S. and Burch M. (1998), "Organising for Europe: Whitehall, the British State and European Union", *Public Administration*, 76, Winter, pp 601-628.

Bulpitt, James (1983), *Territory and Power in the United Kingdom: An Interpretation*, Manchester: Manchester University Press.

Burch, M. and Holliday, I. (1999), "The Prime Minister's and Cabinet Office: an executive office in all but name", *Parliamentary Affairs*, 52 (1) January.

Burns, Jimmy and Ward, Andrew (2000), "Crackdown on soccer hooligans urged", *The Financial Times*, 2 July.

Butler, David (2000), "Apathy may turn out to be PM's big enemy", *Financial Times* 30 June.

Butler, D. and Kavanagh, D., (1997), *The British General Election of 1997*, London: Macmillan.

Cabinet Office (1999), *Modernising Government: Action Plan*, July.

Cabinet Office (1999), *Professional Policy-making for the Twenty-first Century*, September.

Cannadine, David (1998), *Class in Britain*, London: Penguin.

Cassen, Bernard (2000), "Naissance de l'Europe SA", *Le Monde Diplomatique*, Juin, pp 14-15.

Castle, Stephen (2000), "Europe to offer Nato seats to defence bodies", *The Independent*, 17 February.

Carvel,. John (2000), "Heckled, jeered, booed - Blair bombs at the WI", *The Guardian*, 8 June.

Carvel, John (2000a), "Labour stakes credibility on 5-year NHS revolution", *The Guardian*, 28 July.

Charter 1988 (2000), report on constitutional reform, June.

Chirac, Jacques (2000), speech to Bundestag in Berlin, 27 June.

Cohen, Robin (2000), "The incredible vagueness of being British/English", *International Affairs*. 73 (3), pp 575-582.

Colley, Linda (1992), *Britons: Forging the Nation 1707-1837,* London: Pimlico.

Colley, Linda (1999), "Britishness in the 21st Century", Millennium Lecture at 10, Downing St, 8 December, available from http://www.number-10.gov.uk

Conservative Party (2000), *Believing in Britain*, mini-manifesto, 5 September.

Cook, Robin (1997), "The British Presidency - giving Europe back to the people", speech to IEA, Dublin, 3 November.

Cox, Michael, Guelke, Adrian and Stephen, Fiona (eds) (2000), *A Farewell to Arms, From 'long war' to long peace in Northern Ireland,*

Manchester: Manchester University Press.

Coyle, Diane and Castle, Stephen (2000), "Early euro entry would risk stability, says Bank Governor", *The Independent*, 12 April.

Cronin, James E. (1999), "New Labour in Britain: avoiding the past", *Current History*, 98 (627), April, pp 180-186.

Crooks, Ed (2000), "North-south divide widening", *Financial Times*, 21 August.

Currie, David (2000), "The Pros and Cons of EMU", update of February (1997) report, Economist Intelligence Unit.

Curtice, John (2000), "Class acts", *The Guardian*, 22 March.

Curtice, John (2000a), "Heartland Blues", *The Guardian*, 12 May.

Curtice, John (2000b), "Getting things in proportion", *The Guardian*, 6 July.

Curtice, John (2000c), "Voting where it counts," *The Guardian*, 20 October.

The Daily Telegraph (1999), "Most Scots have no wish to separate from their 'fellow-citizens' the English", commentary by Anthony King, 15 April.

The Daily Telegraph, (1999a), opinion poll on Labour government, 5 October.

Dahrendorf, Ralf (1999), "The Third Way and Liberty", *Foreign Affairs*, 78 (5), pp 13-17, September/October.

Davies, Norman (1999), *The Isles, A History*, London: Macmillan.

Davies, Ron (1999), "Devolution: a Process not an Event", address to conference organised by the Institute of Welsh Affairs and Cardiff University, 4 February.

Davies, Peter (1999), "Undoing Britain", *Economist* feature, 6 November.

Denman, Roy (1996), *Missed Chances, Britain and Europe in the Twentieth Century*, London: Cassell.

Denver David and Hands, Gordon (1997), "Turnout", chapter in Norris and Gavin (eds) (1997), pp 212-224.

Department of Trade and Industry (1999), *UK Competitiveness Indicators*, London.

Dodd, Vikram and Watt, Nicholas (2000), "Labour to force pace on euro", *The Guardian*, 30 August.

Donnelly, Rachel (2000), "Regional inequalities in UK are catapulted to the centre stage", *The Irish Times*, 13 April.

Donoghue, Jill and Keatinge, Patrick (1999), *The Security of Europe, Actors and Issues*, Dublin: Institute of European Affairs.

Driver, Stephen and Martell, Luke (1998), *New Labour, Politics after*

Thatcherism, Cambridge: Polity Press.

Duchêne, François (1994), J*ean Monnet, the first statesman of Interdependence*, London and New York: W.W. Norton.

Dummett, Ann (1999), "Citizenship and National Identity", chapter 12 in Hazell (ed) (1999), pp 213-229.

Dungey, J. and Newman, I. (eds) (1999), *The New Regional Agenda*, London: Local Government Information Unit.

The Economist (2000), "The patriot game", 1 April.

The Economist (2000a), "The Ceaucescu moment", 10 June.

Elcock, Howard and Keating, Michael (1998), *Remaking the Union, Devolution and British Politics in the 1990s*, London: Cass.

Elliot, Larry (2000), "Nickels and dimes", *The Guardian*, 15 September.

English, Shirley (1999), "United we stand, divided we fail, Blair tells Scots", *The Times,* 13 November.

Erdem, Esra and Glyn, Andrew (2000), "Northern exposure", *The Guardian*, 4 April.

European Commission, London office (2000), report on British media coverage of the EU, 12 April.

European Council (1999), Cologne Presidency Conclusions, 4 June.

European Council (1999a), Helsinki Presidency Conclusions, 11 December.

Fallessen, Leif Beck (1993), talk on Danish EU policies, Institute of European Affairs, Dublin, 18 March.

Fanning, Ronan (1983), *Independent Ireland*, Dublin: Helicon.

Fanning, Ronan (2000), "John Bull should get red card", *Sunday Independent*, 25 June.

Fenton, Ben (2000), "Britain has much to gain by joining Nafta pact", 12 April.

Financial Times (1999), opinion poll on industry's attitude to the euro, 1 November.

Financial Times (2000), Wales survey, 1 March.

Financial Times (2000a), Regional Development Agency survey, 11 May.

Finlayson, Alan (1999), "Third Way Theory", *Political Quarterly*, 70 (3), July-September, pp 271-279.

Fischer, Joschka (2000), "From Confederacy to Federation - Thoughts on the finality of European integration", speech at Humboldt University, Berlin, 12 May.

Fisk, Robert (1983), *In Time of War: Ireland, Ulster and the Price of*

Neutrality,   London: Andre Deutsch.

FitzGerald, Garret (1991), *All in a Life, An Autobiography*, Dublin and London: Gill & Macmillan.

FitzGerald, Garret (1997), "The Tories who stayed at home", *The Times*, 12 May.

FitzGerald, Garret (1999), "Former ties to US in question as Blair bids to lead Europe", *The Irish Times*, 21 May.

FitzGerald, Garret (2000), "Keeping eye on new ideas for EU integration" *The Irish Times*, 20 May.

FitzGerald, Garret (2000a), "Dilemma over our European and NI policies", *The Irish Times,* 27 May.

Foreign and Commonwealth Office (1999), *Concordat on International Relations.*

Foley, Michael (1999), *The Politics of the British Constitution*, Manchester: Manchester University Press.

Freeden, Michael (1999), "The Ideology of New Labour", *Political Quarterly*, 70 (1), January-March, pp 42-51.

Freedland, Jonathan (1998), *Bring Home the Revolution: The Case for a British Republic*, London: Fourth Estate.

Freedland, Jonathan (2000), "Under pressure", *The Guardian*, 28 June.

Gamble, Andrew and Wright, Tony (eds) (2000), *The New Social Democracy*, Oxford: Blackwell.

Gamble, Andrew and Wright, Tony (eds) (2000), "The End of Britain?", special issue of *The Political Quarterly* 71 (1), January-March.

Gamble, Andrew and Kelly, Gavin (2000), "The British Labour Party and Monetary Union", *West European Politics* 23 (1), January, pp 1-15.

Garton Ash, Timothy (1999), "Ten Years in Europe", *Prospect*, 46, July.

Garvin, Tom (2000), "The French are on the Sea", Chapter 4 in O'Donnell (ed.) (2000).

George, Stephen (1994), *An Awkward Partner: Britain in the European Community*, 2nd ed., Oxford: Oxford University Press.

George, Stephen (1998), *The Intellectual Debate in Britain on the European Union*, Paris: Notre Europe, October.

Giddens, Anthony (1998), *The Third Way*, Cambridge: Polity Press.

Giddens, Anthony (2000), *The Third Way and its Critics*, Cambridge: Polity Press.

Gillespie, Paul (ed.) (1996), *Britain's European Question: the Issues for Ireland*, Dublin: Institute of European Affairs.

Gillespie, Paul (ed.) (1996a), *Britain's European Question: the Issues for Ireland - Seminar Papers*, Dublin: Institute for European Affairs.

Gillespie, Paul (1999), "Multiple Identities in Ireland and Europe", in Ronit Lentin (ed.), *The Expanding Nation: Towards a Multi-Ethnic Ireland*, Department of Sociology, Trinity College, Dublin, pp 8-15.

Gillespie, Paul (2000), "From Anglo-Irish to British-Irish Relations", Chapter 13 in Cox, Guelke and Stephen (eds) (2000).

Gillespie, Paul (2000a), "Optimism of the Intellect, Pessimism of the Will – Ireland, Europe and 1989", *Irish Studies in International Affairs*, vol 11, (2000) forthcoming.

Gillespie, Paul (2000b), "Chirac has set the scene for a 'grand transition' debate", *The Irish Times,* 1 July.

Gould, Philip (1998), *The Unfinished Revolution, How the Modernisers Saved the Labour Party,* London: Abacus.

Gowland, David and Turner, Arthur (2000), *Reluctant Europeans: Britain and European Integration, 1945-1998*, Harlow: Pearson Education.

Grant, Charles (1998), *Can Britain Lead in Europe?* London: Centre for European Reform.

Grant, Charles (1999), "Britain and the EU in (1999)", Centre for European Reform paper for Foreign and Commonwealth Office seminar, 6 January.

Grant, Charles (2000), "Intelligence test", *Prospect* 53, June, pp 21-25.

Grant, Charles (2000a), "Danger of the nuclear umbrella", *Financial Times* 29 June.

Grant, Charles (2000b), *EU 2010: An Optimistic Vision of the Future*, London: Centre for European Reform.

Gray, A.G. and Jenkins, W.I. (1999), "British Government and Administration 1997-98: Modernisation and Democratisation", *Parliamentary Affairs*, 52 (2) April.

Gray, Andrew and Jenkins, Bill (2000), "Government and Administration (1998)-99: Overcoming 'Conservatism' - A Job half Done?", *Parliamentary Affairs* 53 (2), April, pp 219-241.

Gray, John (1997), *False Dawn: The Delusions of Global Capitalism*, London: New Press.

Gray, John (2000), "We need a new electoral system to end our European policy limbo", *The Guardian,* 9 June.

Gray, John and Osmond, John (1997), *Wales in Europe - the Opportunities presented by a Welsh Assembly*, Cardiff: Welsh Centre for International Affairs.

Grice, Andrew (1999), "Blair 'arrogance' is turning off voters, says secret report", *The Independent*, 15 September.

Groom, Brian (1999), "A Federal England?", *Financial Times*, 31 March.

Groom, Brian (1999a), "Regional policy running out of steam", *Financial Times*, 15 December.

Groom, Brian (2000), "Cutting to the core of the problem", *Financial Times*, 14 March.

Groom, Brian (2000a), "Blair plays a New British card amid devolution fears", *Financial Times*, 29 March.

Groom, Brian (2000b), "Blair accused over north-south gap", *Financial Times*, 10 April.

Groom, Brian (2000c), "Tories 'would stay in euro if Labour had taken Britain in'", *Financial Times*, 22 May.

Groom, Brian (2000d), "Caught in the middle of euro debate", *Financial Times*, 7 June.

Groom, Brian (2000e), "Blair calls on national leaders to play more active role in EU", *Financial Times*, 19 September.

Groom, Brian and Brown, Kevin (2000), "Brown wants productivity drive", *Financial Times*, 4 April.

Groom, Brian and Brown, Kevin (2000a), "Mandelson sees stability inside the euro", 17 May.

The Guardian (1999), editorial, "The perils of Europe", 15 December.

The Guardian (2000), editorial, "What is Britishness?", 28 March.

The Guardian (2000), three features on Blair's euro dilemma, 23-25 May.

Guibernau, Montserrat (1999), *Nations without States, Political Communities in a Global Age*, Cambridge: Polity Press.

Guibernau, Montserrat (2000), "Spain: Catalonia and the Basque country", pp 55-68 in O'Neill and Austin (eds) (2000).

Hague, William (1998), "The Potential for Europe and the Limits to Union", speech to INSEAD Business School, Fontainebleau, 19 May.

Hague, William (1999), "Identity and the British Way", Centre for Policy Studies, 19 January.

Hague, William (1999a), "No to a federal Europe", speech in Budapest, 13 May.

Hague, William (1999b), "Strengthening the Union after Devolution", speech to Centre for Policy Studies, 15 July.

Hague, William (1999c), interview with the *Financial Times*, 1

November.

Hall, Stuart (1998), "The great moving nowhere show", *Marxism Today*, November/December, pp 8-14.

Hall, Stuart and Jacques, Martin (1989), *New Times*, London: Lawrence & Wishart.

Halligan, Brendan (1981), "Is Britain on the way out of the Common Market?", *The Sunday Independent*, 7 September.

Halpin, Brendan (2000), "Who are the Irish in Britain? Evidence from Large-scale Surveys", Chapter 5 in Andy Bielenberg, (ed.) (2000), *The Irish Diaspora*, Harlow: Pearson.

Hargreaves, Ian and Christie, Ian (eds) (1998), *Tomorrow's Politics: The Third Way and Beyond*, London: Demos.

Harris, Robert (2000), interview with Tony Blair, *Talk* magazine, April.

Harvie, Christopher (2000), "The Moment of British Nationalism, 1939-1970", *The Political Quarterly*, 71(3), July-September, pp 328-340.

Hattersley, Roy (2000), "The secret socialist at Number 11", *The Guardian*, 13 March.

Hattersley, Roy (2000a), "In search of the Third Way", *Granta* 71, Autumn 2000, pp 229-255.

Hazell, Robert (ed.), (1999), *Constitutional Futures, A History of the Next Ten Years*, Oxford: Oxford University Press.

Hazell, Robert (1999a), "Make up or break up", *Financial Times,* 3 February.

Hazell, Robert and O'Leary, Brendan (1999), "A Rolling Programme of Devolution: Slippery Slope or Safeguard of the Union?", Chapter 3 in Hazell (ed.), (1999), pp 21-46.

Hazell, Robert (2000), "Loose Ends", *Prospect*, 56, October, pp 14-17.

Heffer, Simon (1999), *Nor Shall My Sword: The Reinvention of England,* London: Weidenfeld & Nicholson.

Heisbourg, Francois (2000), "Europe's Strategic Ambitions: The Limits of Ambiguity", *Survival*, Summer, pp 5-15.

Held, David (1998), "Globalisation, The Timid Tendency", *Marxism Today*, November/December, pp 24-27.

Hennessy, Peter (1997), "The Blair Style of Government: An Historical Perspective and an Interim Audit", *Government and Opposition*, 33 (1), pp 3-20.

Hetherington, Peter (2000), "Nudge and Fudge", *The Guardian*, 13 March.

Hetherington, Peter (2000a), "Anger over Livingstone's Nazi

jibe", *The Guardian* , 29 June.

Hetherington, Peter (2000b), "Assemblies all round", *The Guardian*, 26 June.

Hindmoor, Andrew (2000), "Public Policy 1998-99: A Honeymoon Ending?", *Parliamentary Affairs*, 53 (2), April, pp 262-274.

HM Government (2000), *IGC: Reform for Enlargement, the British Approach to the European Union Intergovernmental Conference 2000*, Cm 4595, February.

HM Treasury (1997), *UK Membership of the Single Currency: An Assessment of the Five Economic Tests*, London: October.

HM Treasury (1998), *Pre-Budget Report*.

HM Treasury (2000), *Budget Report*.

Hickman, Mary (2000), "'Binary Opposites' or 'Unique Neighbours'? The Irish in Multi-ethnic Britain", *The Political Quarterly*, 71 (1) January-March, pp 50-58.

Holliday, Ian (2000), "Is the British State Hollowing Out?" *The Political Quarterly*, 71 (2), April/June, pp 167-176.

Hopkins, A.G. (1999), "Back to the Future: From National History to Imperial History", *Past & Present*, 164, August, pp 198-243.

Howorth, Jolyon (2000), "Britain, France and the European Defence Initiative", *Survival* 42 (2), Summer, pp 33-55.

Hughes, Kirsty and Smith, Edward (1998), "New Labour - New Europe?", *International Affairs*, 74 (1), pp 93-104.

Hurd, Douglas (2000), "Decline and fall of a government", *Financial Times*, 14 March.

Hutton, Will (1994), *The State We're In*, London: Cape.

International Monetary Fund (1999), *Global Equilibrium Exchange Rates,* Working Paper 99/175.

Institute of European Affairs (1996), *Intergovernmental Conference: Issues, Options, Implications*. Dublin: IEA.

The Irish Times, (1999), *Scotland and Ireland* supplement, 30 November.

Jenkins Commission (1998), *Report of the Independent Commission on the Voting System,* vols 1 & 2, London: The Stationery Office, 9 December.

Jones, George and Shrimsley, Robert (2000), "PR referendum is not a promise says Blair", *The Daily Telegraph*, 11 January.

Jones, Nicholas (1999), *Sultans of Spin: the Media and the New Labour Government*, London: Gollancz.

Kaletsky, Anatole (2000), "Sending an SOS for the incredible sinking euro", *The Irish Independent*, 24 August.

Kearney, Hugh (1997), "Contested ideas of nationhood", *The Irish Review*, 20, Winter/Spring, pp 1-22.

Kearney, Hugh (2000), "The importance of being British", *The Political Quarterly*, 71 (1), January-March, pp 15-25.

Keating, Michael (1998), "What's Wrong with Asymmetrical Government?", pp 195-226 in Elcock and Keating eds., (1998).

Kellner, Peter (2000), "Summertime blues hit the Tories as Blair jumps back", *The Observer*, 13 September.

Kennedy, Charles (1999), "The British Question", speech to the Scottish Council Foundation, Edinburgh, 30 June.

Kennedy, Charles (2000), "Give power to the regions, or the kingdom could fall apart", *Independent on Sunday*, 9 April.

Kennedy, Dennis (2000), "Acclaimed history gets Ireland alarmingly wrong", *The Irish Times*, 2 October.

Kennedy, Geraldine (2000), "Ahern in constitutional dilemma over suspension", *The Irish Times*, 15 February.

Kite, Melissa (2000), "Scotland 'gets far too much money'", *The Times*, 23 June.

Krieger, Joel (1999), "Beyond the intrigues, Britain, New Labour and the Global Age", *Harvard International Review* XXI (2), pp 42-52.

Krieger, Joel (1999a), *British Politics in the Global Age*, Cambridge: Polity Press.

Krusell, Stuart (2000), IEA briefing by the Executive Director of the World Affairs Council of Boston, 23 March.

Kupchan, Charles A. (2000), "In Defence of European Defence: An American Perspective", *Survival* 42 (2), Summer, pp 16-32.

Kymlicka, Will (1998), *Finding Our Way: Rethinking Ethnocultural Relations in Canada*, Ontario: Oxford University Press.

Laffan, Brigid, Smith, Michael and O'Donnell, Rory (2000), *Europe's Experimental Union: Rethinking Integration*, London: Routledge.

Laffin, M. and Thomas, A. (1999), "The United Kingdom: Federalism in Denial", *Publics: The Journal of Federalism*, 29 (9) Summer 1999, pp 89-107.

Laffin, Martin (2000), "Constitutional Design: A Framework for Analysis", *Parliamentary Affairs*, 53 (3), July, pp 532-41 – Introductin to a section on "Designing a New Democracy: Devolution in the UK".

Lancaster, Thomas D. (1999), "Complex Self-identification and

Compounded Representation in Federal Systems", pp 59-89 in Joanne B. Brzinski, Thomas D. Lancaster and Christian Tuschhoff, (eds) special issue of *West European Politics*, 22 (2), April, on "Compounded Representation in West European Federations".

Leadbetter, Charles (1999), *Living on Thin Air: The New Economy*, London: Viking.

Lee, Joe (2000), "Jack Straw tells it like it is and the 'Brits' don't like it", *The Sunday Tribune,* 16 January.

Leicester, Graham (1998), "Devolution and Europe: Britain's Double Constitutional Problem", pp 10-22 in Elcock and Keating (eds), (1998).

Leicester, Graham (1999), "Questions of image and a new reality", Scotland and Ireland supplement, *The Irish Times*, 30 November.

Lentin, Ronit (ed.)(1999), *The Expanding Nation: Towards a Multi-Ethnic Ireland*, Dublin: Trinity College, Dublin, Department of Sociology.

Leonard, M. (1997), *Britain TM: Renewing Our Identity*, London: Demos.

Livingstone, Ken (2000), "The real national debate that Labour can duck no longer", *The Independent*, 22 August.

Lloyd, John (1999), "Falling Out", *Prospect* 45, October, pp 22-27.

Lockwood, Christopher (1999), "Foreign unit for devolved bodies", *The Daily Telegraph*, 14 January.

Loughlin, John (1999), "Wales: Fractured Nation or Dynamic Region?", paper to roundtable meeting on "Redefining relationships: North-South and East-West links in Ireland and Britain in the new Millennium", Department of Politics, University College Dublin, 8 January.

Lynch, P. (1999), *The Politics of Nationhood: Sovereignty, Britishness and Conservative Politics*, London: Macmillan.

Lynch, Philip (2000), "The Conservative Party and Nationhood", *Political Quarterly*, 71 (1), January-March, pp 59-67.

Maclay, Michael (2000), "A mission for Britain", *Prospect*, 50, March, pp 22-26.

McKibbin, Ross (1999), "Mondeo Man in the Driving Seat", *London Review of Books* 21 (19), 30 September.

McKibbin, Ross (2000), "Make enemies and influence people", *London Review of Books* 22 (14) 20 July.

McKibbin, Ross (2000a), "New Labour: Treading Water?", *New Left Review* 4, second series, July/August, pp 69-74.

McLaughlin, Dan (2000), "UK euro entry would ease Irish inflation", 24 August.

Major, John (1999), *The Autobiography*, London: HarperCollins.

Maples, John (2000), "Dear William: what you're doing wrong", *The Times*, 15 February.

Marquand, David (1999), "Pluralism v. populism", *Prospect* 42, June, pp 27-31.

Marquand, David (2000), *The Progressive Dilemma, from Lloyd George to Blair*, London: Phoenix.

Marquand, David (2000a), "Revisiting the Blair Paradox", *New Left Review* 3, second series, pp 73-79.

Marr, Andrew (2000), *The Day Britain Died*, London: Profile.

Marr, Andrew (2000), "Just when you thought it was safe…", *The Spectator*, 5 February.

Mawson, John (1998), "English Regionalism and New Labour", in Elcock and Keating (eds), (1998), pp 158-175.

Meehan, Elizabeth, (1999), "The Belfast Agreement – Its Distinctiveness and Points of Cross-fertilisation in the UK's Devolution Programme", *Parliamentary Affairs*, 52 (1).

Meehan, Elizabeth (2000), *Free Movement between Ireland and the UK: from the "common travel area" to The Common Travel Area*, Studies in Public Policy 4, Dublin: The Policy Institute.

Meehan, Elizabeth, (2000a), "Europe and the Europeanisation of the Irish Question", in Cox, Guelke and Stephen (eds), (2000).

Millar, Frank (2000), "Devolved 'New Britain' must tackle the English question", *The Irish Times,* 11 January.

Millar, Frank (2000a), "Mo's palace remarks do not presage republican plot", *The Irish Times*, 29 June.

Millar, Frank (2000b), "Polls show protests have dealt Labour a blow", *The Irish Times,* 18 September.

Miller, William L. (1998), "The Periphery and its Paradoxes", pp 167-196 in Berrington (ed.) (1998).

Miller, William L. (1999), "Modified Rapture All Round: The First Elections to the Scottish Parliament", *Government and Opposition*, 33 (2), (1999), pp 299-322.

Milne, Kirsty (2000), "The Lib Dems need a bit of spin", *The Observer*, 9 April.

Mitchel, James and Leicester, Graham (1999), *Scotland, Britain and Europe, Diplomacy and Devolution*, Edinburgh: Scottish Council Foundation.

Modood, Tariq (1999), "New Forms of Britishness: Post-immigration Ethnicity and Hybridity in Britain", in Lentin (ed.)

(1999), pp 34-40.

Moscovici, Pierre (1999), address to Institute of European Affairs, Dublin, 7 July.

Mulgan, Geoff (1998), "On a Whinge and a Prayer", *Marxism Today*, November/December.

Nairn, Tom (1994), *The Enchanted Glass, Britain and its Monarchy*, London: Vintage.

Nairn, Tom (1998a), "Nations – breaking up is hard to do", *Marxism Today*, November/December, pp 40-2.

Nairn, Tom (2000), *After Britain: New Labour and the Return of Scotland*, London: Verso.

National Centre for Social Research (1999), *British Social Attitudes* survey, 30 November.

New Statesman (2000), issue featuring debate on the monarchy and a republic, 4 August.

Nicoll, Alexander (2000), "Defence orders go to Europe", *Financial Times*, 17 May.

Nicholson, Mark (2000), "Scotland and Wales 'unhappy with devolution'", *Financial Times,* 23 February.

Norris, Pippa and Gavin, Neil P. (1997), *Britain Votes 1997*, Oxford: Oxford University Press.

North Atlantic Council (1999), Washington summit *communique* issued by the Heads of State and Government, 23 and 24 April.

North Atlantic Council (1999a), "The Alliance's Strategic Concept", approved 23 and 24 April.

O'Brien, Patrick (1999), "Imperialist Balance Sheet", *New Left Review,* 238, November/December, pp 48-80.

The Observer (1999), opinion poll on the Labour government, 26 September.

The Observer (2000), opinion poll on the health service, 16 January.

The Observer (2000a), editorial on the monarchy and a republic, 23 July.

OECD (1988), *UK Economic Survey*, Paris.

OECD (1999), *Economic Outlook*, December.

OECD (2000), *OECD Economic Surveys: United Kingdom.*

O'Leary, (1999), pp 24-26.

O'Leary, Brendan (1999a), "The Nature of the British-Irish Agreement", *New Left Review*, 233, pp 66-96.

O'Leary, Brendan (1999b), "Four options, one way forward", *Financial Times*, 11 November.

O'Leary, Brendan (2000), constitutional aspects of suspension, *The Irish Times,*

O'Neill, Michael (2000), "Great Britain: From Dicey to Devolution", in O'Neill and Austin (eds) (2000), pp 69-95.

O'Neill, Michael and Austin, Dennis (2000), "Democracy and Cultural Diversity", special issue of *Parliamentary Affairs*, 53 (1), January.

Osborn, Andrew (2000), "EU support hits new low", *The Guardian*, 25 July.

O'Toole, Fintan (2000), "Britain on the brink", interview with Tom Nairn, *The Irish Times*, 15 January.

Owen, Geoffrey (1999), *From Empire to Europe*, London: HarperCollins.

Parekh, Bhiku (2000), "Defining British National Identity", in Gamble and Wright (eds) (2000), pp 4-14.

Parekh Report, The (2000), *The Future of Multi-ethnic Britain*, London: Profile Books/Runnymede Trust.

Partridge, Simon (1999), *The British Union State – imperial hangover or flexible citizens' home?*, London: Catalyst, pamphlet 4, January.

Partridge, Simon (1999a), "The Irish diaspora and devolved democracy in the British-Irish islands", *Times Change*, Summer.

Partridge, Simon (2000), "The many Englands: implications for UK devolution, the Council of the Isles and a more federal Europe", paper to Friedrich Ebert Foundation/University of Tubingden symposium, 1 July.

Paul, William (1999), "Blair must settle score", *Scotland on Sunday*, 19 December.

Paxman, Jeremy (1998), *The English: a portrait of a people*, London: Penguin.

Peston, Robert (1999), "Blair hits out at Eurosceptic press", *Financial Times,* 14 December.

Pickard, Jim (2000), "Growth of devolution needs 'patient' nurturing", *Financial Times*, 27 March.

Pike, Alan (2000), "Call to prevent erosion of council powers", *Financial Times*, 28 June.O'Donnell, Rory (ed.) (2000), *Europe, The Irish Experience*, Dublin: Institute of European Affairs.

Prescott, John (2000), "Narrowing the north-south divide", *Financial Times,* 22 August.

Pricewaterhouse Coopers (2000), *European Economic Outlook*, London.

Qvortrup, Mads (1999), "Spain's rolling programme of devolution", in Hazell and O'Leary (eds) (1999).

Rawnsley, Andrew (2000), "Forty-eight hours from meltdown", *The Observer,* 17 September.

Rayner, Jay (2000), "London's choice: a second term: I'll be London", *The Observer*, 30 April.

Redwood, John (1999), *The Death of Britain?* London: Macmillan.

Rees-Mogg, William (2000a), "Why Tony Blair really fears Livingstone", *The Times*, 15 May.

Rhodes, R. A. W. (2000), "New Labour's Civil Service: Summing-up Joining-up", *Political Quarterly* 71 (2), April/June, pp151-166.

Riddell, Peter and Fletcher, Martin (1999), "Prodi calls Britain in from the cold", *The Times*, 14 December.

Riddell, Peter, (2000), "Worries at the front of Blair's mind", *The Times*, 7 January.

Riddell, Peter (2000a), "Stay-at-home voters to turn backs on Labour", *The Times*, 31 March.

Riddell, Peter (2000b), "Blair fails to bridge class divide", *The Times*, 29 June.

Riddell, Peter (2000c), "[Electoral] Issue goes to the heart of 'the project'", *The Times*, 29 June.

Riddell, Peter (2000d), "Tories lead Labour on law and pensions", *The Times*, 28 July.

Ritchie, Murray (2000), *Scotland Reclaimed, the Inside Story of Scotland's First Democratic Parliamentary Election*, Edinburgh: The Saltire Society.

Robbins, Keith (1998), "Britain and Europe: devolution and foreign policy", *International Affairs*, 74 (1), pp 105-118.

Robertson, George (1999), "The Alliance and military capabilities for European security", address to 50th anniversary conference at the United Services Institute, London, 8 March.

Royal Institute of International Affairs (1997), *An Equal Partner: Britain's role in a changing Europe*, final report of Commission on Britain and Europe.

Ryan, Alan (1999), "Britain: Recycling the Third Way", *Dissent*, Spring, pp 77-80.

Sabin, Philip A.G. (1996), "Britain in Europe: Defence and Security Aspects", in Gillespie (ed.) (1996a), pp 157-168.

Safran, William and Maiz, Ramon (eds) (1999), *Identity and Territorial Autonomy in Plural Societies*, special issue of *Nationalism and Ethnic Politics* 5 (3&4), Autumn/Winter.

Salmond, Alex (1999), "Scotland - a European Nation", address to Institute of European Affairs, Brussels, 16 February.

Saloman Smith Barney (2000), *Sterling Weekly*, 4 January.

Sassoon, Donald (1999), *The New European Left*, London: Fabian Society.

Schake, Kori, Block-Lainé, Amaya and Grant, Charles (1999), "Building a European Defence Capability", *Survival* 41 (1), Spring, pp 20-40.

Schonfield, Andrew (1972), *Europe: Journey to an Unknown Destination*, London: Allen Lane.

Schröder, Gerhard and Amato, Giuliano (2000), "We are serious about the future of Europe", 28 September.

Schwend, Joachim (1999), "The federal option for the UK", paper to British Council "Looking into England" conference, available at www.britishcouncil.org/studies/england/schwend.htm

Seitz, Raymond (1998), *Over Here*, London: Trafalgar Square.

Seymour-Ure, Colin (1997), "Newspapers: Editorial Opinion in the National Press", chapter in Norris and Gavin (1997), pp 78-100.

Shrimsley, Robert (2000), "Blue is the colour, power is the aim," *Financial Times*, 7/8 October.

Siedentop, Larry (2000), *Democracy in Europe*, London: Allen Lane, The Penguin Press.

Smyth, Patrick (1999), reports on Florence Third Way summit, *The Irish Times*, 29 October

Smyth, Patrick (2000), "'Core group' ideas alter Irish-EU perspective", *The Irish Times*, 20 June.

Solana, Javier Madariaga (1999), "Nato's new roles and missions", address to the Nato 50th anniversary conference at the United Services Institute, Whitehall, 8-9 March.

Solana, Javier Madariaga (1999a), Washington summit statement, 24 April.

Solana, Javier Madariage (2000), "The Development of a Common Foreign and Security Policy and the Role of the High Representative", address by the Secretary-General of the European Council and High Representative for the EU Common Foreign and Security Policy, Institute of European Affairs, Dublin, 30 March.

Sparrow, Andrew (2000), "Gap between the rich and poor grows under Blair", *The Daily Telegraph*, 13 April.

Sparrow, Nick (1999), "Decisions, decisions", *The Guardian*, 9 December.

Straw, Jack (2000), "Human rights and political wrongs", *The Observer*, 13 August.

Stephens, Philip (1999), "Liberated by Europe", *Financial Times*, 26 February.

Stephens, Philip (1999a), "Think Euro-politics", *Financial Times*, 18 June.

Stephens, Philip (2000),"A dangerous lack of direction", *Financial Times*, 31 January.

Stephens, Philip (2000a), "Behind the mask of Blairism", *Financial Times*, 28 April.

Stephens, Philip (2000b), "The revenge of Middle England", *Financial Times*, 31 August.

Studler, Donald T. (1999), "Unwritten Rules - Britain's Constitutional Revolution", *Harvard International Review* XXI (2), pp 48- 52, Spring.

Sylvester, Rachel (1999), "How Blair's 'secret burden' in bringing Labour to a halt", *The Independent on Sunday*, 18 July.

Talbott, Strobe (1999), "A new Nato for a new era", address to the Nato 50th anniversary conference at the United Services Institute, Whitehall, 9 March.

Talbott, Strobe (1999a), "America's Stake in a Strong Europe", remarks at Chatham House conference, 7 October.

Taylor, Alan ed. (2000), *What a State! Is Devolution for Scotland the End of Britain?* London: HarperCollins.

Timmins, Nicholas (2000), "Gap shifts between the haves and the have-nots", *Financial Times*, 27 January.

Tomaney, John (1999), "New Labour and the English Question", *The Political Quarterly* 70 (1), January-March, pp 75-82

Tomaney, John and Mitchell, Michelle (1999), *Empowering the English Regions*, London: Charter 88, Reinventing Democracy, Paper no. 6, September.

Tonra, Ben (ed) (1997), *Amsterdam, What the Treaty Means*, Dublin: Institute of European Affairs.

Toolis, Kevin (2000), "Race to the right", *The Guardian*, 20 May.

Travis, Alan (2000), "Labour's troubles pile up", *The Guardian*, 19 January.

Travis, Alan (2000a), "Support for royal family falls to new low", *The Guardian*, 12 June.

Travis, Alan (2000b), "Labour slump puts Tories ahead", *The Guardian*, 19 September.

Travis, Alan (2000c), "Britain becoming more equal, voters say", *The Guardian*, 17 October.

Vaz, Keith (1999), speech to Wilton Park conference on "The EU after 2000", 1 November.

Verhofstadt, Guy (2000), "A Vision for Europe", speech to European Policy Centre, Brussels, 21 September.

Wainwright, Hillary (2000), "Silencing the left", *The Guardian*, 24 July.

Walker, David (2000), "Northern slights", *The Guardian*, 22 June.

Wallace, Helen (1997), "At Odds with Europe", *Political Studies*, XLV, pp 677-688.

Ward, Lucy (2000), "Kennedy warns Blair on electoral reform", *The Guardian*, 20 March.

Watkins, Alan (2000), "Rover and poll reform may rebound on Mr Blair", *The Independent on Sunday*, 19 March.

Watkins, Alan (2000a), "Blair won't take a lead on Europe until after election", *The Independent on Sunday*, 21 May.

Watt, Nicholas (2000), "Personal feuds fire Labour's euro dispute", *The Guardian*, 17 June.

Watt, Nicholas and Ward, Lucy (2000), "Hague to champion NHS and schools in centre bid", *The Guardian*, 22 June.

Webster, Philip and Riddell, Peter (2000), "Cook push for early euro poll", *The Times*, 30 June.

Weir, Stuart (2000), "Beyond our Ken", *Red Pepper* 70, April.

Wellings, Ben (2000), "England's Occluded Nationalism", *Arena journal*, no. 14 (1999)-(2000), pp 99-112.

White, Michael (1999), "Blair hails middle class revolution", *The Guardian*, 15 January.

White, Michael and Elliott, Larry (2000), "Tories attack Labour's underspending", *The Guardian*, 1 July.

White, Stuart (1998), "Interpreting the Third Way': Not one road but many", *Renewal*, Spring.

Whitehead, A. (1999), "From regional development to regional devolution", in Dungey and Newman (eds), (1999).

Whiteley, Paul (1999), "Quids in – or out", *The Guardian*, 22 June.

Whiteley, Paul (2000), "Paper politics", *The Guardian*, 11 April.

Whiteley, Paul (2000a), "Vote tote", *The Guardian*, 1 June.

Whiteley, Paul and Seyd, Patrick (1999), "A question of priorities", *The Guardian*, 27 September.

Whiteley, Paul and Seyd, Patrick (2000), "Vote winners", *The Guardian*, 11 January.

Whiteley, Paul (2000), "If apathy rules", *The Guardian*, 18 February.

Whiteley, Paul (2000a), "Euro choice", *The Guardian*, 29 August.

Wintour, Patrick (2000), "Labour tries to reclaim the flag", *The Guardian*, 28 March.

Wintour, Patrick (2000a), "Ministers urged to respect rank and file", *The Guardian*, 8 May.

Wintour, Patrick (2000b), "Blair urged to delay election", *The*

Guardian, 8 May.

Wintour, Patrick (2000c), "The rhetoric and the reality: how ministers' claims of success check out", *The Guardian*, 14 July.

Wintour, Patrick (2000d), "Class-ridden UK exposed in new study", *The Guardian*, 12 July.

Wintour, Patrick, Keller, Peter and Browne, Anthony (2000), "Poll deals tax and health blow to Blair", *The Observer*, 16 January.

Wright, Tony and Chen, S. (2000), *The English question*, London: Fabian Society.

Wring, Dominic Baker, David and Seawright, David (1999), "Panel games", *The Guardian*, 9 November.

Wolf, Martin (2000), "A decisively indecisive policy towards the euro", *Financial Times*, 10 January.

Worcester, Robert (2000), *How to Win the Euro Referendum: Lessons of 1975*. London: Foreign Policy Centre.

Young, Hugo (1998), *This Blessed Plot, Britain and Europe from Churchill to Blair*, London: Macmillan.

Young, Hugo (1999), "Blair must stop acting dumb and speak out on Europe", *The Guardian*, 15 June.

Young, Hugo (1999a), "Blair will fight for the single currency. Eventually", *The Guardian*, 17 June.

Young, Hugo (1999b), "Cook (almost) rushes in where Brown fears to tread", *The Guardian*, 7 September.

Young, Hugo (1999c), "The only answer is yes", *New Statesman*, 1 November.

Young, Hugo (2000), "Procrastinating Blair risks humiliation by his enemies", *The Guardian*, 13 January.

Young, Hugo (2000a), "What is Britishness? Tories dream while Labour defines", *The Guardian*, 28 March.

Young, Hugo (2000b), "Never mind the economics, the euro is a political issue", *The Guardian*, 4 July.

THE INSTITUTE OF EUROPEAN AFFAIRS (IEA)

Patron: Mary McAleese, President of Ireland

Comité d'honneur: An Taoiseach Bertie Ahern; David Byrne; John Bruton; Albert Reynolds; Patrick Hillery; Garret FitzGerald; Charles J. Haughey; Richard Burke; Padraig Flynn; Ray MacSharry; Michael O'Kennedy; Peter Sutherland.

The Institute of European Affairs is an independent self-governing body which promotes the advancement and spread of knowledge on the process of European integration and, in particular, on the role and contribution of Ireland within Europe.

The Institute provides a permanent forum for the identification and development of Irish strategic policy responses to the continuing process of European integration and to the wider international issues which impact on Europe. The main aim is to provide objective analysis of the key political, economic, social and cultural issues for those charged with representing Irish views within the European policy-making structures. This is done by facilitating policy discussion with inputs from all relevant sectors, assembling information on key topics and disseminating research results.

As an independent forum, the Institute does not express an opinion of its own. The views expressed in publications are solely the responsibility of the authors.

The legal form of the Institute is that of a company limited by guarantee and not having share capital. It is funded by annual membership subscriptions from companies, organisations, institutions and individuals. A number of foundation members enable the Institute to operate on a financially secure basis.

Institute of European Affairs

FOUNDATION MEMBERS

A & L Goodbody
Aer Lingus
Aer Rianta
AIB Bank plc
An Post
Arthur Anderson
Bank of Ireland
Bord Failte
Bord Gais
Bord na Mona
CERT
CRH plc
Deloitte & Touche
Eircom
Electricity Supply Board
Enterprise Ireland
Ericsson
Esat Telecom
FBD Insurances plc/
   Irish Farmers Journal/IFA
FEXCO
First Active
FitzPatrick Hotel Group
Forbairt

FORFAS
Glen Dimplex
Goldman Sachs
Guardian PMPA
Guinness Ireland Ltd
IBEC
IDA Ireland Ltd
Independent Newspapers plc
Irish Dairy Board
Irish Distillers
Irish Life & Permanent plc
Kerry Group plc
National Irish Bank
National Treasury Management
Agency
RTE
Siemens Limited
SIPTU
Smurfit (Ireland) Limited
Tesco Ireland Ltd
The Irish Times
Ulster Bank
VHI
Waterford Crystal plc

Institute of European Affairs

CORPORATE MEMBERS

Agriculture and Food,
  Department of
All Party Oireachtas
  Committee on the
  Constitution
Amárach Consulting
Arthur Cox
Arts, Heritage, Gaeltacht and
  the Islands, Department of
ASTI
Attorney General/Chief State
  Solicitors Office, Office of
  the
British Embassy
Central Bank
Church of Ireland Working
  Group on Europe
Clissman H & Sons
Citibank
Committee on European
  Affairs of the Irish
  Episcopal Conference
Construction Industry
  Federation
Defence, Department of
Defence Forces Library
Dept. of History UCC
Director of Public
  Prosecutions, Office of the
Dublin City University
Dublin Corporation
EBS
Education and Science,
  Department of

Embassy of the Czech
  Republic
Embassy of Greece
Embassy of the Republic of
  Cyprus
Embassy of the Republic of
  Hungary
Equality Authority
Enterprise, Trade and
  Employment, Department
  of
Environment and Local
  Government, Department
  of the
European Commission Library
  Service
European Foundation for the
  Improvement of Living &
  Working Conditions
FÁS
Finance, Department of
Foreign Affairs, Department
  of
Fyffes
Government of Quebec
  London Office
Health and Children,
  Department of
Higher Education Authority
ICOS
ICTU
IMPACT
INTO
Irish Bankers Federation

Irish Ferries
Irish Intercontinental Bank
Irish Management Institute
Justice, Equality and Law
	Reform, Department of
Leargas
Local Government
	Management Services
Marine and Natural Resources,
	Department of the
McCann FitzGerald,
NCB Group
NESC
NorDubCo
Northern Ireland Public Sector
	Enterprises
Office of the Director of
	Telecommunications
	Regulation
Ombudsman, Office of the

Public Enterprise, Department
	of
Revenue Commissioner, Office
	of the
Royal Danish Embassy
Royal Norwegian Embassy
Ryan Hotels plc
Social, Community and Family
	Affairs, Department of
Taoiseach, Department of the
Teagasc
Tipperary Rural Business
	Development Institute
TSB Bank
UCC
UCD
Udaras na Gaeltachta
University of Dublin Trinity
	College
University of Limerick
Wavin Ireland Ltd

Institute of European Affairs

PUBLICATIONS

STUDIES IN EUROPEAN UNION

The New Third Pillar: Cooperation Against Crime in the European Union (2000)
Editor: Eugene Regan
ISBN 1-874109-53-2, 228 pages, IR£15.00/€19.00

Europe: The Irish Experience (2000)
Editor: Rory O'Donnell
ISBN: 1-874109-48-6, 233 pages, IR£15.00/€19.00

Original Sin in a Brave New World (1998)
By Bobby McDonagh
ISBN: 1-874109- 40-0, 249 pages, IR£15.00/€19.00

Amsterdam: What the Treaty Means (1997)
Editor: Ben Tonra
ISBN: 1-874109-35-4, 224 pages, IR£15.00/€19.00

Justice Co-operation in the EU (1997)
Editor: Gavin Barrett
ISBN 1-874109-33-8, 244 pages, IR£15.00/€19.00

European Security: Ireland's Choices (1996)
Editor: Patrick Keatinge
ISBN 1-874109-24-9, 224 pages, IR£15.00/€19.00

Britain's European Question: The Issues for Ireland (1996)
Editor: Paul Gillespie
ISBN 1-874109-22-2, 224 pages, IR£15.00/€19.00

Constitution-Building in the European Union (1996)
Editor: Bridgid Laffan
ISBN 1-874109-21-4, 239 pages, IR£15.00/€19.00

Social Europe: EC Social Policy and Ireland (1993)
Editor: Seamus Ó Cinnéide
ISBN 1-874109-06-0, 176 pages, IR£15.00/€19.00

Maastricht and Ireland: What the Treaty Means (1992)
Editor: Patrick Keatinge
ISBN 1-874109-03-6, 180 pages, IR£10.00/€12.69

Economic and Monetary Union (1991)
Editor: Rory O'Donnell
ISBN 1-874109-01-X, 148 pages, IR£12.95/€16.44 (**out of print**)

Political Union (1991)
Editor: Patrick Keatinge
ISBN 1-874109-00-1, 200 pages, IR£12.95/€16.44 (**out of print**)

IMPLICATIONS FOR IRELAND

Agenda 2000, Implications For Ireland (1999)
ISBN 1-874109-44-3, 122 pages, IR£15/€19.00

Ireland and the IGC (1996)
Dermot Scott ISBN 1-874109-19-2, 54 pages, IR£3.95/€5.00

EMU and Irish Fiscal Policy (1993)
Donal de Buitléir and Don Thornhill
ISBN 1-874109-05-2, 74 pages, IR£7.50/€9.52

Political Union (1991)
Paul Gillespie and Rodney Rice
ISBN 1-874109-02-8, 60 pages, IR£5.00/€6.34

UNDERSTANDING EUROPE

Eastern Exchanges
Interchange of Education, Training and Professional Formation between Ireland and Czechoslovakia, Hungary and Poland.

Miriam Hederman O'Brien
ISBN 1-874109-04-4, 48 pages, IR£5.00/€6.34

Managing the Finances of the EU: The role of the court of auditors (1996)
Editor: Barry Desmond
ISBN 1-874109-25-7, 80 Pages, IR£7.50/€9.52

OCCASIONAL PAPERS

No. 1 Irish Public Opinion on Neutrality and European Union (1992)
Michael Marsh IR£4.00/€5.07

No. 2 The Economic Consequences of Maastricht (1992)
Paul Tansey IR£5.00/€6.34

No. 3 Subsidiarity: Its Application in Practice (1993)
Ciaran F. Walker
ISBN 1-874109-07-9 IR£5.00/€6.34

No. 4 Ireland's Contribution to the European Union (1994)
Dermot Scott
ISBN 1-874109-08-7, 48 pages, IR£7.50/€9.52

No. 5 Knowledge of the European Union in Irish Public Opinion: Sources and Implications (1995)
Richard Sinnott
ISBN 1-874109-09-5, 48 pages, IR£7.50/€9.52

No. 6 Citizenship of the European Union (1995)
Niamh Hyland, Claire Loftus and Anthony Whelan
ISBN 1-874109-13-3, 64 pages, IR£7.50/€9.52

No. 7 The Role of the Commission and Qualified Majority Voting (1995)
John Temple Lang and Eamonn Gallagher
ISBN 1-874109-14-1, 48 pages, IR£7.00/€8.88

FINAL REPORTS

Sustainable Energy and the Environmental Imperative (1999)
Editors: David Taylor, Brian Motherway
ISBN: 1-874109-50-8, pages 120, IR£15.00/€19.00

The Security of Europe - Actors and Issues (1999)
Editors: Jill Donoghue, Patrick Keatinge
ISBN: 1-874109-47-8, 123 pages, IR£15.00/€19.00
IGC Conference Report (1997)
Edited by Ben Tonra
ISBN 1-87109-32-X, 80 pages, IR£5.00/€6.34

The 1996 Intergovernmental Conference: Issues, Options and Implications (1996)
ISBN 1-874109-18-4, 288 pages, IR£30.00/€38.00

What Price CAP? Issues and Challenges Facing Agricultural and Rural Policy in the European Union (1995)
Editor: Brendan Kearney
ISBN 1-874109-15-X, IR£30.00/€38.00

Maastricht: Crisis of Confidence (1992)
Paul Gillespie, Brendan Halligan, Philip Halpin, Patrick Keatinge and Bridgid Laffan, IR£4.00/€5.07

INTERIM REPORTS

**The World Trade Organisation – Issues for the Millennium Round
A Preliminary Report Prior to the Seattle Ministerial Conference (1999)**
ISBN: 1-874109-50-8, 30 pages, IR£10.00/€12.69

Towards a Safer Europe – Small State Security Policies and the European Union: Implications for Ireland (1995)
Editor: Patrick Keatinge
ISBN 1-874109-11-7, 160 pages, IR£30.00/€38.00

Europe – Community and Continent: The enlargement of the European Union and its relationships with its continental neighbours (1994)
Tony Brown
250 pages, IR£12.50/€14.27

SUMMARY OF INTERIM REPORTS

A European Cultural Identity: Myth, Reality or Aspiration (1997)
Ben Tonra and Denise Dunne
ISBN 1-874109-10-9, 32 pages, IR£5.00/€6.34

Social Policy and the IGC. Flexibility, Institutional Reform and the Third Pillar (1997)
Joe Larragy, ISBN 1-874109-28-1, 32 pages, IR£5.00/€6.34

EMU - The Third Stage (Treaty and Non-Treaty basis of EMU) (1997)
Gavin Barrett, ISBN 1-874109-31-1, 104 pages, IR£15.00/€19.00

Hungary, Ireland and the European Union (1997)
Editor: Martin O'Donoghue, ISBN 1-874109
32 pages, IR£5.00/€6.34

SEMINAR PAPERS

EMU: 'One Year On' Conference 21 February 2000
ISBN: 1-874109-52-4, 75 pages, £10.00/€12.69

EMU: Duisenberg Conference 10 November 1998
ISBN: 1-874109-43-5, 33 pages, £15.00/€19.00

EMU: Conference 18 May 1998
ISBN: 1-874109-42-7, 29 pages, £5.00/€6.34

The Euro & The US Dollar: Conference 29 May 1998
ISBN: 1-874109-42-7, 81 pages, £15.00/€19.00

The Legal and Constitutional Implications of the Amsterdam Treaty - Conference 27 November 1997
ISBN 1-874109-3-9, 76 pages, IR£15.00/€19.00

EMU: Prospects & Problems: Seminar 9 July 1997
ISBN: 1-874109-36-2, 103 pages, IR£15.00/€19.00

EMU: Final Preparations: Conference 18 November 1997
ISBN: 1-874109-37-0, 28 pages, IR£5.00

Britain's European Question: the Issues for Ireland-Seminar papers (1996)
Editor: Paul Gillespie
ISBN 1-874109-23-0, 176 Pages, IR£20.00/€19.00 (**out of print**)

Recent Changes in Multilateral Security 1995
Foreword: Patrick Keatinge Facsimile pages, IR£10.00/€12.69

SEMINAR REPORTS

The Irish Presidency of the Council of Ministers (1997)
IR£4.00/€5.07

The Netherlands' Presidency of the Council of Ministers (1997)
Dr. Ben Tonra (Rapporteur)
15 pages, IR£4.00/€5.07

Norway and the European Union (1996)
Tony Brown (Rapporteur)
ISBN 1-874109-20-6, 48 pages, IR£7.50/€9.52

Austria our New Partner (1995)
Tony Brown (Rapporteur)
ISBN 1-874109-15-X, 44 pages, IR£7.50/€9.52

Sweden in the European Union (1995)
Tony Brown (Rapporteur)
ISBN 1-874109-17-6, 48 pages, IR£7.50/€9.52

Finland in the European Union (1995)
Tony Brown (Rapporteur)
ISBN 1-874109-16-8, 48 pages, IR£7.50/€9.52

SUMMARIES OF INTERIM REPORTS

Europe: Community and Continent (1994)
Tony Brown
ISBN 1-874109-10-9, 48 pages, IR£4.00/€5.07

Towards a Safer Europe
Patrick Keatinge
ISBN 1-874109-11-7, 56 pages, IR£7.50/€9.52

WORKING PAPERS

The Third Stage of EMU: Procedures and Timetable (1997)
Brendan Halligan, ISBN 1-874109, 14 pages, IR£5.00/€6.34

PUBLISHED ON BEHALF OF THE EUROPEAN COMMISSION REPRESENTATION IN IRELAND

European Social Policy – Options for the Union
David Gardner (Rapporteur): Free distribution

CONTEMPORARY/HISTORIC DOCUMENTS ARCHIVE

European Document Archive
Editor Tony Brown
c. 64 pages an issue, 297 x 210 mm, ISSN 0791-8097.
Annual subscription (4 issues) IR£40.00/€50.78
Back issues available – current issue No. 24, Summer 2000.
The European Document Series has ceased to be a print on paper publication. It is now published exclusively on the Institute's web site www.iiea.com

NEWSLETTER FOR MEMBERS

IEA News
Editor: Conall Quinn
Quarterly, current issue No. 23, Summer 2000.

GERMAN COMMENTARY

Volume No. 1, Spring 1997,
Jill Donoghue
ISBN: 1-874-109-30-3, IR£5.00/€6.34

Volume No. 2, October 1997,
Jill Donoghue
ISBN: 1-874109-30-3, IR£5.00/€6.34
Volume No. 3, April 1998
Jill Donoghue
ISBN: 1-874109-39-7, IR£5.00/€6.34

Volume No.4 December 1998
Jill Donoghue
ISBN: 1-874109-45-1, IR£5.00/€6.34

Volume No. 5 December 1999
Jill Donoghue
ISBN: 1-874109-51-6, IR£5.00/€6.34

WTO UPDATE

Issue Number 1, October 1999
Editor: Seamus Bannon

ENLARGEMENT UPDATE

Issue Number 1, October 1999
Editor: Jill Donoghue

Issue Number 2, November 1999
Jill Donoghue

EMU REVIEW

Issue No. 1, January 2000
Editor: Jill Donoghue

INDEX